FROMMER'S
1987–1988 GUIDE TO ATLANTIC CITY & CAPE MAY

by Gloria S. McDarrah

Published by Prentice Hall Press
A Division of Simon & Schuster, Inc.
Gulf + Western Building
One Gulf + Western Plaza
New York, NY 10023

ISBN: 0-671-62349-4

Manufactured in the United States of America

Although every effort was made to ensure the accuracy
of price information appearing in this book
it should be kept in mind that prices
can and do fluctuate in the course of time.

CONTENTS

MAPS

INFLATION ALERT: We don't have to tell you that inflation has hit the United States as it has everywhere else. For that reason it is quite possible that prices may be slightly higher at a given establishment when you read this book than they were at the time this information was collected in late 1986. Be that as it may, we feel sure these selections will still represent the best travel values in Atlantic City, Cape May, and environs.

ATLANTIC CITY

ATLANTIC CITY is on a winning roll. If you had the foresight to bet that the old Queen of the Seaside Resorts would once again enjoy a brand-new reign, you're raking in the chips.

The whole world seems to have rediscovered Atlantic City. Since 1976—when the state of New Jersey passed the casino gambling referendum—it's become the most visited vacation destination in the United States.

Greeting this record-shattering number of visitors (29.5 million in 1985) are two breathtaking "Gold Coasts." One is an oceanfront lineup of nine magnificently appointed skyscraping casino-hotels, the other boasts two luxuriously spread-out bayfront properties, both representing an investment of some $2 billion. But even as this is being written, construction activity is skyrocketing—in fact, more than the broad sandy beaches, the saltwater taffy, or even the Miss America pageants that traditionally symbolized Atlantic City, the giant construction crane better represents the exciting spirit that is transforming the old seaside spa into a dazzling city of the future.

Atlantic City's renaissance has finally begun to spill over from the Boardwalk to the quiet streets behind the oceanfront. Fine, world-class restaurants are opening in modest, two-story frame houses on neglected streets that were suffering the inner-city decay so common in the 1950s and 1960s. This movement will give you just a hint of the eventual transformation the city fathers hope to effect with the funds garnered from the massive influx of tourists since the crucial year of 1977 when gambling was introduced.

Make no bones about it—gambling is what it's all about in Atlantic City today. In casinos the size of football fields (or at Resorts International, two football fields), day melts into night. In these windowless expanses there are no clocks and the chandeliers' glitter is repeated in the reflections on mirrored tile ceilings and columns. The throbbing, colored lights and ceaseless electronic ringing of the slot machines beat a nervous rhythm for the higher stakes being wagered at the felt-covered blackjack tables, where maximum bets on one hand can be $1,000.

The glamour game in Atlantic City casinos is baccarat. It's played in ritzy-looking baccarat alcoves that are set off from the other casino activities with velvet ropes. The casinos treat the players (and other games' biggest spenders) to expensive meals and other kinds of courtesies, including luxurious hotel suites and free transportation. Craps, big six, and roulette are the other Atlantic City casino games, and whether your stake is a measly roll of nickels or a high-rolling stack of thousands, complimentary drinks on the casino floor are available to all. Cocktail waitresses circulate the room, fetchingly attired in costumes so brief that it seems amazing that they take the customers' eyes from the tables for no more time than the brief seconds needed to ask for a beverage (or pack of cigarettes).

Outside, along the Boardwalk, the strikingly modern architecture of the casino-hotels gives us a glimpse of a future world. Bally's pinkish-gray granite front glitters in the strong sunlight. The Atlantis Casino Hotel's glass-paneled skyscraper façade mirrors ocean and clouds. The jaggedly sawtoothed concrete of the oceanfront Trump Casino Hotel, with its astonishingly placed penthouse some 30 stories above the ground, looks like a space shuttle perched on a mountain of the moon.

At night top entertainers perform in the casino-hotels' showrooms: Frank Sinatra, Joan Rivers, the Pointer Sisters, even Luciano Pavarotti have been headliners. The hotels are brilliantly lit. The Sands' orange logo gleams high up on the building's façade, across the street from the stunningly spotlit classical tower of the Claridge. Bally's purple awnings take on a Day-Glo brilliance, and farther up the Boardwalk, Resorts' orange awnings are outlined with strings of white lights.

The Boardwalk is always a prime attraction, that 60-foot-wide wooden promenade that links the flash and elegance of the new with the one-story pizza parlors, fudge shops, fast-food outlets, souvenir stores, restaurants, and game arcades that have survived from Atlantic City's pre-gambling era. Boardwalk bikers, shoppers, joggers, and strollers enjoy the incomparable sea air in a never-ending parade that goes on year round. For the less athletic, motorized trams ply the Boardwalk from the Golden Nugget to the Garden Pier, moving slowly enough for you to enjoy the bustling scene. Atlantic City's old rolling wicker chairs are occasionally available for a ride along the Boardwalk.

Boardwalk concerts (remember the Beach Boys?), art shows, bayside marinas for excursion boats and fishing parties, golf courses, the huge Ocean One shopping gallery in the shape of an ocean liner—added to the excitement of gaming tables and slot machines—keep the action going. Atlantic City has come a long way since Memorial Day heralded the opening of the season and the Miss America Pageant was able to lengthen the season by just one week after Labor Day.

While you're here, take some time also to go outside Atlantic City proper and spend the day in some of the historic towns nearby, explore the semi-wilderness of the million-plus acres of the Pine Barrens, track birds in the self-drive eight-mile auto tour of the Brigantine National Wildlife Refuge, visit the local wineries (yes, wineries in south Jersey), and tour the museums and historic houses of nearby Ocean City.

It's all here—the world-famous Boardwalk, the glamorous nightlife, the stunning casino-hotels, and of course the traditional attractions of swimming and sunning on the wide, gently sloping, white sand beaches, as inviting as they have been since 1854, when a few casual visitors astonished the locals by deciding to spend the night in Millie Leeds's Cottage, thus inaugurating Atlantic City's first hotel.

ABOUT NEW JERSEY: Long before the spacious ocean beaches of south Jersey became the most highly developed resort area of the East Coast, the state of New Jersey was the stronghold of the Lenni-Lenape Indians, part of the loosely organized group of tribes belonging to the Delaware Nation. The area between the Hudson and Delaware Rivers was first claimed by the Dutch explorer Henry Hudson in 1609 as part of the New Netherlands settlement. The Dutch relinquished the region in 1664, when the colonizing English seized control. James, Duke of York, was granted title to New Netherlands by his brother, King Charles II. The duke awarded proprietorship of the lands between the two rivers to two of his loyal followers: Lord John Berkeley, first Baron of Stratton, whose domain was in the south and west of the region, and Sir George Carteret, who became proprietor of what is now northern and eastern New Jersey.

The original land grants that separated Jersey into two parts ran roughly along a line from Little Egg Harbor in the southeast to the Delaware Water Gap in the northwest. The split in proprietorship continued, in one form or another, until 1702, when the colony of New Jersey was recognized as one entity by the crown. Oddly enough, the growth of the state has followed along the lines of the old grant to Berkeley and Carteret. Northern New Jersey has been closely connected in its economic development to New York, and southern New Jersey to Philadelphia.

One of the original 13 colonies, the small state of New Jersey (46th in size among all the states) is surrounded by water on all sides except its New York State northern border. On the east are the Hudson River and the Atlantic Ocean; on the south and west, Delaware Bay and the Delaware River. The elongated strip of barrier beaches that have become the great playground of the East Coast separate the mainland from the Atlantic Ocean.

All too often the state has been given a bum rap, its superior highway system crossing through the heavily industrialized eastern section of the state that borders New York City is the part most familiar to motorists hurrying by. But there's a lot more to the Garden State than you'll see speeding along on the turnpike, and the millions of vacationers who annually flock to the 127 miles of New Jersey beaches from Sandy Hook to Cape May Point know it.

ATLANTIC CITY—HOW IT ALL BEGAN: To the Lenni-Lenape Indians, the ten-mile-long windswept island strip now occupied by Atlantic City and its southern neighbors Ventnor, Margate, and Longport, was Absegami (variously translated as Big Water, Little Water, or more poetically as Place of Swans). No doubt that Indian name was too complicated for English tongues to curl around, so we find the first recorded owner of Absecon Island to be Thomas Budd, an Englishman who came here in 1678. The briar-covered island was included in a huge parcel of some 15,000 acres deeded to Budd in settlement of a claim for $6250 he had against the proprietors who ruled the royal grant. It was quite a bargain he acquired. The beach lands were valued at 4¢ an acre, those on the mainland at about 40¢.

Until 1800 there was little attempt at a permanent settlement on Absecon Island, which was separated from the mainland by some five miles of marshes and bays. A historian writes of that period, "On the beach nothing interrupts the monotonous sough of the seas but the quack of the wild geese, the cry of the curlew or the shrill scream of the gull." No one came to the shore except some hunters, or occasionally an adventurous beach party crossed over the old Indian trail or turnpike (today's Florida Avenue). On this island of peaceful solitude, the odds that the stupendous development of the next 100 years would ever take place appeared slim.

By 1838 the first glimmerings of civilization came to Absecon

Island in the person of one Jeremiah Leeds, whose unprepossessing cottage was the unlikely precursor of Atlantic City's splendid future. Jeremiah's grandfather had actually built the first house on the island in 1783, on the Baltic Avenue site now occupied by the Municipal Bus Terminal. By mid-century, the official surveyor's map still showed only shanties on Absecon Island. But a turn in the tides of Atlantic City's fortunes was near.

TRACKS TO GLORY: A far-sighted doctor who lived on the mainland, Jonathan Pitney, and Richard Osborne, a civil engineer, are credited with the genius of hatching an idea that would link Philadelphia's teeming urban streets with the healthful sea air of an ideal watering place. Perhaps they were intoxicated by the exhilarating ozone. "Build a railroad," they urged, and their reasoning seemed so logical and persuasive that people wondered why the idea had never been advanced before. Investors lined up eagerly, anxious to buy shares. By 1852 construction of the Camden & Atlantic Railroad—and promotion of the resort—had begun.

Osborne is also credited with naming the city he and Pitney had conceived when he presented a plan for the city's streets to the railroad's board of directors. The streets running parallel to the beach he named for the world's great seas—Pacific, Atlantic, Arctic, Baltic, Mediterranean. For streets running east and west from the sea to the marshes, he used the names of the states. And the rush was on!

The city was incorporated in 1854, and in the same year, on July 5th, the first train took a speedy 2½ hours to arrive in Atlantic City from Camden. Although the first hotel had yet to be completed, the resort's future had arrived. Land profiteering was the order of the day, and the railroad's land company was in the forefront. Imposing hotels like the United States and the Surf House were soon full of tourists, and the first rooming houses began to take in the overflow of visitors. By 1878 one railroad was unable to handle the passengers from Philadelphia to the shore, and another railroad line, the Narrow Gauge, was completed.

THE GREAT WOODEN WAY: The Boardwalk was a triumph of Yankee ingenuity over a vexing problem encountered with one of Atlantic City's most pervasive elements—the sand. Unable to keep it out of hotel lobbies or the railroad coaches, Alexander Boardman, a conductor on the Camden & Atlantic, and Jacob Keim, a local hotelier, got together and asked the City Council in 1870 to build the first wooden footwalk, and thereby keep the sand out of everybody's shoes. Built the very same year, the Boardwalk cost $5,000 (half the city's tax revenue); it was eight feet wide, and was laid on the sand in sections that could be taken up and stored for the winter. By 1880 a new Boardwalk had to replace the worn-out original walkway. A hurricane in the fall of 1889 wrecked the new walk, but the idea had taken hold, and the Boardwalk has become as important to Atlantic City as the ocean itself.

Today's version is 60 feet wide and six miles long. The raised walk has a substructure of concrete and steel that is covered with planks laid in a herringbone pattern. Steel railings make good leaning bars to watch the ocean waves and keep strollers from falling off the Boardwalk, a common problem in earlier versions. Some of the rolling wicker chairs that were once so much a part of the scene on the Boardwalk still ply the walkway.

On one side of the Boardwalk, in accordance with the City Council decree, were the hotels (now casino-hotels), restaurants, and shops. On the other side were the amusement piers—the Steel Pier, Steeplechase Pier, the Million Dollar Pier, and others —where thrilling rides and refreshments, vaudeville shows and circus performers, provided Atlantic City crowds with a kaleidoscope of entertainment. The only survivors of these wooden structures that jutted out into the ocean are the Garden Pier, at New Jersey Avenue where the arts and historic museums are, and the pier used by Resorts as a helicopter landing pad.

ELEPHANTS, AIRPLANES, AND ORANGES: The magnetism of Atlantic City was intensified by the promotional stunts thought up to keep the tourists amused and, perchance, make page one of some newspaper and attract even more tourists to Atlantic City in the short three months of the season—Lucy the Margate Elephant (see Chapter VI) is still drawing visitors. There were all kinds of animal acts on the piers, but the one that spread Atlantic City's fame throughout the world was a dive on horseback by a young woman named Lorena Carver, who did it for 25 years from high on a tower on the Steel Pier.

Another wacky feat distinguished the famous air show in July 1910. During this carnival of the air, Glenn H. Curtis dropped oranges from a height of 100 feet onto a yacht to demonstrate how to bomb a target. Marathon dance contests were a natural for promoting the Boardwalk; it was not uncommon for a winning couple to spend more than 100 days in the arms of Terpsichore.

There is one contest, held in Atlantic City since the 1920s, that still holds millions of Americans enthralled.

THERE SHE IS . . . : In recent years the song may be different, but the melody lingers on. Why? Certainly the continued popularity of the Miss America Pageant defies rational explanation. In this era of raised consciousness, one would think that a beauty contest would be good-naturedly ignored until it quietly packed its tent and stole away, but no . . .

Although the Miss America Pageant sponsors emphasize the $2½-million scholarship money awarded to contestants and winners, and the importance of talent, character, and personality, there's no doubt that essentially the pageant is of direct lineal descent to that eight-contestant beauty contest won by a pretty 16-year-old Washington girl in 1921. That first Atlantic City contest was a resounding success, and received nationwide recognition. The contest continued to be held, intermittently between 1930 and 1935, when it gained strong business backing, and it's been on the boards ever since, and since 1940 at the Convention Hall. Today it's an American icon, as much a part of the national psyche as apple pie, hot dogs, and the Fourth of July.

A paid staff of only 12 people, supplemented by volunteers from all over the country, run the nonprofit corporation that sponsors the pageant. First there are the over 3,000 local contests leading to the state titles, and then the main event in Atlantic City, now held the week after Labor Day weekend. Past contestants include the actress Joan Blondell (1926); Bess Myerson (Miss America 1945), who has been active in New York State politics; and Phyllis George (Miss America 1971), now a prominent entertainment personality. If you're interested in the history of the Miss America Pageant phenomenon and the shenanigans of the contests, Frank Deford's *There She Is* provides all kinds of interesting anecdotes in his well-researched book on the contest.

QUEEN OF RESORTS, THEN AND NOW: The aura of glamour generated in Atlantic City's heyday in the first half of the 20th century was symbolized by the luxurious hotels—the Haddon Hall, the Dennis, the Traymore, the Shelburne, the Marlborough-Blenheim—that overlooked the Boardwalk. Through the 1950s a stay at one of these grand palaces was a vacation to remember.

But after World War II America seemed to grow out of its love affair with Atlantic City. Some sources say that the increase in national air travel, the continued demographic shift westward, and the deterioration of Atlantic City itself combined to create a climate of slow decline. Others feel the decline was simply a product of the more sophisticated tastes that found the honkytonk side-show attractions of the piers out of date compared to such modern amusement centers as Disneyland. Hard times beset Atlantic City; fewer visitors meant layoffs for the local people employed by the big hotels. And gradually unemployment took its inevitable toll as city neighborhoods deteriorated.

From the early 1970s it became clear that the city could only sustain itself by tourism, and that tourists could only be attracted after massive renovation and infusions of capital. The crucial year was 1977—it was decided that the introduction of casino gambling would turn around the city's fortunes. Ten short years later, the growth has been phenomenal—11 new casinos (with ground broken for several more), a virtually new skyline, top entertainment nightly, outstanding growth in convention bookings for the late 1980s, and a pervasive sense of growth and progress. Locals try to avoid a comparison with Las Vegas, but even physically Atlantic City seems to hold the advantage, with its fine oceanfront and walkability.

Atlantic City's greatest natural advantage (aside from the Atlantic Ocean) is its location on the East Coast, where some 54 million people live within a 300-mile radius of the resort. This nearby population has comprised the bulk of Atlantic City's tourists since the turn of the century, and it now appears that casino gambling is bringing them back to rejuvenate the celebrated Baghdad by the Sea.

Chapter I

GETTING TO AND AROUND ATLANTIC CITY

GEOGRAPHICALLY, Atlantic City is on the Northeast Corridor, centered along the Boston–Washington axis. It's easy to get there now via public transportation, by air or bus, and promises to become even easier. Preliminary approval of a train station to be built at the foot of the Atlantic City Expressway portends speedy Amtrak service to New York and Philadelphia. New Jersey's superb road system welcomes those arriving by car.

Getting There

BY AIR: Bader Field (Atlantic City Municipal Airport) is actually in the city itself; the entrance to the field is on Albany Avenue (U.S. 40). **Allegheny Commuter** (tel. 609/344-7104 or toll free 800/428-4253), affiliated with USAir, provides frequent direct flights between Bader and Philadelphia's International Airport (25 minutes), New York's JFK and LaGuardia Airports (50 minutes), and Washington, D.C.'s National Airport (50 minutes). Off-peak, one-way fare is $49 to New York or Washington and $29 to Philadelphia. Regular fare to New York is $76, to Washington $84, both one way.

Twelve miles (about 20 minutes) from Atlantic City the **International Air Terminal** on Tilton Road, Pomona (tel. 609/645-7895), serves charter passenger lines.

Helicopter service between New York City and Atlantic City is provided daily by **Resorts International Airlines** (tel. 212/972-4444 or 609/344-0833); one-way fare is about $79.

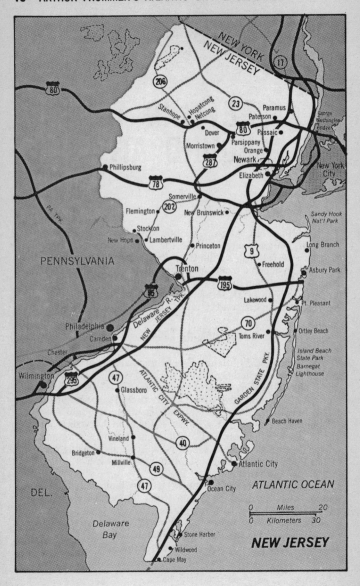

NEW JERSEY

Limos or a taxi can bring you into town. Metro's Rapid Rover (tel. 344-0100) car service provides 24-hour-a-day, door-to-door shuttle service for about $5.

BY BUS: Buses are often the budget way to travel, especially if you like the idea of leaving the driving to them. For Atlantic City, in fact, there's no cheaper way to go. If you happen to live within 150 miles of Atlantic City, I'm sure you must know about the bonanza of freebies offered to one-day bus trippers by the casinos, in conjunction with various bus lines. It hardly pays to stay home when you examine some of the promotional schemes, and apparently lots of people agree, because on any given day some 800 to 1,000 buses are unloading passengers at the casino-hotels for a day of the action.

Greyhound, for example, was recently offering a $23 round-trip ticket ($24.75 on weekends and holidays) that you could use in a three-day period—with at least $10 in coin returned to you by a casino representative who boarded the bus in Atlantic City. If you took the Greyhound bus on a less-busy hour—say Monday through Thursday at 2 p.m.—you'd be rewarded by $17.50 in coin and a $5 deferred coupon to be credited on a future trip. That would bring the cost of the trip down to a cool 75¢. Buses leave from New York City's Port Authority Bus Terminal at Eighth Avenue and 41st Street almost every half hour from 8 a.m. to 8:30 p.m. weekdays, till 10:30 p.m. Friday and Saturday.

Domenico Tours (tel. 212/757-8687) is one of the private bus operators that was advertising $23 bus trips to Harrah's Marina—with a $15 cash rebate, a $3 food/beverage credit, plus a $5 deferred voucher. Your local newspaper and/or bus station will have the latest information on casino bus trip special offers.

Atlantic City's **Municipal Bus Terminal** is at Arkansas and Arctic Avenues. Regular express and/or local service is provided by Greyhound (tel. 609/345-5403), Trailways (tel. 609/344-4449), and New Jersey Transit (tel. 609/344-8181).

BY CAR: Although driving may be the most convenient way for you to get to Atlantic City, once you're there a car may be difficult to park. Keep in mind that Atlantic City is very compact, that the oceanfront casinos are all within a 20-block strip along the Boardwalk, and that public transportation (see below) is cheap and frequent.

If you do decide to drive, the trip will take about 2½ hours from New York City, 4½ hours from Washington, D.C., and 1½ hours from Philadelphia. The most direct route into town from all major arteries is the Atlantic City Expressway. Two other highways, U.S. 30 and U.S. 40, feed into Atlantic City, but unless you're planning to stop for a bite to eat or look for a motel, you'll find these routes too congested with trucks and stoplights.

From New York City, the most direct route is via the New Jersey Turnpike, southbound, to the Garden State Parkway, southbound to shore points, which intersects with the Atlantic City Expressway. From central Philadelphia (and points west via I-95), the classic route is the Atlantic City Expressway from the Benjamin Franklin Bridge. Coming from the south, I-95 and U.S. 40 from Washington, D.C. (or U.S. 13 and 9 from the Norfolk area to the Cape May–Lewes Ferry).

Whichever direction you're coming from, you'll find that the friendly people at the **New Jersey State Tourist Office** have provided Information Centers on the Garden State Parkway (at Cape May Court House), on I-287 (at Morristown), and at other key locations.

Parking

Once in the city you'll be faced with the problem Atlantic City's popularity has caused—the dearth of parking spots. Most motels include free parking in their rates, and many run vans to the more distant casinos. In the hectic summer season (and more and more frequently in spring too) you may find that the most centrally located motels have to park your car at an off-premises lot and will charge you an extra $2 or so every time you want to use your car during your stay.

Parking policies vary widely among the casino-hotels. Out in the marina section, Harrah's and Trump Castle provide free self-parking in vast concrete garages connected to the hotels with closed-in walkways (valet parking also available). Casino hotels in town offer free self- or valet parking to guests staying at the hotels. Others can use the parking facilities for a limited number of hours. Resorts International offers their guests valet parking or a guarded self-parking open lot (free) about two blocks from the hotel, plus a free shuttle bus to transport you to and from the hotel.

I've noted parking policies of the casino-hotels and motels with their descriptions in the next chapter.

Downtown, there's metered parking on the streets perpendicular to the beach and there are parking lots along Pacific Avenue. Expect to pay $6 to $8 for an evening's parking near the casinos, more on weekends. As an inducement to drivers, the casinos may offer to "validate" your parking receipt for a certain number of hours—which means you won't have to pay anything at all for parking if you take your parking receipt into a casino to be stamped. Lots that offer validated parking are so posted. You're more likely to find that kind of offer in the winter.

Getting Around

JITNEYS: I've always thought that Atlantic City's jitneys were the perfect solution to urban mass transit problems, and I haven't found any reason to change my mind. They're small (only about 15 passengers), clean, frequent, and cost only 75¢ per ride. Jitneys run along two routes—Pacific Avenue is one; the other goes from Brighton Park, near Park Place and the Boardwalk, to Harrah's Marina and Trump Castle via Indiana Avenue and Brigantine Boulevard.

BUS: Along Atlantic Avenue a more conventional-looking bus services a route all the way to Longport (the last community on Absecon Island), going through Ventnor and Margate. Minimum bus fare is 70¢.

TRAMS: For an oceanfront ride on the Boardwalk that's as much sightseeing fun as it is a transportation option, motorized trams offer an easy-on, easy-off $1 trip (75¢ for seniors) from Albany Avenue to the Garden Pier. They run from 10 a.m. to about 9 p.m. during the week, to midnight on weekends and in summer.

TAXIS: Taxi line-ups are easy to find at casino-hotel entrances and airports. If you're at another location, a phone call will bring you good service. **Yellow Cab Co.** (tel. 344-1221), **Dial Cab** (tel. 344-3452), and **Mutual** (tel. 345-6111) are among the numerous companies in town. The current tariff is $1.35 for the first one-fifth of a mile, 20¢ for each additional fifth of a mile, and 20¢ for each additional passenger.

CAR RENTALS: Budget Rent-A-Car, 3003 Pacific Ave. (tel. 345-0600), offers inexpensive and dependable service, including pick-up at Bader Field to their in-town location (only from 8 a.m. to 8 p.m. Monday to Friday, to 5 p.m. Saturday and Sunday). Rates range from $30.95 to $49.95 per day, unlimited mileage, depending on size of car. **Avis** (tel. 345-3246, or toll free 800/331-1212) offers similar service. **Hertz** (tel. 646-1212, or toll free 800/654-3131) has a desk right at the airport.

Having a car in Atlantic City is a mixed blessing, since parking can be a problem. If you're just going to be doing a minimum of traveling around, you might consider using public transportation. But if you're really going to tour, visiting out-of-town sights and restaurants in nearby areas, then you'll certainly want to have a car. Unlimited-mileage arrangements are the most economical way to go, unless you get sufficient free mileage with the "cents per mile" deal to keep your expenses down.

Orientation

Atlantic City occupies the northern end of Absecon Island, which is part of the system of reefs, islands, and lagoons that separate the mainland from the Atlantic Ocean intermittently along this country's eastern shores. Although Atlantic City gets most of the press, the downbeach communities of Ventnor, Margate, and Longport occupy the southern reaches of Absecon Island. One limited-access highway (the Atlantic City Expressway) and two major routes (U.S. 30, locally dubbed the White Horse Pike, and U.S. 40, the Black Horse Pike) join Atlantic City to the mainland.

If you've ever played Monopoly, the names of Atlantic City's streets and avenues will be hauntingly familiar. (One of the best-selling games ever, Monopoly was invented in 1930 by Charles Darrow, a Philadelphian whose Atlantic City vacations were immortalized in this now-classic board game based, first, on chance, the roll of the dice and the draw of a card—if you pick up the card that tells you "Do not pass Go, do not collect $200," your luck has run out—and second, on the buying and selling of real estate. Both elements seem greatly prophetic of Atlantic City's fortunes!)

The Boardwalk, along the Atlantic Ocean beachfront, has always been a pedestrian and tram-car mall. The beaches are rigorously cleaned and the water attracts thousands of summertime bathers with its gently sloping bottom and low waves.

Behind the Boardwalk, the neatly patterned grid of Atlantic City's streets are easy to follow. The avenues, named for the world's great seas—Pacific, Atlantic, Baltic, Mediterranean—are parallel to the Boardwalk. At its northern end (Inlet section) Baltic becomes Madison Avenue; at its southern end (downbeach) it's called Fairmount. With some few exceptions, the streets perpendicular to the Boardwalk are named for the states, roughly in geographic order; northernmost is Maine, then New Hampshire, Rhode Island, and so on.

Jutting out from the Boardwalk into the ocean are what remain of the famous piers whose carnival attractions were so much a part of Atlantic City's history. The Garden Pier, near New Jersey Avenue, has the recently rebuilt museum building. The Steeplechase Pier, now owned by Resorts International casino-hotel across the Boardwalk, is undergoing a major refurbishing. The Central Pier, near Kentucky Avenue, has suffered storm and fire damage. Directly across from Caesars casino-hotel near Arkansas Avenue, on the site of the old Million Dollar Pier, is the shopping center called Ocean One, arrestingly shaped like an ocean liner. Aboard this "vessel" are three levels of shops, restaurants, entertainment, and some of the best ocean views in town.

Nine spectacular oceanfront casino-hotels stand along the Boardwalk, with construction for additional properties already under way (see Chapter II), and on the bay side of the island stand Trump's Castle and Harrah's Marina.

And now it's time to preview what's in store for you at these fabulous casino-hotels whose exciting entertainment and recreational facilities have made Atlantic City the most visited resort destination in the United States.

WHERE TO STAY IN ATLANTIC CITY

SOMEWHERE IN ATLANTIC CITY there's a hotel or motel that's exactly right for you. The casino-hotels are the most celebrated, and charge corresponding rates. Their multi-room suites boast original artwork, museum-caliber modern or antique furniture, Steinway pianos, Oriental rugs, fully stocked bars and kitchens, Jacuzzis, private saunas, and incomparable ocean views. In these ultra-luxurious surroundings movie stars, Greek shipowners, and oil-rich billionaires feel right at home. Prices for these super-deluxe suites begin at around $275 per night, and some ascend to the stratospheric atmosphere of $700 daily. (Should you be willing to pay the prices, don't be surprised if none of these suites is available. All the casino-hotels like to keep these palatial suites free so the hotel can bestow them as gifts to high rollers.)

In these very same casino-hotels, though, there are also standard rooms at prices that are comparable to New York's or San Francisco's leading first-class hostelries. And if you don't mind paying from $90 to $140 a night for a room, you'll enjoy the privilege of proximity to the casino floor, plus a few other mitigating factors to help you rationalize the expense.

If you stay at a casino-hotel, you'll have a very comfortable and luxurious place to bunk, an intriguing variety of good to fabulous restaurants under the same roof, and easy access to lounges, cabarets, and showroom entertainment, plus spa and health-club facilities, a pool an elevator ride away, and of course, an on-site casino.

Along Pacific Avenue, roughly between Albany and Pennsylvania Avenues, are many of the noncasino hotels and motels, where you can find accommodations for a nightly tab of $40 to

$95. Need I say that the $40 would be during the winter season, the $95 in summer. I've tried to select the best and most reputable motels. In the summer months even the less desirable are booked solid, so it's imperative to reserve ahead as far in advance as you can. Many motels insist on a night's payment as a deposit in advance of your arrival. In any event, be sure that you have the rate in writing from the motel, as many Atlantic City horror stories hinge on an unannounced rate hike.

If you don't mind an out-of-town location, there are some very comfortable accommodations in the new motels that are opening up along Routes 30 and 40 near Atlantic City. Some of the older motels along these routes are sprucing up and offer decent rooms at a moderate rate. I've noted several in the motel section below.

Package Plans for Savings

Special room/entertainment/dining packages will deal you a midweek bargain vacation. They grant considerable price reductions for short stays in Atlantic City. I've described some of these plans in my previews of the hotels (below), but there may be different—even better—packages offered by the time you arrive. Be sure to inquire when you reserve a room whether a package plan is available.

Another possibility that offers not only rooms but complete kitchen facilities and other amenities are the condo/hotels that have recently made their appearance on the Atlantic City scene. Two are right in town, one at the foot of Route 30.

Another option you might like to investigate would be staying outside Atlantic City in a nearby community. Somers Point and Ocean City, for example, are less than ten miles away. (Check the Ocean City section below for recommendations there.) In any of these outlying communities (even as far away as Cape May, some 40 miles south) there is limousine service to Atlantic City daily, at reasonable rates, and you'll probably save a bundle on hotel and restaurant costs.

No matter where you'd like to spend the night, you're taking a risk by not reserving in advance, with the possible exceptions of the months of January, February, and March. But even then, you have to remember that Atlantic City is a big convention town,

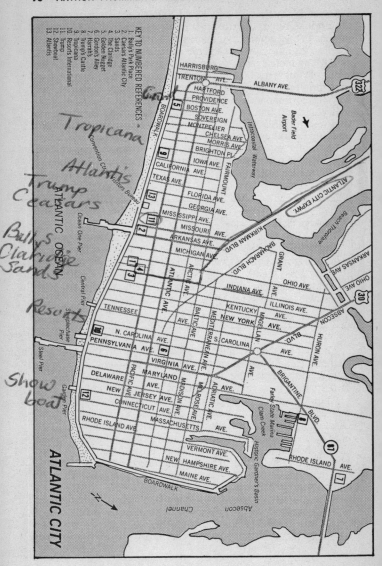

KEY TO NUMBERED REFERENCES:
1. Bally's Park Place
2. Caesars Atlantic City
3. Sands
4. The Claridge
5. Golden Nugget
6. Gordon's Alley
7. Harrah's
8. Trump's Castle
9. Tropicana
10. Resorts International
11. Trump
12. Showboat
13. Atlantis

and you may find to your consternation that every available bed in town has been commandeered by visiting conventioneers.

ABOUT THOSE CRANES . . . : Within the last ten years casino-hotels have been built along the Boardwalk and at bayside. At last count, Atlantic City only had some 7,000 first-class hotel rooms, with about 3,000 more in the offing (after the completion of current construction projects).

The builders, many of them already owners of one casino-hotel property, apparently know a good thing when they see it, for even more hotel rooms are on the drawing boards. Resorts International, first of the casino-hotels in 1978, has broken ground for Resorts II, directly north of its present property.

The Golden Nugget plans to build a 500-room casino-hotel at the marina area, and of course the Showboat Hotel Casino should be completed by the time you read this, in early 1987. Two other Boardwalk projects, the Dunes (at Albany Avenue) and Penthouse (at Missouri Avenue), have been undertaken, but no completion date has been announced for either of these.

And that's not all! In addition to the brand-new construction going on all over town, many of the present casino-hotels have started a variety of expansion projects, which I'll detail below in the descriptions of the individual properties.

A NOTE ABOUT THIS CHAPTER: Since in Atlantic City the hotel-casino complex is not just a place to stay but the reason for coming, many guests hardly leave their hotels. And that's how the hotels like it—each offers a full range of eating establishments, nightlife, the gambling casino, and other resort facilities. So, along with the descriptions of accommodations, I'm listing in this chapter each of the casino-hotels' dining options as well. In descending order of price category, noncasino hotels and motels are listed in the last part of this chapter. Chapter III details restaurants outside the casino-hotels. Nightlife and sports (both in the casino-hotels and elsewhere) are described in subsequent chapters.

The Casino-Hotels

As I indicated earlier on, you'll have a choice of two prime locations—oceanfront or bayside—and each has its own advantages. If you opt for bayside, you'll be just about two miles, or a ten-minute jitney ride, from the Boardwalk. It's a quiet area, for the casino-hotels by the bay are very much self-contained resorts, set in a subtly colored, marshy landscape, with expansive views of the wetlands, the Intracoastal Waterway, and the channel between Atlantic City and Brigantine. At the oceanfront, or just a few steps back (Sands and Claridge), you'll be able to walk out of your hotel onto the Boardwalk, whose myriad attractions and distractions, including the ocean beach, are just steps away, as are the casinos and facilities of the other Boardwalk properties. Easier access to free parking facilities has given the bay side a bit of an edge to drivers, but the downtown hotels are beginning to address this problem with more lots (I've noted parking facilities throughout).

Each of the casino-hotels has a very distinct personality, as expressed in their individual decors, casinos, restaurants, and other facilities. This preview of their accommodations and dining options should help you choose from among these very exciting offerings.

You'll undoubtedly note that none of the casino-hotels has fewer than 500 rooms—and there's a very good reason for that magic figure. When the New Jersey gambling referendum was passed in 1977, permitting gambling only in Atlantic City, very strict regulations controlling all phases of gambling also passed into law. Gambling was permitted only on a casino floor (not in the lobby, in supermarkets, or any other retail establishment, including laundromats, as in Las Vegas), and casinos were only permitted in establishments that provided at least 500 sleeping rooms. (The reason for these restrictions, of course, was to create more jobs in Atlantic City, the motivation for bringing gambling into the state in the first place.) Other gaming regulations even set out the permissible size of the rooms, and the personnel who can be employed in any part of the casino-hotel—even busboys and chambermaids, absolutely *everybody* who works there, must be licensed by the Casino Control Commission, as must the vendors servicing the hotels. Casinos may be open from 10 a.m. to 4 a.m. on weekdays, from 10 a.m. to 6 a.m. on weekends, and the minimum age for admittance to the casino floor is 21.

In my opinion this kind of tight regulation has given Atlantic City gambling a very classy kind of atmosphere. The casinos' ambience tends to dramatize the excitement of the games and, conversely, the other attractions of Atlantic City provide a very relaxing alternative to the thrill of wagering. It's a combination that's hard to beat.

RESORTS INTERNATIONAL: Resorts International, North Carolina

Avenue and the Boardwalk, Atlantic City, NJ 08401 (tel. toll free 800/GET-RICH, or 609/344-6000).

Resorts, the first of the Atlantic City casino-hotels to open, and the first to obtain a permanent license, prides itself on size, variety, top entertainment, and slickness. The initial investment was $140 million, which included providing licenses of varying degrees for each of the 4,000 employees. With nine restaurants, 15 shops, the largest casino in town, a parking capacity of 4,500 ($8 per day for valet parking, free if you park yourself), and the opulent Superstar Theater, Resorts possesses a competitive, casino-oriented attitude. A luxurious new health club with separate facilities for men and women, including sauna, steam room, Jacuzzis, a year-round swimming pool, sundeck, squash courts, and numerous cocktail bars and lounges, fully qualify Resorts as a complete, self-contained vacation destination.

To my mind, Resorts offers the quintessential gaming resort experience, incorporating the architectural grandeur of traditional Atlantic City with the glitz and glamour generated by big-name entertainers, a flashy glass/brass/marble decor, and the siren sounds of a croupier's call. Originally, Resorts acquired the grand old Chalfonte-Haddon Hall; it later sold the Chalfonte, but kept the architecturally superb old Haddon Hall.

At night, Resorts' brick and limestone tower, its red neon sign ablaze with light, is visible from the mainland. If you're closer at hand, the orange awnings over the street-level monumental windows and high storefronts are electrically outlined with a string of white lights. The glass-walled, burgundy-red-carpeted lobby has two levels, glass-sheathed columns trimmed with brass, brass planters with seasonal floral displays mixed with other greenery, and a brilliant array of chandeliers, whose zillions of tiny bulbs burn night and day.

The casino's chandeliered precincts can be entered from the lobby floor or the Boardwalk hotel entrance. In its 60,000 square feet of space, 2,850 gamblers can be accommodated at 1,728 slot machines (including the outsize Big Berthas that tower over seemingly child-size players), 82 blackjack tables, 20 craps tables, 14 roulette and 4 big-six wheels, and 3 baccarat tables. Did you know that each blackjack table uses 16 decks of cards daily (Resorts disposes of 490,000 decks of cards and 73,000 dice a year)? All this wear and tear necessitates changing felt on the tables every four to six weeks ($35 per blackjack table, $100 per craps table). On any given day there are $25 million worth of chips on the premises. The baccarat customer is the premium gambler, and the richly decorated "pit" is sunken and railed off from the rest of the floor. But Resorts doesn't forget the slot machine customers. In addition to the usual "fruit salad" machines, there are video blackjack, poker, and dice—plus the so-called progressive slots, whose jackpots advance by so much per minute, to a healthy $1 million maximum. Only 20% of the casino tables allow minimum bets below $5 during peak hours. On the casino floor, a staff of cocktail servers, trays in hand, will provide complimentary drinks at your request.

But let's talk about rooms and rates before we return to the hotel's other attractions. There are 686 guest rooms, 518 in the main wing and 168 in the North Tower, adjacent to the casino. Six elevators, trimmed in red and brass, with low control panels for handicapped guests, service the main wing, whose rooms have been undergoing extensive redecoration. In the floors newly redone thus far, cheerfully wallpapered corridors are color coordinated with the turquoise and silver Art Deco patterned carpet; the waiting areas for the elevators on each floor all have mirrored walls.

The standard guest rooms have a king-size or two double beds, and the color schemes, some in pastel shades, others in a bolder mode, all have a contemporary flair. In some rooms I saw pink, rose, and white furnishings dramatically accented with shiny black-lacquer pieces and gleaming brass trim. Black-and-white-print bedspreads and shiny black headboards were set off by white walls and a rosy-pink rug. Two contemporary armchairs, their curves outlined with brass, were convivially placed at a glass and brass round table, thoughtfully decorated with a bud vase holding fresh flowers. Another thoughtful touch is the nightly turndown service, complete with chocolates on your pillow. The color TV was on a black enamel base, which concealed a refrigerator. Many TVs (not all) have remote-control tuning. The turquoise tile bath has a host of take-away amenities: shampoo, French milled soap in tortoise-shell case, shower cap, shoe mitt, etc.—all cunningly presented in a wicker basket. There's a digital-readout doctor's scale in the bathroom, should you have brought along your diet on vacation too. The closet is room size, and offers a free overnight shoeshine. All rooms have direct-dial phones (one in the bathroom too), and individually controlled heat/air conditioning.

Standard rooms cost $90 to $145 a night for king-size or two double beds; with a larger sitting area the price is higher. In summer the room cost rises to $105 to $160. Ocean views (full or partial) and larger seating areas are what escalate the prices. If you want to have an extra cot, it will cost $10. The maximum number of persons per unit is four, but there's plenty of room (thanks to the Haddon Hall's spacious legacy). No pets are allowed, and all rates are based on double occupancy.

Note on Room Rates
   Atlantic City has a 12% luxury tax that is charged by all casino-hotels. Rates given here do *not* include the tax.

Sumptuous suites range from $245 to $400. A big Advent TV screen, wet bar, and private Jacuzzi are some of the extras the suite dweller gets.

The Resorts Bonanza Package Plans, available Sunday through Thursday nights, are offered year round for one, two, or three nights. The least expensive time of year is November through February, when a one-night package is $39.95, two nights are $83. In the most expensive season—July 1 to August 31—it's one night for $76, two nights for $127, and three nights for $192. All prices are per person, based on double occupancy, and taxes are additional. You'll get room, buffet meal(s), admission to the show in the Carousel Cabaret, a free visit to the health spa and use of all its facilities, and a round-trip tram ride on the Boardwalk.

The main entrance to Resorts is on North Carolina Avenue, where a uniformed doorman stands ready to greet you under the sidewalk-sheltering marquee. You'll find the registration desk right inside the revolving doors, facing the street. You won't be bored as you stand in line to register, though, as there are a house mime (Geordie) and a "robot" whose sole purpose is to entertain in the front lobby and outside the restaurants. A concierge/information desk up a few steps to your right will also hold your baggage.

The biggest names in American entertainment have performed at Resorts' 1,700-seat Superstar Theater: Johnny Mathis, Liberace, Julio Iglesias, Melissa Manchester, Don Rickles, Tom Jones, and Engelbert Humperdinck have packed in the crowds. The New York Philharmonic has appeared here, and in a historic performance, Luciano Pavarotti sang in a specially designed amphitheater tent. Nationally televised sports events—boxing matches and the Jimmy Connors tennis tournament—are also Resorts sponsored. Besides revue shows and headliners, there's live entertainment in the Rendezvous Lounge (lobby level) and the Casino Royale (off the casino floor).

Resorts' health-club facilities are on the third level, as is the swimming pool, whose retractable glass dome ensures year-round use. You can relax, winter or summer, in the yellow and white lounge chairs amid green plants and look out at the great ocean view. Universal-type machines will give you a strenuous workout, under skilled supervision; then you can unwind in the sauna or the unusual steam room, where Patti Lupone, among others, has inhaled the eucalyptus-oil-scented steam. Six private massage rooms ($35 for a half hour) complete the indoor facilities. Resorts' Dutch Treat cabaña is open on the beach from 10 a.m. to 6 p.m., June to September.

If there's extra change jangling in your pocket, go to the lobby level where boutiques purvey an expensive array of designer sportswear, shoes (Andrew Geller), jewelry, perfume, gifts. There's a James's saltwater taffy store on the Boardwalk. Up the escalator on the second level is a charming Antiquarian shop that has old posters, prints, and books, as well as all kinds of china, glass, and other small antiques.

Restaurants

Resorts' nine restaurants offer a variety of dining to suit your mood. The most expensive restaurants are on the third (dining) level, as is the pretty blue-and-white Wedgwood buffet room; the other eateries are on the lobby level. The consumption of food and beverages at Resorts is on a truly mind-boggling scale. In one year, for example, the popular menu items throughout the casino-hotel were shrimp (115,200 pounds), filet mignon (48,000 pounds), and a whopping 900,000 clams. For breakfast, a hearty 2½ million eggs and 101,600 pounds of bacon were served to hungry gamblers. A side dish of 644,000 pounds of potatoes (fried, baked, and mashed) was also consumed. But aside from these great quantities, Resorts food has great quality too.

Le Palais, the premier French restaurant, has a turn-of-the-century luxurious ambience. At the entrance you'll pass through two round-arched doorways flanked by potted flowers and trees. The room is beautifully appointed; there is a red tulip on each white-cloth-covered table, and white china with gold edging gleams. Red marble and mirrored columns shimmer with the reflected glow of the wall sconce/chandeliers that are spaced around the room. Across from the entrance, a white grand piano paired with a violin provide a soft accompaniment to the elegant meal.

The food is a combination of French classicism and fresh local produce, and it's really good. For example, first try the fresh baby scallops sautéed with mushrooms and Oriental spices ($7) or a traditional Caesar salad prepared tableside for two ($9). Recommendable main dishes include roast duckling with green cabbage and spicy apricot sauce ($20) or a grilled veal chop with endive and avocado butter ($24). You might opt for cheese and fruit or an airy soufflé for dessert. The dessert trolley, with chocolate mousse, fresh strawberries, and hand-whipped cream, and an array of freshly baked and decorated cakes and fruit tarts, is a severe temptation.

Le Palais is open for dinner only, from 6 p.m. to midnight Tuesday to Saturday. Reservations (tel. 340-6400) are advisable. Expect to pay about $90 and up for dinner for two.

A discreetly striped awning, an étagère gaily bedecked with plants and flowers, and a hand-wrought-iron door that could lead into the garden of an Italian villa mark the entrance to **Capriccio's.** A black-and-white-tile floor and a shiny espresso machine at the bar of the cocktail lounge precede your entrance into the first of three airy rooms. Walk past the pink-and-white-striped banquettes and the wall murals of 18th-century Italy to the oceanfront room, where stone statuary decorates the spaces between the round arched windows. At each table there's a pretty fringed lamp. Your meal might begin with a delicious antipasto or roasted peppers. You'll have a considerable choice of main courses. Among them are veal scaloppine topped with eggplant, tomatoes, and mozzarella ($21); chicken breast with scampi and capers in a cognac sauce; or tagliolini verdi carbonara (green noodles with prosciutto). Seafood entrees feature broiled swordfish, lobster tail in a spicy tomato sauce, or Mediterranean fish soup with lobster, mussels, scampi, clams, and vegetables. Thick slices of fresh honeydew melon provide a refreshing dessert. Or if you decide to throw caution to the winds, there's a three-tiered dessert trolley with calorie-laden pastries and creamy cakes. A full-bodied demitasse of Italian espresso coffee is the perfect end to this Roman banquet.

Capriccio serves dinner only, from 6 p.m. to midnight every night except Wednesday and Thursday. Per-person cost, with wine, will probably be at least $40. Reservations are recommended (tel. 340-6457).

Resorts carries on the tradition of the old Haddon Hall with **Camelot,** a Tudor-inspired dining room with high-backed chairs.

A green and blue tartan rug, the suits of armor standing in museum-like splendor, and lots of carved wood evoke the baronial setting of a medieval banquet hall. You may begin your feast, appropriately enough, with sliced sirloin Worthington, an impressive presentation of paper-thin slices of smoked beef, garnished with red onions, cornichons, and capers ($7.25). Prime rib, steaks, and lobster are the room's specialties. Calf's liver with crisp bacon and fried onions ($12.75) and baked salmon ($18.50) are other English-inspired entrees. Sherbet and ice cream, fresh fruit, or an attractive trolley full of desserts can add a sweet grace note to your meal; an Irish coffee is a fitting conclusion. With entrees ranging up to $29, you might pay from $40 for a full dinner.

Camelot is open for dinner from 6 p.m. to midnight. Closed Monday and Tuesday. Call 340-6450 for reservations.

The **House of Kyoto**, which has expansive ocean views, serves sophisticated Japanese cuisine for lunch (1 to 2:30 p.m.) and dinner (6 to 11 p.m.). Waitresses in kimonos walk softly among the wooden slat screens, stone lantern pedestals, and light-wood tables and chairs. All the authentic Japanese dishes—including tempura—are served. A sushi bar offers a fixed-price dinner assortment of 12 artfully arranged raw fish and vegetable tidbits for $12.50. A full dinner will cost about $25 and up per person.

The **Wedgwood Pavilion** offers sumptuous buffet-style dining. The menu changes daily, and there are seasonal and holiday special menus. A typical buffet lunch in the pretty blue and white surroundings might include an array of appetizing salad ingredients with dressings, cold meats and cheeses, several hot entrees, vegetables, fresh fruit, cakes, and beverages. Quite a spread for the price! A breakfast buffet is featured from 7 to 11 a.m. ($7.11); lunch is 11 a.m. to 6 p.m. and dinner is from 6 to 10 p.m. Sunday to Thursday, to midnight on Friday and Saturday ($9.50 and $12.50 respectively).

Outside the **Celebrity Deli,** set in concrete blocks along the Boardwalk are the handprints and handwritten comments of some of the celebrities who've played at Resorts. "Are you sure this is cake mix?" asked Joan Rivers. Rodney Dangerfield said, "I hope they don't put the rest of me in this." "Better my hands than my seat," commented Alan King. Inside, the colorful orange leather seats and green walls provide a cheerful backdrop for a raft of celebrity photos that will watch while you happily consume deli sandwiches (hot pastrami is $6.25), served with coleslaw, a stuffed cabbage platter ($6.95), or a therapeutic bowl of chicken soup with matzoh balls ($2.25). Smoked fish, eggs, salad platters, bagels with the usual accompaniments are also offered, not to mention apple strudel, New York–style cheesecake, and Dr. Brown's Cel-Ray tonic.

The Celebrity Deli (tel. 340-6452) is open from 11 a.m. to 10 p.m. weekdays, to 2 a.m. on Friday and Saturday.

Also conveniently accessible from either the Boardwalk or the Resorts' lobby, the **Frusen Gladjé Ice Cream Parlor** (tel. 340-6807) is all spick-and-span white-tiled floors and white ceilings, with chrome and sky-blue chairs at little round ice-cream tables. All sorts of sweet treats, concocted from tart sorbets (lemon, orange, and raspberry) or creamy ice-cream flavors, are what's on here.

All the casino-hotels have at least one 24-hour eatery, and Resorts' is just five steps away from the casino floor. Bright yellow walls, yellow and green print booths, hanging plants, and white globe lamps give this coffeeshop a summery and sunny feeling. In addition to the obligatory coffeeshop sandwiches, soups, and breakfast fare, the **Café Casino** has some Chinese specialties— lemon chicken and pepper steak with tomatoes, to name a few of the entrees, which range in price from $7 to $19. American-style entrees are also offered for dinner.

The **Oyster Bar** is also near the casino floor, right next to the Rendezvous Lounge. You can get a quick snack of clams or oysters ($4.75 a half dozen), oyster stew ($5.50), or clam chowder ($1.75 and $3). If seafood isn't your favorite snack, you can have a tasty bowl of chili ($3).

The Oyster Bar is open noon to midnight on weekdays, to 4 a.m. on weekends.

Future Projects

Envisioned for Resorts' future is a 42-story hotel tower extravaganza to be built across Pennsylvania Avenue from the present site. Resorts II would have a casino projected to be the largest in the world, nine restaurants, convention facilities, and a disco. An enclosed bridge over the Boardwalk will lead to a renovated Steel Pier family entertainment center.

There's little doubt that Resorts' owners are keeping their bets on Atlantic City.

HARRAH'S MARINA: Harrah's Marina, 1725 Brigantine Blvd., Atlantic City, NJ 08401 (tel. toll free 800/2-HARRAH'S, or 609/441-5000).

Harrah's was the first casino-hotel to take advantage of the lovely marshland area at Absecon Inlet. The graceful concrete structure sits on 11 bayfront acres by Brigantine Boulevard, with the pleasure craft of summer docking practically at the front entrance. Jitneys offer a ten-minute connection to the Boardwalk at Brighton Park, and Harrah's is worth the trip. Or else you can drive directly—one of Harrah's strong points is free parking, valet or self, for guests. A 2,400-car covered garage gives convenient, sheltered access to the hotel via a second-floor walkway.

A wall mural of blue and white sailboats reminds you of Harrah's nautical setting as you approach the white pipe-rack and glass marquee at the main entrance. Harrah's own boardwalk, a baywalk, skirts the waterfront where the dockside marina (tel. 441-5315) has slips for about 110 boats. These boating guests can use all the hotel's facilities, including room service, even though they sleep aboard ship. Docking fees vary according to the size of the boat, and slips are available on a daily, monthly, or seasonal basis.

Added to the original 506-room hotel is a 15-story Atrium Hotel Tower, which has 250 suites. In each suite the bedroom overlooks either the Atlantic City skyline or the bay area, and the living rooms face an enclosed courtyard atrium. Harrah's has a relaxed, modern ambience. You'll enter past two sets of glass doors, each eight panels wide, to the lobby concourse. The registration area is to your right, the casino a few steps down to your left. Behind the pink marble counter with an incised shell motif border, stretches a rough-textured wall hanging irregularly banded with pastel swaths of blue, pink, yellow, and orange. You won't have much time to ponder whether you're gazing at an abstract land- or seascape, as the service is quick and attentive. On an earlier visit to Harrah's I saw superb antique cars from Harrah's world-famous collection in Reno on display in the lobby. More recently the front lobby held a display of old slot machines. One, dating back to 1938, was called Trap the Snake; three snakes took the jackpot (20 nickels). Later I came upon two shiny antique models behind the shopping arcade.

The casino itself is a conventional, single-level box of dark reds and deep green, with polished wood paneling and brass trim. A row of tivoli lights—great clusters of pencil-thin tubes of tiny lights—illuminates the casino's center aisle. The minimum bets on table games range from $3 to $500. Harrah's has slot machines of every coin denomination except pennies, and it also has all the latest variations of the basic slots theme: video slots, video blackjack, video poker, and a special area for progressive slots, with a moving neon sign that lets you watch the jackpot ante moving up. On the 44,698-square-foot casino floor there are 2 baccarat tables, 3 big-six wheels, 12 roulette tables, 22 craps tables, 60 black-jack tables, and 1305 slots.

Slot machine players near the Bay Cabaret can pull the handle in tune with the continuous live music that's so close to the casino floor. Service there begins at 1 p.m. and continues till casino closing. At the other end of the casino the Winner's Circle lounge also purveys drinks, but you can slake your thirst right on the casino floor from the cocktail servers whose complimentary offerings are just a request away. Harrah's also offers entertainment in the Atrium lounge and the 850-seat Broadway-by-the-Sea Theater (tickets are available at a special box office). Seven restaurants can satisfy your every dining whim.

Also on the lobby floor are a giftshop that sells newspapers and magazines, a jewelry store, and emporia for men's and women's sportswear. And that's not all the facilities Harrah's has to offer! There's a beauty salon on the third level, reachable by escalator or elevator. Teenagers and children of Harrah's visitors have an especially attractive place to go—Lucy's Marina Fun Center. It's a good-size area with comfortable red leather seating, all kinds of games (tabletop shuffleboard, pinball, video), a wide-screen television set, and a snackbar stylishly furnished in blond wood and yellow leather. Next door to Lucy's is a supervised children's center where youngsters from ages 2 to 8 are cared for, free of charge, from 10 a.m. to 6 p.m. There are three paddle tennis courts, an enclosed, heated swimming pool, and an exercise room with the latest Nautilus equipment on the fourth floor, as are six shuffleboard courts and a sundeck for open-air lounging. If golf's your game, the guest services department will set you up at the nearby Brigantine Golf Club.

The standard guest rooms at Harrah's are all decorated in pastel tones of green, blue, or yellow. Matching draperies and bedspreads, rugs, club chairs, cable color TV/radio units, and expansive views make for comfortable and attractive accommodations. There are marble vanities in the color-coordinated bathrooms and a good supply of amenities, including shower caps, shoe mitts, special soaps, etc.

A standard room, with either one king-size or two double beds, costs from $80 to $115 in the winter, $90 to $125 in spring and summer. You can expect to pay the higher rates on weekends and on higher floors. Midweek packages are available; be sure to ask for the current offering. Atrium Tower one-bedroom suites are $110 to $135 in winter, $120 to $155 in spring and summer.

In the VIP suites (all on higher floors) the one-bedroom offerings have sophisticated mauve and gray furnishings. Round couches, glass breakfronts, concealed entertainment centers with TV, etc., and wet bars are some of the extras that command a $300-per-night price tag.

Although Harrah's is not equipped to house your pet, there is a nearby kennel they'll contact for you.

Restaurants

Dinner in an elegant French restaurant? Or do you hunger for a sizzling steak? Or does an all-you-can-eat buffet in a snappy modern room sound appealing? You can try all that—and more —right here at Harrah's by sampling the fare at its seven restaurants.

The Meadows, located on the second level, is well known for deft service, fine food, and a breathtaking window wall with a view to neighboring Brigantine. The decor is elegant, with plushly upholstered armchairs, wall coverings, and carpeting in harmonizing shades of beige, plum, and deep blue. These colors are picked up in the pretty watercolors of lily pads that adorn the end walls. The room has two levels, and each level has leather banquettes and smaller tables. There are pots of mums and wicker-covered pots of ivy between the two levels, and hanging plants along the window wall.

When you see your water glass being filled (and refilled) with Evian water, your sweet butter served in the shape of a jolly duck atop crushed ice in a little silver bowl, and a warm loaf of sourdough bread wrapped in a white napkin and presented on a neat little butcher-block board, you'll know this will be no ordinary "gourmet" meal. Appetizers, hot or cold (priced from $7 to $12), come first, and you might choose a classic, French escargots or frogs' legs. Soups and salads are offered next ($3.25 to $4.75). Preceding your entree is a complimentary sorbet. The entree might be salmon, veal with mushrooms, or tournedos Rossini ($17 to $38). A special wine list and dessert, from the pastry cart, a special house crêpe, or imported cheeses, round out the meal.

The Meadows is open for dinner from 6 p.m. to midnight, seven days a week. Reservations are suggested (tel. 441-5050).

Andreotti's purveys northern Italian cuisine in a relaxed setting highlighted by decorative latticework. The chef specializes in homemade pastas, and ravioli stuffed with red snapper is one of the unique offerings. From antipasto to dolce, the menu offers top quality. Expect to pay from $40 up for a three-course meal. Open Friday to Tuesday for dinner only from 6 p.m. to midnight; reservations are encouraged (tel. 441-5000).

The Steakhouse, in a setting of dark-wood paneling and etched glass, has the traditional American favorite—beef—plus a choice selection of seafood and some lamb entrees as well. If you opt for a steak, it will be prepared over a mesquite grill that imparts a delicious smoky savor to the meat. There's an unusually good selection of domestic wines to complement the all-American fare. Open for dinner Wednesday through Sunday 5:30 p.m. to 12:30 a.m.

The Deli, on the first floor of the hotel, typifies the warmth of the New York delicatessen. Matzo ball soup, corned beef and pastrami sandwiches, chicken or flanken in a pot, and real potato pancakes have that old-time taste. Open for lunch and dinner daily 11 a.m. to 11 p.m., until 2 a.m. Saturday and Sunday.

Bring a hearty appetite to **The Buffet** so you can do justice to the lavish spread at this colorful, contemporary room. It's an open, airy place, with glazed red ceramic tile walls, light-colored bentwood chairs with red leather seats, and light-wood tables with red tile tops. Once you've paid for your lunch ($8.95) or dinner ($11.95), and have been shown to a table, head right for the buffet, where one night's dinner consisted of mixed green salad, tomatoes, cottage cheese, creamed herring, egg salad, meat salad, fresh fruit salad, macaroni salad, broccoli, mashed potatoes, sausages with peppers, breast of chicken, roast beef, Oriental rice, stuffed flounder, chocolate mousse, carrot cake, fruit tarts, and all the coffee you could drink. On Friday a seafood buffet with shrimp, king crab, etc., costs $12.95 at lunch, $15.95 for dinner. The Buffet's all-you-can-eat champagne brunch every Sunday from 9:30 a.m. to noon is justly famous at $9.95.

The Buffet's lunch is served from 11 a.m. to 5:30 p.m. daily; dinner is from 5:30 to 11 p.m.

The **Food Bazaar** is the best-looking fast-food, self-service restaurant I've ever seen. The view is just super—it's below the Meadows and has the same expansive vista at street level. The food counters are color-coded: green is over the deli section; blue at soups, sandwiches, hot dogs, and burgers; purple leads to pizza; orange at beer and wine; and yellow is ice cream and desserts. There's white garden-type furniture, and snake plants separate the self-service counters from the dining area. Sandwiches cost $5 to $6, and a hot-fudge sundae is $1.95. (Don't ask how I know that last one!)

Marina Garden is the requisite 24-hour coffeeshop, offering everything from chicken in a basket and fried flounder to blueberry pancakes, and freshly baked pies and cakes. Dinner entrees range from $8 to $17.50. You can watch the boats docking as you munch away if you sit near the floor-to-ceiling windows.

GOLDEN NUGGET: Golden Nugget, Boston at Pacific Avenues on the Boardwalk, Atlantic City, NJ 08401 (tel. toll free 800/257-8677 or 609/347-7111).

The man whose vision and financial acumen launched the Golden Nugget, Steve Wynn, now chairman of the board, oversees his kingdom with a real showman's flair. As we went to press most of the lobby was under wraps, in a state of refurbishing that was slated to become "the most exquisite shops in Atlantic City." We have no doubt that it will emerge exactly as promised.

At night the Nugget's two-story-high round arched windows are lit up around an entire ocean blockfront, as is the central hotel tower.

The Golden Nugget has 514 guest rooms and suites, and every last one of them has an ocean or bay view. The standard rooms have either a king-size or two double beds in a decor based on a variety of tropical pastel hues.

Rates go from $110 to $180 in the winter (mid-September to March), from $120 to $190 in summer (April to mid-September). Children under 12 may sleep in their parents' room at no extra charge; otherwise there is an extra-person charge of $10 for each guest over double occupancy.

Probably the ultimate bargain offered is the package plan called the Elegant Escape, from Sunday to Thursday, November to March. Accommodations for one night and two days at the Golden Nugget, one $10 food and beverage credit coupon redeemable in any on-premises restaurant, and $5 in tokens are $49 per person, double occupancy. Deluxe accommodations for one night in a high-priced room makes this worthwhile. Then there's also a 50% discount on admission to the Opera House Theater, hotel room tax included (and that's a hefty 12%, remember), and free use of the pool, sauna, steam bath, and exercise room. If you have three days, I can't think of a better buy than the Victorian Vacation package, for a Sunday to Thursday, three-day/two-night stay at $99 per person, double occupancy. This package must be prepaid before you arrive, but here's what will be waiting for you: two $10 food and beverage credits, $5 in tokens, a Golden Nugget T-shirt, plus other complimentary services (not least of which is that the hotel room tax is included).

These prices are reasonable for what you get. Rooms are cheerful and bright with tropical colors on a restful beige background. They are illuminated by the brilliant ocean view or, at night, the handsome chandeliers. Each room has a bedside telephone (plus one in the bathroom), lots of table lamps, a cable color TV/FM/AM unit, and colored lithographs. The closets have mirrored sliding doors. Luxury continues into the bathroom, where a large marble corner sink displays a bountiful supply of guest amenities—shampoo, hand lotion, perfumed soaps, a sewing kit, shoe horn, etc.—that are replenished daily.

Suites range from $160 to $200 and up. The Gatsby suites, on floors 16 to 19, are an Art Deco symphony in peach and black, with every last detail in keeping with the period theme. These cost $250 per unit.

For true sybarites, the two end suites on the 22nd floor are the epitome of sophistication in a snazzy combination of black glass and brass, not to mention the 12 super-large suites, each themed to a different sign of the zodiac. In the zodiac suites you can expect to loll beneath a glass ceiling on a bed with a Lalique glass headboard. Most luxurious of these ultra-opulent digs are the Oriental-motif President's Apartment and the Chairman's Victorian Apartment. The lucky occupants of these two splendiferous suites can wallow in personalized bathrobes, individual component stereo systems, remote control TVs in each bedroom and living area, a Jacuzzi, private saunas, and a king's ransom in art and antiques. And . . . there's a butler in attendance 24 hours a day.

Six restaurants, several cocktail lounges, and a wide variety of entertainment options, including renowned headliners, are some of the facilities that the Nugget offers. And that's not the whole story.

The casino, which takes up the major portion of the ground floor, is mythic Americana, ragtime version. There's a Victorian-print red carpet under foot and a ceiling above with a mirrored-tile recessed coffer from which the most elaborate chandeliers in town hang. The gaming tables are red topped and brass trimmed; even the slot machines are brass. It seems to be all golden in tone. The casino takes up 40,717 square feet, and holds 57 blackjack tables, 20 craps tables, 10 roulette wheels, 2 baccarat tables, and 4 big-six wheels. Thirty percent of the casino's square footage is devoted to the 1,200 slot machines. The slots have the latest progressive jackpot machines in various denominations. There's a separate video poker room. One of the world's largest jackpots, I'm told, $1¼ million, was paid here. Many of the employees are in costume, which heightens the period-decor effect, and there is a lounge near the casino floor, the Rangoon Saloon.

There's no dearth of sports facilities here. The enclosed swimming pool, 28 by 40 feet, is protected from the elements by windowed walls and a white roof with a recessed skylight that is bordered by a lovely mural of flowered garlands. Hanging plants with pink and white flowers, white stone statuary and urns of flowers, white beach chairs and tables, and a white brick floor around the pool provide a wonderful garden-like setting for your swim. Also on the third floor, the health-club facilities have Universal gyms, large saunas, whirlpool tubs and steam baths—with separate but equal facilities for men and women. A sundeck and snackbar complete the floor.

There's fun for all ages in the Arcade, which has a good selection of electronic games near the Boardwalk. Across the lobby near the casino entrance at the Garden Court is the Emporium, specializing in newspapers, magazines, T-shirts, and other sundries and small gift items.

Restaurants

The high-quality food at the Golden Nugget is famous in Atlantic City. The food is excellent, whether you're enjoying one of the culinary productions at the Victoria or helping yourself to the abundant salad bar at Charlie's steakhouse or the popular Cornucopia Buffet. This last is so popular, in fact, that double lines during lunch and dinner hours extend around the second floor. (If you're a guest at the hotel, step up and tell the hostess; you won't have to wait in the longer line.)

Victoria's is the fine French restaurant here, located on the second floor. The decor is elegant, the mood restrained. A maître d' is on hand to greet you in the entrance foyer, which is covered with a stained-glass dome. The opulence of gold and mirrored columns standing among huge banks of flowers is counterbalanced by the subtly colored woven wall tapestries and dark-green shaded bulbs of the crystal chandeliers.

The menu is divided into eight mouthwatering categories: savouries, silver tureen, fresh greens, fish and crustaceans, lamb and beef, specialties, dessert and cheeses, and *les cafés*. In case you haven't guessed by now, savouries are appetizers, and you'll choose from the likes of baked clams, lobster with red caviar sauce, or frogs' legs niçoise (in Nice they prepare frog legs like this: pan fried with shallots and garlic, deglazed with lemon juice, finished in brown butter, a sprinkle of crushed croutons and parsley, and served with a tomato fondu flavored with basil). Now that's a culinary production! Your silver tureen could hold consommé Monte Carlo, velouté of mushroom, or (my favorite) Beefeater gin tomato. A gourmet salad may please—heart of palm, or radicchio, Boston and lamb's lettuce, perhaps. Seafood comes sautéed (sole) or poached (an interesting fresh lobster and vegetable combination). Lamb and beef entrees are simply prepared and very hearty. As for the specials, there are casserole of pheasant, duckling Chambord, and breast of chicken with a secret sauce. All entrees are garnished with potatoes and the best of the day's market vegetables. After this kind of feast, I'd opt for fruit for dessert. The less-disciplined, of course, could opt for a chocolate mousse, an ice-cream parfait, or a moist and rich slice of cake from the artistically bedecked pastry cart. Spanish, Brazilian, Victorian, espresso, regular, or decaffeinated coffee are *les cafés*. The wine list is extensive—and expensive. In fact, with savouries in the $10 range, main dishes at least $20, and desserts around $6, dinner, without wine, will be about $50 and up, and worth it.

Victoria's is open for dinner seven days a week from 6 p.m. to 1 a.m. Call for reservations (tel. 340-7230).

Stefano's has a delightful Italian garden setting. It's bright and cheerful with huge hand-painted Italian ceramics, ivy plants, and white columns decorated in the manner of a Tuscan villa. The appetizer trolley offers an interesting selection of hors d'oeuvres, which you might follow with a classic fettuccine Alfredo. Fish, veal, and chicken entrees all are prepared with an Italian flair, and you may want to have the toasted garlic bread as an added treat. Top off your feast with cassata ice-cream cake, and you may just have enough room for a swallow of strong Italian espresso. Expect to pay from $40 and up for your meal. Stefano's is open for dinner from 6 p.m. to midnight.

Lillie Langtry's doesn't sound Chinese, but it is, and it serves some of the best Cantonese food anywhere. The dining room is exquisitely decorated—hand-painted wallpaper depicts scenes of Chinese court life of some imaginary dynasty, and there are authentic antique Chinese porcelains placed around the room. The colors are deep red—the Oriental rug, tablecloths and napkins—and a contrasting tan—the gold-banded dinner service. Handsome wooden columns, etched-glass panels, and plush banquettes add to the feeling of opulence.

The staff here is exceptionally welcoming, and when the food arrives you'll know you're an honored guest. You might start with crab Rangoon, a deep-fried wonton filled with crabmeat, cream cheese, and chopped scallions, or have a taste of everything with assorted tidbits (spare ribs, fried shrimp, eggroll, paper-wrapped chicken, and crab Rangoon). Shark's-fin soup is a specialty, and you'll have a wide selection of beef, poultry, and seafood specialties. Ba chen duck is one possibility; it's braised boneless duck, served with barbecued pork, shrimp, sea scallops, and vegetables. Fried bananas, lichees and Chinese gooseberry cake are among the desserts. Tsingtao beer from China and plum and dry white Chinese wines are stocked. Entrees start at $10, and a full dinner could be about $30.

Open for dinner daily from 6 p.m. to 1 a.m., Lillie Langtry's suggests you call and reserve your table (tel. 340-7220).

Across from Lillie Langtry's is **Charlie's,** the Golden Nugget's 168-seat steakhouse. It's all rawther British, with a small-paned glass front, and a mural of an English country landscape that appears to be right outside. Waiters are in 1890s outfits, which seem to go well with the hammered-copper canopies and brass-leaved oak tree that is Charlie's logo. Chippendale chairs, wooden tables with polished tops and red placemats, and attractive table lamps reinforce the English tone.

Whatever you choose to eat, your meal will include rolls, soup of the day (help yourself from the copper kettle), and crisp greens and such from the salad bar. If you just want soup and salad bar fixings, your tab will be $7.25. The menu also includes prime beef cuts—T-bone, filet mignon, sirloin, rib, etc.—plus fish and lobster. Desserts are substantial too: peanut butter or banana cream pie, chocolate swirl cheesecake, to name a few. There's draft beer and a house wine to accompany the meal. A full dinner at Charlie's could range from $35 upward.

Charlie's is open for lunch from 11:30 a.m., for dinner from 6 p.m., seven days. You can reserve ahead (tel. 340-7480).

The **Cornucopia Café,** which has a bright ocean view, shares its cheerfully executed Victorian space with the adjacent Cornucopia Buffet. From ceiling to floor of both these establishments there's not an inch of ungilded, unpainted, unmuraled, unbeflowered space. Blue wrought-iron chairs, blue floral banquettes, little pots of ivy on the tables, are in the Buffet. The Café has a stunning stained-glass ceiling inset; the rest of the ceiling is encrusted with decorative gold wreaths and vines, with glass chandeliers taking up the slack.

The 24-hour Café has it all—from a good all-day breakfast menu (eggs Benedict, omelets, corned beef hash) to hearty deli sandwiches or a good tuna melt (topped with mozzarella), lots of salads, pastas, steaks and other entrees, and desserts—either at the counter or tables. Your breakfast could be as little as $3, your dinner not much more than $20, and there are a lot of choices in between.

The **Cornucopia Buffet** offers a brunch from 10:30 a.m. to 3

p.m. for $9, and dinner from 5 p.m. to late evening
One recent evening the all-you-can-eat spread consist
green salad, coleslaw, potato salad, lentil salad, cold win
sliced ham and turkey, cheeses, fried chicken, rice, spareribs,
corn, roast beef, seafood Newburg with great chunks of crabmeat, lobster, and shrimp, Jell-O, strawberry cake with whipped
cream, apple crumb cake, bread pudding, fresh fruit, cheesecake, and chocolate cake. Shall we loosen our belts?

In summer the Buffet sometimes has special spreads—
Chinese, ranch barbecue, and seafood have been featured.

On the Boardwalk you can kiss (or have a snack) in the **Sweetheart Café,** open 11 a.m. to midnight. If thoughts of love pro-
voked by a red and white decor of lovebirds and hearts etched in
glass don't make you forget to eat, you can have great fried chick-
en nuggets, pizza, burgers, and such here.

If your idea of romance is spelled Häagen-Dazs, the **Cream-
ery,** right across the way from the Sweetheart Café, is a picturesque turn-of-the-century style ice-cream parlor. From a scoop
to a sundae, what's your pleasure?

**TROPICANA: Tropicana, Iowa Avenue at the Boardwalk, Atlantic
City, NJ 08401 (tel. toll free 800/228-2828, or 609/340-4000).**

Like a ziggurat married to an air control tower, Ramada's
Tropicana steps up and away from the Boardwalk in a series of
white concrete and dark glass horizontal bands, balconies, and
terraces. The exciting configuration incorporates much of the
steel framework of the former Ambassador Hotel as well as the
site of the old Diplomat Hotel. There's lots of space here, at this
desirable Boardwalk location where the Tropicana occupies two
oceanfront blocks. The Trop's dual hotel heritage has be-
queathed it a private street entrance, between Iowa and Brighton
Avenues, over which the unified new hotel rises. On one side of
this sheltered street is the hotel lobby entrance, where you can
leave your car for valet parking (free for guests) or have a bell-
man take your bags into the lobby while you park at the public
garage (free for hotel guests) at Brighton and Pacific Avenues.

Across the private street from the lobby is Tropicana's Promenade, an attraction in itself. From the cowboy boots, Stetson
hats, and suede and leather garments at J.C. Western Wear to the
handmade sequined sweaters at Talk of the Walk and the fine col-
lectibles at Abel's jewelers, you'll see lots of unique specialty
items at the Promenade shops.

Not much happens in the rosy-marbled lobby area (except for
hotel registration). It's furnished handsomely but sparingly with

few Chinese pieces. There are few seats—we all know where the management would like you to hang out. The casino is an escalator ride up from the lobby, on the second level where you'll find the hotel's restaurants. The Chinese Jade Beach Restaurant is on the Boardwalk level near the shopping Promenade. There are three lounges on the second level and a showroom is on the third level. A comedy room that showcases new talent is near the lobby, on the first floor. Twenty floors up (I'd go on one of the three glass-walled elevators that give you a ride equalled only by the glass elevators of the Eiffel Tower in Paris) is the fourth lounge, Top of the Trop, where a cocktail at sunset is one of Atlantic City's most thrilling experiences. The view, from all four sides, is just magnificent.

Back down on earth, but not earthbound, is a dramatic, six-story, skylit atrium that provides space for the gaily striped display of enormous cold air balloons. The atrium provides lots of light and air for the casino, which is, by Atlantic City standards, not very splashy, although it does have mirrored columns, golden lights, a red-figured carpet, and a chandelier or two. The casino is among the larger in town, 50,873 square feet, and has 1,452 slot machines, including video poker, and progressive slots with mounting jackpots and mini Berthas. There are 119 gaming tables: 76 blackjack, 26 craps, 11 roulette, 3 big-six, and 3 baccarat. There is a slot machine lounge overlooking the casino floor.

To keep its day bus-trippers' patronage in the winter, the Trop has a Coach Club that offers discounts on bus tickets, cash bonuses, and shopping credits redeemable from November to February. To join the "Club," there's no membership fee, you just have to be a regular bus patron. Drive-in guests or locals can join Trop One Diamond Club. For a $25 membership fee they receive discounts on rooms, entertainment, dining, or Promenade shopping. Gaming tournaments are also popular at the Trop.

The Tropicana opened in 1981 with 515 guest rooms, including 52 theme suites: American modern, California, Dallas, French, Italian, Scandinavian, traditional English, and Oriental. I peeked into the gray-and-plum-colored magnificence of the duplex American modern suite and saw acres of chrome, glass, and steel. The Italian suite was a vision of black marble with all the accoutrements of a luxury apartment. (Rates given on request.)

The standard rooms are extremely attractive, handsomely furnished, and offer ocean views either to the south or north. The color scheme is sophisticated and low key. Some have plum, soft gray, or blue upholstery and matching bedspreads and draperies printed in an abstract design using the aforementioned colors.

Many standard rooms are large enough to accommodate a sofa and coffee table, along with the writing desk, chair, and dresser. There are mirrored sliding doors for the closet and a separate dressing room area with a roomy vanity sink outside the bath for added convenience. The Tropicana is right up there with the guest amenities—aloe vera shampoo, bath gelée, and cocoa butter soap are among the luxurious extras. Every room has color TV, phone, and individual heat and air-conditioning controls.

Room rates are based on time of year and Monday to Thursday versus weekend occupancy. In winter the rates are $95 midweek, $125 weekend. Summer rates are $135 midweek, $155 weekends. Fall and spring rates are $105 and $135. There's a $10 charge for an additional person in your room; children under 18 may sleep free in a room with an adult.

The Tropicana offers several package plans. The Winter Adventure is available Sunday through Thursday, November to April, priced at $48.50 for one night and $84.50 for two nights, based on double occupancy. The package includes accommodations, meal credits ($10 or $20), $10 casino bonus, a Trop gift, and other discount coupons; also included are taxes, tips, and baggage handling. Spring and fall packages are also offered at about $10 more per person per night.

Right at the Tropicana are two outdoor tennis courts, paddle tennis, and an outdoor pool overlooking the ocean on the sixth floor. The health-club facilities include a Universal exercise machine, Exercycle, solarium, and sauna.

Restaurants

Les Paris is a real jewel of a restaurant. Its colors are gray and pink, and there's perfection in every last detail, from the Lenox china to the crystal wine and water goblets and the striking fresh flower arrangements that are the centerpieces of this softly lit, 54-seat room. There's a handsome lounge for predinner imbibing and, as you might expect, prices match this rarified ambience. Appetizer prices, for example, fall in the $9 to $14 category, like smoked Scottish salmon or terrine of pheasant. There are tempting fish, meat, and poultry entrees. Among your choices are Dover sole, roast duck, veal with morels. Desserts are classically French—fruit jubilee, chocolate or Grand Marnier soufflés, or pastries. With entrees ranging from $22 to $40, the tab for two would be around $100, not including wine.

Les Paris is open for dinner only, 6 p.m. to midnight. Call 340-4060 for reservations.

The **Regent Court** adjoins Les Paris, and it's a somewhat less formal room—and the price is a bit less intimidating too. The setting is reminiscent of an English country manor: handsome brass chandeliers, blue banquettes, an open fireplace. The tables are set with English ironstone with pewter accessories, like the little vase with fresh flowers on each table and the pewter water goblet. Each table is served an individual loaf of fresh warm bread and a bountiful crock of butter. Steak and seafood are the fare here, with some other typically English entrees like lamb chops. From the traditional appetizers, shrimp cocktail, or seafood chowder, for example, to the calorie-laden desserts, such as a slice of chocolate cake with vanilla rum sauce, you'll pay about $35 to $45 for a satisfying meal. Two strawberries freshly dipped in chocolate are the house's way of saying thank you for dropping in.

The Regent Court is open seven days a week for dinner only, from 6 p.m. to midnight. Reservations are requested (tel. 340-4080).

Il Verdi means "the green" in Italian, and that should be your clue to finding the way to Tropicana's restaurant that features northern Italian cuisine. The setting is lush and relaxing. At the entrance is a green marble fountain, ornately carved wall mirrors reflect green upholstered chairs, and plants and fine china help keep Il Verdi green. Hot or cold appetizers can start you off in the right direction. Mussels in marinara sauce is a good starter. Pasta is a specialty, and you'll have a hard time deciding among linguine with clam sauce, tortellini in cream sauce, or fettuccine Alfredo. A spinach salad might precede your entree. There are some unusual dishes and some tried-and-true favorites here. Seafood lovers would enjoy the shrimp in a garlic wine sauce. Carnivorous types would find the tender sirloin of beef pizzaiola a tasty morsel, or perhaps veal scaloppine with shallots and mushrooms would be a tempting choice. Zabaglione is a fitting conclusion for this hearty meal; also available are fruit compote, strawberry mousse, a tempting display of tarts and pastries, and assorted ice cream and sherbet flavors. With entrees in the $25 range, a full dinner here will be at least $40 minimum.

Il Verdi, like the Tropicana's other top restaurants, is open for dinner only, 6 p.m. to midnight. Phone 340-4070 for reservations.

Summerfields Buffet is recommended for big eaters; there is a lunch spread from 11 a.m. to 4:45 p.m. for $8.95, and dinner is laid out from 5 p.m. to late evening for $12.95.

Here's what I found at their all-you-can-eat table one evening: assorted salads and cold cuts, roast beef, chicken, stuffed cabbage, flounder, vegetables, and assorted cakes, pies, and puddings. When you take a breather, you'll have a fine ocean view to admire in this very handsomely decorated room of light wood, beige and green print banquettes, and very accommodating servers who bring around the wine or coffee or tea that is included in the price of your meal.

At the **Back Stage** you'll find New York–style deli fare. A wall of windows lets you watch the ocean and Boardwalk below as you enjoy an overstuffed sandwich or hot platter. The Back Stage's specialties include homemade soup and deep-dish beef stew. Hearty hot sandwiches like a pastrami or corned beef, or a smoked fish platter, or chef's salad, are really a complete meal in themselves. Open from 11 a.m. to 10 p.m. (around 6 p.m. in slower times), the Back Stage has prices from $1.50 for that bowl of soup to $6.95 for the beef stew. Very reasonable indeed!

The **Brasserie Coffee Shop** is open 24 hours and has a pleasant, garden-like setting with white trellises at the entrance. It's very crowded at mealtimes, and you'll probably have to wait in line for a table. At any hour of the day or night you can order sandwiches or an all-American steakburger (all are $5.75 each). Chicken in the basket, broiled fish, and other entrees range from $7 to $17 (for sirloin steak). There are also salads, eggs, and omelets. And for dessert, apple strudel and cheesecake can't be beat.

C. W. Sweet, the famous ice-cream, sundae, milkshake, and cookie emporium, is on the street level at the Boardwalk.

ATLANTIS CASINO HOTEL: Florida Avenue and the Boardwalk, Atlantic City, NJ 08404 (tel. toll free 800/257-8672, or 609/344-4000).

No longer are those familiar rabbit ears affixed to the 22-story glass-sheathed tower at Florida Avenue and the Boardwalk. In March 1984 Playboy Enterprises relinquished control of its Atlantic City hotel-casino to the Elsinore Corporation, and the new owners changed the property's name and logo in the summer of 1984.

A multi-million-dollar renovation underway when the new owners took over has been completed. The hotel complex actually consists of two structures: the six-story theater building on one side of Florida Avenue and the 22-story tower building across the street. Two 57-foot-long glass-enclosed skywalks (one for guests, one for services) connect the two buildings. Inside the tower building's Boardwalk entrance, the lobby decor, in shades of rose and burgundy, Italian marble floors, glittering chandeliers, and glass and brass-trimmed columns emblazoned with a shell motif, gives visitors a palatial welcome. The lobby is long on dazzle but short on seats, so unless you want to pop into the lobby-level Garden State Café, the 24-hour coffeeshop, you'll go along to the escalator, where you'll have a fine window view of the ocean as you're wafted up to casino levels I, II, or III.

Due to the small-sized lot on which the hotel was built, the tower building has three small casino levels instead of the wide-open spaces other casinos have chosen. Seeking to take best advantage of its trilevel casino with three different gaming experiences, Atlantis has on level III the Salon, which is set aside for the higher limit players. The salon is richly decorated. You'll see gold leaf, rose-colored marble, etched glass, the hand-cut prisms of Venetian crystal chandeliers, and the seashell motif on the walls, carpets, and upholstery in tones of peach, rose, and burgundy. In the Salon Privé are the traditional table games: 2 baccarat, 1 roulette, 4 craps, and 14 blackjack, plus a slots area. Within a few steps is a cocktail lounge, Le Club.

The **Shangri-la Casino** on level II is handsomely adorned with all sorts of Chinoiserie—great Fu dogs, including a beautiful green ceramic one made in China for the casino, Oriental lattice-work, lamps, and screens.

On casino level I the hotel would like you to feel as though you're in 1910 New Orleans aboard a Mississippi riverboat, and a gigantic riverboat "movie set" heightens the illusion. Hand-painted murals, ship's-wheel patterned carpet, and stained-glass domes give authenticity to the decor. All three casino levels total 51,516 square feet, and there are a total of 92 table games—61 blackjack, 16 craps, 9 roulette, 3 big-six, and 3 baccarat—plus over 1,300 slot machines.

If your game is slots, Atlantis has a club for players of their Reel Winners slot machines. Tokens are dispensed at regular intervals during play and ten Reel Tokens makes you a member. Club members may then exchange Reel Tokens for booklets with discount certificates for the hotel's restaurants, lounges, and even hotel accommodations.

Atlantis's guest rooms are on floors 6 through 21. The rates for a room with either a king-size or two double beds range from a low of $80 (November to February, midweek, bayview) to a high of $145 (June 29 through September 2, ocean view, weekend). Higher rates, in general, apply to summer, on weekends, and ocean views. Add $12 for a third person occupying a room. The guest rooms feature color TV, individually controlled air conditioning and heat, and phones in bedroom and bath. Contemporary and comfortable are the buzz words for the rooms; there are soft rugs, deep armchairs, roomy closets, and well-lit vanities throughout. Some rooms have Murphy beds that disappear into the wall so you can have a parlor in the daytime, a bedroom at night. It's also possible for a family or party of four to get adjoining rooms and create a suite with a convertible parlor and regular bedroom. (Rates are given on request.)

The ultra-luxurious suites are concentrated on the 21st floor. They're rarely available to the general public (the hotel likes to keep them for high rollers' use), but when they are, winter rates are from $300 a night and up. The Victorian Suite carries out the period theme with a carved Victorian sofa and chairs, brass lamps, marble-topped tables, and a flowered carpet. Other themed suites—like the Jamaican, art deco, Old English, Egyptian, and Moroccan—offer you the chance to feel as though you're really in another time or place. Facilities, however, are strictly up to date: tub shower baths with bidets, separate powder rooms, wet bars, clock radios, and cable color TV units in every room.

A two-night package plan, called "Players Choice," is priced at $103 a person, double occupancy ($179 per person single occupancy), for Sunday to Friday arrivals. It includes a variety show, $20 per person in dining coupons, valet parking, and use of health-club facilities. Taxes are included.

The breathtaking view of the ocean is a relaxing extra at the 22nd-floor health club. Swim in the heated pool in a tropical setting of plants, beige and white lounge chairs, and glass-topped tables. You can pamper yourself in the warm, swirling water of a whirlpool or sit in the sauna or steam room. A coed exercise room has machines plus a staff to supervise their use. Two racquetball courts are available at $10 for a one-hour session.

At the 800-seat Cabaret Theater, in the theater building, headliner entertainment is featured.

The London Arcade, on the Boardwalk level of the theater building, has oak veneer and diamond glass-paned fronts that lead into gift stores and boutiques.

There's valet parking for hotel guests. If you prefer self-parking, check out the free (with casino validation) 24-hour facility at the end of the Atlantic City Expressway. A free shuttle bus every 10 minutes gives easy access to the casino-hotel.

Restaurants

Look for a new Chinese restaurant serving Cantonese fare at affordable prices on the fifth floor, in an exotic setting of shimmering pools and waterfalls to be added to the facilities I'll describe below. In addition to the pools and floating lily pads with an arching bridge that leads to the green marble pagoda that is the maître d's station, the new **Empress Restaurant** will feature an inlaid marble floor, silk-screen partitions, and luxurious Oriental appointments.

Ready to serve you now is the hotel's steakhouse, the **Golden Steer,** but the ambience is much more romantic and intimate than the steakhouse label might lead you to expect. From the chocolate-brown and white china, custom-made for the Golden Steer, to the soft, mushroom-colored banquettes of the enclosed booths, all the appointments are low key and sophisticated.

I'd recommend starting with oysters Rockefeller. Possible entree choices are Eastern sea scallops or grilled breast of chicken with mushrooms, in addition to the prime beef selections. With assorted desserts from $3.50, and entrees around $25, the dinner tab will be in the $35 to $40 range, without tax, wine, or tip.

The Golden Steer, on the fifth floor, is open from 6 p.m. to midnight for dinner. Call 441-2650 for reservations.

One of the prettiest coffeeshops in town is the **Garden State Café,** on the lobby level where you can sit and watch the passing parade on the Boardwalk while you eat. Artfully decorated with trellises, hanging plants, and white and green chairs, tables, and booths, the café serves up breakfast 24 hours a day. Fresh-squeezed juice ($1.90), eggs and omelets with ham, bacon, or sausage, or lox and onion ($3 to $11), plus breads, toast, and beverages make getting up seem worthwhile. There's usually a breakfast special that includes much of the above (juice or fruit, two eggs any style with bacon, ham, or sausage, and hash browns, toast or croissant, and coffee, tea, or milk) for $7.95.

From 11 a.m. to 7 a.m. the menu broadens to include sandwiches (deli, plus the likes of a Philly cheese steak for $7.25), soups, salads, and hamburgers (served with french fries). Dinner entrees, such as fried shrimp ($10.50), will satisfy a hearty appetite. I can vouch personally for the Black Forest cake ($2.55). Bar drinks are available here all day.

The **Galley Buffet,** on the first floor right downstairs from the Riverboat Casino, offers a very reasonably priced alternative for $6 to $8. One day the lunch included crab cakes, barbecued chicken, roast beef, turkey, vegetables, a salad, desserts, and coffee or iced tea.

TRUMP PLAZA CASINO HOTEL: Trump Plaza Casino Hotel, Mississippi Avenue and the Boardwalk, Atlantic City, NJ 08401 (tel. toll free 800/441-0909, or 609/441-6000).

Smack-dab in the center of town, the Trump Plaza Casino

Hotel, owned by a partnership of Harrah's (a subsidiary of Holiday Inn) and the Trump organization of New York City, has a 39-story, $220-million presence on the Boardwalk. The angular white concrete and dark reflecting glass façade has been artfully designed to give each of the 614 guest rooms a view of the sea. The tower is set back from the Boardwalk on a seven-story pedestal building, whose rooftop affords the space for a glass-enclosed pool, health spa, snackbar, and tennis courts.

An enormous porte cochère entrance from Pacific Avenue shelters the drive-through access. As you step out of your car, you'll see hand-cut cobblestones in a fishtail pattern paving the driveway, which will give you an inkling of the fastidious attention that has been paid to every detail of this building's interior appointments. The main lobby is monumental in scale, with a three-story-high atrium that is highlighted by a multi-coffered brass ceiling. Giant polished brass and mirrored columns soar 37 feet high, and escalators link the lobby with the casino.

Crystal chandeliers (rumored to have cost in excess of $100,000), strings of tivoli lights, and polished brass slot machines with electrically lit bases enliven the casino. Its 60,000 square feet encompass 82 blackjack, 22 craps, 12 roulette, 6 big-six, and 3 baccarat tables and 1,688 slot machines.

You can slake your thirst or just relax in six lounges, ranging from **Swizzle's,** adjoining the casino floor, to the ocean view **Skyway Lounge** on the third floor and Trump's, which has lively musical entertainment, also on the Casino level. A purple and orange color scheme, brass lighting, and headliner stars like Bill Cosby, Crystal Gayle, and Sammy Davis, Jr., are on view in the hotel's 750-seat theater.

Younger guests can take advantage of the hotel's nursery, available for children 3 to 8 years old, and a teen center features video games, a pool table, and a video jukebox.

Standard accommodations in this modern concrete tower have either two double or one king-size bed. The decor is simple, but the composition of the furnishings—the satin or velvet bedspreads, the burled veneer of the dressers, and the custom made wallpaper wall—betokens the fine quality of the pieces. Dramatic burgundy, blue, or green are the principal colors used as accents, along with marble, brass, or polished chrome lamps to add color to the predominantly soft beige of the rooms. Color TV, phones, and the expansive ocean views are in every room. The tile baths have large vanities and built-in lighting.

Rates for standard rooms are $100 at midweek, $120 on weekends in winter, rising to $125 midweek and $145 on weekends in summer. Add $10 for an additional occupant.

The premium duplex penthouse suite, which juts out over the rest of the tower, has a commanding view from its window-walled living room of a vast oceanscape. It is truly magnificent. The suite can be expanded to six bedrooms, has a private Jacuzzi, and fittings of cream, brass, and onyx. There are ten duplex suites and about 75 single-level suites.

Without stepping outside you can go to the Convention Center via a skywalk.

Restaurants

Ivana's, the gourmet French restaurant, is decorated in sophisticated tones of brown and cream. Unusual glass tubes encasing delicate glass flowers provide a touch of color in this elegant room. You'll dine to the accompaniment of piano music at a table set with pink tablecloths and gold-trimmed china. The entrees, featuring the likes of lobster, sole, salmon, and steak Châteaubriand, are prepared with a French flair. Desserts are all made on the premises. Dinner will cost from $45. Open daily from 6 p.m. to midnight, Ivana's says reservations are necessary (tel. 441-6400).

Maximilian's has traditional fare—prime ribs, fresh lobster—in a traditional, clubby setting of wood paneled walls, stained glass, and plush seating. The dessert cart features the hotel's homemade cakes and pastries. Expect to pay $40 and up for dinner. Open from 6 p.m. to midnight, and reservations are requested (tel. 441-6420).

Harvey's Deli has authentic New York delicatessen fare, from cold borscht ($2.25) to a Reuben sandwich ($6.25). Smoked fish platters, blintzes, and hot entrees like knockwurst or stuffed cabbage, round out the menu. New York–style cheesecake is, of course, an appropriate ending. Harvey's is open from 11 a.m. to 2 a.m. daily.

Trump Plaza's 24-hour coffeeshop, **The New Yorker,** has a wonderful black marble replica of the Chrysler Building at the entrance. A full range of standard coffeeshop fare is on hand: breakfast is served around the clock, lunch and dinner from 11 a.m. to 2 a.m. seven days.

Le Grand Buffet has a grand ocean view plus an all-you-can-eat spread whose daily themes follow a schedule—Sunday, champagne brunch; Monday, Oriental; Tuesday, Mediterranean; Wednesday, American; Thursday, French; Friday, seafood; and

Saturday, Italian. Stopping in on a Monday, I noted a spread of beef and tomatoes, sweet-and-sour chicken, shrimp lo mein, fried rice, dumplings, egg rolls, spareribs, fresh fruit, assorted cakes, and that grand ocean view. Lunch is 11 a.m. to 5 p.m. and costs $9.95; dinner is served from 5 to 10 p.m. and costs $12.95.

A **Casino snackbar,** off the casino floor, provides a quick bite from 11 a.m. to 11 p.m. Monday to Friday, 11 a.m. to midnight on weekends.

Scoops, a pretty pink-and-green ice-cream parlor, features Häagen-Dazs treats of every sort. Open seasonally seven days, 11 a.m. to 11 p.m.

CAESARS ATLANTIC CITY CASINO/HOTEL: Caesars Atlantic City Casino/Hotel, Arkansas Avenue and the Boardwalk, Atlantic City, NJ 08401 (tel. toll free 800/257-8555, in New Jersey 800/582-7600, or 609/348-4411).

Caesars incorporates the old Howard Johnson Regency, and until recently the name was incorporated too, and the hotel was known as Caesars Boardwalk Regency, but no more. Now it's Caesars Atlantic City.

Not only has Caesars shed its former name, but it's shed its skin as well! The hotel's gold wrap-around exterior is gone, and there's an aluminum skin that, at night, is sparked with red neon marquees. An 18-foot-tall statue of Caesar Augustus has a hand raised in welcome at the Boardwalk.

If you've been here before, you'll find Caesars Roman in motif, like its sister properties in Las Vegas and Lake Tahoe. Reproductions of classic statuary, *Hercules* and a *Winged Victory* in the lobby, and a 17-ton replica of Michelangelo's *David,* in the casino; two burnished brass profiles of Caesar are set over the glass entrance on Pacific Avenue; and the hotel has enough pink, black, and white marble in balustrades, columns, and other appurtenances to have seriously depleted Italy's famed marble quarries.

The Boardwalk entrance has room for monumental white marble columns that seem to disappear a floor or two higher behind gleaming metal curtains, all this forming a suitable backdrop for the shiny black and brass-trimmed casino doors. The main lobby, with guest services and registration, is entered via Pacific Avenue; it has a new porte cochère to keep the incoming customers protected from the elements.

Inside the casino, a rich color scheme is accented with black glass columns, brass, and Art Deco patterns on the rug, columns,

s. The gaming area offers 114 table games: 72 blackjack, ... 10 roulette, 4 big-six, and 4 baccarat. There are 1,600 slot machines, about 480 in a Slot Lounge a few steps up from the casino floor.

Caesars Circus Maximus Theater offers headliner entertainment (more about that in Chapter V), and the Arena and Forum lounges also offer musical entertainment. But that's not quite the whole show!

On the second level, you should stroll along the shopping promenade (with the clearest explanations of where you are, geographically, of any of the casinos). C. W. Sweets, an ice-cream parlor and chocolate factory rolled up into one proper ball, is a sure and pleasurable bet for cash. You might donate some of yours to a thick ice-cream crêpe ($5.95), chocolate-fudge sundae ($2.95), or a box of fudge to take home. Next door is the Electric Company, all shiny, electronic, and buzzing with various electronically produced sounds. The arcade is open from 10 a.m. to midnight. This is the day-care version of a casino, and it's great. Next, you'll come to the adult stuff: a Gucci's, women's apparel boutique, Tiberius for men's tailoring, and so on. Don't miss the chrome-and-glass skylight, with its aerial view of the casino (and the fourth floor's aerial view of you).

For those who want to get some exercise and keep up their daily fitness routine, Caesars is a good place to be. On the hotel's beach are two volleyball courts, and if you've brought the children along, you can leave them in a supervised beach play area while you take a swim or a nap in the sun. Caesars Beach Club has its own experienced lifeguards, and the area is set off with brightly colored cabañas. The hotel also furnishes free bicycles to guests for Boardwalk cycling in the morning from April to November. The health spa has Universal equipment, a steam room, sauna, and Jacuzzis.

You won't have to leave the premises to enjoy sports facilities. On site are three tennis courts, two year-round platform tennis courts, and an outdoor pool.

Caesars has queen- and king-size and double-bedded rooms. Winter rates are $95 to $145; in summer the range is $140 to $175. Call ahead as far as possible for the best selections.

There are a variety of color schemes in either contemporary or traditional veins. A particularly attractive room had a king-size bed with round headboard, matching bedspreads and draperies, a desk and chair to sit at while you calculate your winnings, color TV and phone. The suites tend to be starkly modern, often monochromatic in a relaxing gray, with all the amenities that make for a luxurious stay. If you're not that big a spender, be sure to ask about the midweek package plans that offer savings on entertainment tickets, food, and rooms.

Restaurants

Fine Chinese cuisine served in the elegant **Oriental Palace** is the top of the line at Caesars. While you might stay faithful to the old favorite Cantonese and Szechuan dishes on the menu, if you're feeling more adventurous why not sample one of the unusual Mongolian specialties, Mongolian hotpot (a tasty mélange of meat and seafood) among them. A full dinner will cost from $25 and up. Call for reservations (tel. 340-5940). The Oriental Palace is open for dinner only.

In **Le Posh** the atmosphere is sophisticated and elegant; you'll dine graciously indeed, seated on a comfortable banquette in a setting reminiscent of a '30s-era nightclub. Appealing appetizers include escargots in pastry or cold asparagus vinaigrette. Entrees featuring seafood, veal, chicken, or beef are prepared with light cream sauces or more chastely grilled. Fresh vegetables and a basket of rolls accompany the dinner. The dessert cart has several tiers laden with temptations. Dinner will cost from $45. Le Posh is open daily from 6 p.m. to midnight; reservations are suggested (tel. 340-5914).

Primavera's luxurious old world setting will put you in the likes of a Venetian palazzo for dinner. From the antipasti, zuppe, pasta, and insalata to the meat and fish entrees and dolci, it's northern Italian cuisine all the way. For starters I'd recommend the sautéed shrimp on a bed of spinach, for dessert the smooth zabaglione—in between the choice is yours! Call 340-5917 for reservations.

Side by side are **Caesars' Hyakumi Japanese Restaurant** (tel. 340-5455) and the **Imperial Steakhouse** (tel. 340-5452). Although the decor in the Imperial is Oriental, you enter via a footbridge over a landscaped rock garden and pond, you'll dine on New England lobster and thick cuts of sirloin and porterhouse steak. The Imperial is open daily from 6 p.m. to midnight.

In the Hyakumi the food is prepared in full view of the diners according to the ancient art of teppanyaki cooking. The dinner is a seven-course, fixed-price menu at $34.50. You could start with a choice of soups, kenchin juru (vegetable soup with beans) or sumashi (chicken broth with rice). Tempura and sunomono (a salad of marinated cucumbers and shredded crabmeat) are next. Three entrees are chicken, steak, or baby lobster meat. Assorted Japanese vegetables, steamed rice, and green tea accompany the meal. Fresh fruit and special ices are a refreshing conclusion. The room is decorated simply. On the walls are a handsome display of Japanese works of art and kimonos.

The **Boardwalk Café** has an extravagant salad bar—I counted 25 bowls of salad ingredients, and they all looked fresh and appealing. At lunch you can take your pick of a sandwich buffet or just browse along the salad bar. Every night there's a prime rib buffet ($11.95), preceded by that salad bar, with potatoes, fresh bread, and dessert. A panoramic view of the Boardwalk and the Ocean One pier expand the space of this very pleasant room. The tables are beige Formica-topped, the seats a comfortable tan wicker with bright red with white polka-dot cushions. The lunch buffet ($8.95) goes from 11 a.m. to 4:30 p.m.; dinner is 5 p.m. to 9 p.m., seven days.

Milt & Sonny's, patterned after a classic New York deli, has all the dishes that deli lovers yearn for. A waist-high divider of green plants separates the deli from the rest of the third floor. Wooden seats, ceiling fans, and Tiffany-look lamps evoke a turn-of-the-century eatery.

Open 24 hours, its menus offer breakfast, lunch, and dinner. Two eggs, any style, served with french fries or baked beans, and toast or bagel with cream cheese, are $3.75. Sandwiches run the gamut from salami and liverwurst to pastrami, and are served with potato salad. Deli platters offer some great alternatives like a Nova Scotia salmon platter with tomato and Bermuda onion or a chopped chicken liver plate with potato salad, hard-boiled egg, and onion. Burgers (one-third pound) come plain, with cheddar cheese, or with cheese and bacon. Milt & Sonny's offers the classic New York deli beverage, Dr. Brown's Cel-Ray Tonic.

In a rustic New England coastal setting, the **Sand Bar** serves oysters and clams on the half shell, jumbo shrimp, and clam chowder. A pitcher of cold beer is the perfect accompaniment. Your light bite should cost less than $5. The Sand Bar is open from noon to 2 a.m.

Nearby on the third floor, **Señor Pedro's** has the expected Mexican specialties at reasonable prices that should satisfy your appetite for something hot and spicy.

Ambrosia seems too splendid for a 24-hour coffeeshop, with its shiny blue enamel, etched glass, and brass trim. But its eclectic menu offers traditional coffeeshop fare. Hot entrees are served with the vegetable of the day, and assorted breads. Desserts, beer, and wine are on tap. From a snack to a full meal, Ambrosia is a convenient place to go (it's right near the Pacific Avenue entrance).

BALLY'S PARK PLACE: Bally's Park Place, Park Place and the Boardwalk, Atlantic City, NJ 08401 (tel. toll free 800/225-5977, or 609/340-2000).

In their haste to make Bally's Park Place the third casino-hotel to open in Atlantic City, their renowned architects, Skidmore, Ownings and Merrill, appear to have forgotten to take fullest advantage of the hotel's oceanfront location, and, sad to say, few of the 510 rooms have ocean views.

Two classically elegant hotels, the Marlborough and the Blenheim, were demolished on the site where you'll see the sprawling six-story structure that houses the casino, restaurant promenade, convention space, and the main lobby. The U-shaped hotel wing, formerly the old Dennis Hotel, has a street-level entrance on Pop Lloyd Boulevard, a nicely landscaped thoroughfare that runs through the complex. Most of the guest rooms are in the hotel wing, which rises 11 stories in its central section, and seven stories on either side.

At night the pink and gray granite of the six-story casino building is overshadowed by its building-height glass-enclosed stairwells that are outlined with tivoli bulbs. Bally's signature purple awnings with green and red accent stripes are also aglow at night.

Bally's Park Place uses a stylized tree as its logo and theme, and the accent throughout is on greenery and fresh flowers. In the lobby, huge round planters display flowers of the season and also provide comfortable benches. The burgundy and gold casino's focal point is a giant 93-foot-high escalator flanked by a cascading waterfall on either side. This design concept certainly makes it convenient for gamblers to head up to the restaurant level and back down again. (Nongamblers can take the elevators.) A handsome fountain at the top of the escalator makes inspired use of gargoyles, seashells, and turtles salvaged from the demolished Blenheim Hotel. You can stroll around or find a seat along the restaurant-level promenade and admire the flowers and potted trees strung with lights that turn the space into a veritable indoor park.

The casino floor, carpeted in burgundy with the Bally tree in gold printed all over it, extends through 60,000 square feet, and it encompasses 117 table games: 76 blackjack, 22 craps, 12 roulette, 4 big-six, and 3 baccarat. Bally's 1,596 slot machines were, in a manner of speaking, homemade—by Bally Mfg. Corp. of Chicago. A prime slot area, 7th Heaven, is devoted to $1 machines, and its 57-foot-long neon sign, the largest neon indoor sign in the U.S. was first turned on by George Burns.

The Dennis Room, on the casino level, is a charming survivor of the old Dennis Hotel. Its high, round-arched windows framed by silk shades have an expansive view. Used as a sitting area, its handsome black marble fireplace, intricately carved ceiling, and 75-year-old grand piano bring back a touch of traditional elegance. A cocktail lounge just steps from the casino floor not only has drinks and music, but a stock market ticker flashing over the bar. Bally's long-running revue show, *An Evening at La Cage,* is in its second year at the Park Cabaret, and Upstairs at the Park, on the restaurant level, has music.

At Bally's Boardwalk and Park Place corner, the store is occupied by Reese Palley, "merchant to the rich," whose fine porcelains, hand-carved furniture, and objects d'art make memorable gifts. Clothing boutiques and a small gift shop that carries newspapers and magazines as well are in the hotel lobby.

Bally's spa is state-of-the-art, with four racquet ball courts, an aerobics exercise room, swimming pool, whirlpool "park," and a health-food bar and grill.

Valet parking is available free for hotel guests. There are also lots of parking lots nearby.

The guest rooms at Bally's are handsomely decorated, although it is a bit jarring to come upon a brilliant-red bathtub (in harmony with the old color scheme) in a chamber that has been recast in a more subtly colored mode. Sparkling metallic wallpaper—in gold, teal, or rose—complements the like-colored tones of the bedspread, draperies, and rug. King- and queen-size and two-double-bedded rooms are available, as well as rooms with round beds and mirrored ceilings. Marble vanities and well-lit makeup mirrors are added features. You'll find all the comforts expected—armchairs, TV, phone, and roomy closets with sliding doors. Room rates range from $105 to $135 mid-September to mid-June; the price goes up to $125 to $145 from mid-June to mid-September. Children under 12 may occupy their parents' room at no extra charge. For each person over double occupancy the extra person charge is $15 (maximum of four guests per room).

Suites that have the high rollers in mind are generously endowed and furnished in art deco, Oriental, or French themes. On the seventh and eighth floors, mansard loft suites have an ocean view.

Bally's has several package plans available. Their Jackpot Package guarantees you a jackpot (just kidding, folks). It does offer two nights accommodations, valet parking, one breakfast, $10 in quarters, a gaming guide, tax, and gratuities, for $105 per person, double occupancy, for Sunday to Thursday arrivals between September 16 and June 14.

Restaurants

Bally's restaurants have high standards. Menus change three times a year.

On the top floor of the casino building, Bally's restaurant row is headed up by **Prime Place,** named for its mouthwatering specialties—T-bone ($29), sirloin ($27), and filet mignon ($22.50). Broiled to your order and accompanied by your selection from the bountiful, polished brass-and-wood salad bar, it's America's favorite dinner. The barbecued baby back ribs are always a good appetizer, or else a colossal shrimp cocktail. Even the black bean soup with rice and onion makes an interesting beginning. Other recommended main courses, besides the steaks, include double breast of capon with sauce diable ($17) and lobster tail tempura in sauce orientale. Of course everything tastes better with a glass of wine, and there's a good selection of imported and American wines.

On the separate dessert menu there's a tempting selection of chocolate fondues, flambé fruits, and original creations, like strawberries Dorothy, fresh sliced strawberries, sautéed in butter and sugar, with a touch of crème de Noyeaux and white crème de cassis, flamed with brandy and served with vanilla ice cream. The tab here could well be $50 per person, not including tip.

Prime Place overlooks Brighton Park, and in summer it's especially lovely to watch the lit fountain as well as the fine ocean view. The restaurant is a roomy, comfortable space, with wine-colored velvet banquettes, crystal chandeliers, and cut flowers on each table. The stained-glass doors at the entrance are brilliantly colored.

Prime Place (tel. 340-2709) is open for dinner from 6 p.m. to midnight. Closed Wednesday and Thursday in winter, open seven days in summer.

Sunday brunch (Saturday too, in season) from 9 a.m. to 2 p.m. in Prime Place is a lavish spread. Priced at $16.50 usually it includes roast beef, ham, bacon, fish, hot cereal, fruit soup, egg dishes from omelets to eggs Benedict, blintzes, lyonnaise potatoes, desserts, and beverages.

Another fine dining choice on the sixth floor is **By the Sea,** where you'll also have a window-wall ocean view. Blue (for the sea) and beige (for sand) make a relaxing and appropriately nautical setting, although seafood dishes are only half the menu offerings.

A repast might begin with a flourish—a full array of cold seafood appetizers called the Cart Royale—or creamy lobster bisque has a faithful following. Especially recommended are broiled bay scallops with lemon butter ($18.50). Some special entrees are prepared tableside. Prime Place and By the Sea share the dessert menu (see above). Here the tab will be in the $50 range.

By the Sea (tel. 340-2709) is open seven days in season, Wednesday to Saturday in winter, from 6 p.m. to midnight year round.

Music from the Upstairs at the Park lounge, and the beautiful stained-glass-topped gazebo, will keep you amused as you wait in line for the fabulous seafood buffet at the **Sidewalk Café** (I assure you, it's worth waiting for). Red tile floor, brass-trimmed columns, white tables and yellow-cushioned chrome chairs, and dashing yellow banners hanging from the ceiling make a bright and lively setting. The buffet, which costs $15.99 per person, plus tax and gratuities, is laid on from 5 to 10 p.m. Friday, 2 p.m. to midnight on Saturday, and 2 to 10 p.m. on Sunday.

A mural of Atlantic City in the 1920s is the backdrop for this superb spread, which includes clam chowder, an array of cold salads, cold appetizers (like poached salmon filet, smoked whitefish, and a huge bowl of unpeeled shrimp), hot entrees (seafood Newburg, mussels marinara, clams steamed in white wine, linguine in clam sauce), vegetables, ice creams with toppings, mousse, cakes, plus beverages. If you like seafood, this is the best buy in town.

Ice cream is treated with the respect this delectable confection deserves at **Sundae's Ice Cream Parlor,** which presents the Häagen-Dazs and Bassett flavors in glittering cut-glass dishes, with no plastic plates or spoons anywhere in sight. Ice-cream floats, milkshakes, frozen yogurt, gourmet toppings—this place has them all. And you'll enjoy the setting too; Casablanca fans, globe lights, white tile floors, and red leather accents. Open 2 p.m. to midnight Sunday, till 2 a.m. on Friday and Saturday. Hours are subject to change.

Park Place Deli is on the casino level, near the Boardwalk entrance. There are sauerkraut, pickled tomatoes, and cherry peppers on the tables. Giant plastic transparencies of oldtime movie stars hang from the ceiling in this replica of a New York deli. High marks go to the deli sandwiches, as well as such oldtime favorites as chicken in the pot, stuffed cabbage, and cheese blintzes. Prices range from $8 to $12 for main dishes, about $4.95 to $7 for sandwiches. The deli's hours are 11:30 a.m. to 11 p.m. Sunday to Thursday, to 2 a.m. on Friday and Saturday.

A green and white garden-like setting, enhanced by white trellises, hanging plants, and a view of the hotel wing's courtyard, make the **Greenery** a pleasant place to eat, whether you're having a quick bite or a full meal. On the first floor, this pleasant spot features a breakfast buffet ($8.95) and a dinner buffet ($13.95), along with all the expected coffeeshop offerings. A typical breakfast buffet includes juice or fruit, bagels, lox, eggs, French toast, blintzes, sausages, other hot entrees, hot breads, and beverage. Meats for the dinner buffet—roast beef, ham, or turkey—are carved to order.

The **Lone Star,** the fastest snackbar this side of Texas, is self-service, and it's got soup and hot dogs, burgers, and other sandwiches, including the local favorite Philly cheese steak ($3.99). Hours are noon to 4 a.m. Sunday to Thursday, until 6 a.m. on Friday and Saturday. The Lone Star is right off the casino floor.

Cafeteria-style service prevails at **Jib's Oyster Bar.** This small but popular room is nattily decorated in white and blue with chrome to add some shine. Bluepoint oysters and cherrystone clams are 95¢ each, gulf shrimp run $1.50 each, and bay shrimp cocktail is $2.95. Clam chowder and hot seafood like clams casino or oyster stew are also served. There are beer, wine, and soft drinks. Jib's is open noon to 2 a.m. Sunday to Thursday, to 4 a.m. on Saturday and Sunday.

THE CLARIDGE: The Claridge, Indiana Avenue at the Boardwalk, Atlantic City, NJ 08401 (tel. toll free 800/257-8585, in New Jersey 800/257-5277, or 609/340-3400).

Half a century ago, the Claridge meant international elegance in Atlantic City. At a cost of $140 million, Del Webb Hotels has returned the 26-story landmark to prominence. The English motif is strong and pleasant, beginning with the nicely landscaped shrubbery and the handsome fountain (lit at night) in Brighton Park, which lies between the hotel and the Boardwalk. At night the illuminated façade and spotlit white tower lend a traditional elegance to the skyscape. At the front lobby entrance, a white limestone porte cochère assures you of a grand, and dry, entrance. Old-world elegance is the hallmark of the lobby too, in the crystal chandeliers, well-polished wood paneling, and brass fixtures. It resembles the lounge of an upper-class English men's club, except for the lack of seats—there are none.

The five-level casino greets you with an ambience worthy of a

James Bond movie. Counting all the alcoves and nooks and crannies of this multilevel space, the casino totals 34,752 square feet. The 70 table games break down into: 48 blackjack, 12 craps, 6 roulette, 2 big-six, and 2 baccarat. There are 984 slot machines of various types, an outsize Big Bertha, two mini-Berthas, progressive jackpot, even a zodiac slot machine where you can play your sign. The effect in toto is intimate and even genteel, with a blue ceiling, warm paneling, burgundy carpet, and tivoli lights. If you're looking for a casino that's easy on the glitz, look no further.

The hotel guest rooms occupy floors 7 through 24 of the Renaissance-style brick and limestone tower. Don't forget your room number; the keys are coded and bear figures that do *not* correspond with your room number. There are rooms with two double beds or one king- or queen-size bed. If you can reserve a room far enough in advance, you can have your choice of city, bay, or ocean views. Blue or burnt orange are the dominant colors. The bedrooms are nicely decorated along traditional lines. Color-coordinated bedspreads, draperies, carpets, and ceramic-base lamps are effectively set off by the warm wooden tones of the dressers and night tables. All rooms have good bedside lamps, phones, clock/radio, cable color TV with HBO, and mirrored sliding-door closets. Baths are bright with Art Deco print silvery wallpaper in pretty shades of peach, brown, and tan. You'll find the little gift amenities on your vanity counter—a sewing kit, perfumed soap, shower cap, etc. The hallways are excellently maintained.

The price of the rooms depends on view and, of course, time of year. From November to April the cost is $75 to $85 Sunday to Thursday, $95 to $105 on Friday and Saturday; from the end of April through June and mid-September to the end of November, $95 and $105 weekdays, $115 to $125 weekends; from the end of June to mid-September, $120 to $130 weekdays, $140 to $150 weekends. Children under 12 may occupy their parents' room free. The extra-person charge is $10 for each guest over double occupancy (maximum of four guests per room).

Corner rooms are especially luxurious; some even have their own Jacuzzis. The rooms on the highest floors are reserved for special suites (rates on request).

The Claridge's current three-day-two-night package is called the Midweek Winner's Choice. For $92 (per person, double occupancy) you get baggage handling, one visit to the health spa, one free admission to the Palace Theater, complimentary parking, and $10 in coin per person.

On the eighth floor, the health club's facilities include a glass-enclosed pool area invitingly surrounded by orange lounge chairs and hanging plants. Fitness buffs will make use of the Universal exercise machine; less active types have a bronzing room, steam room, sauna, and Jacuzzi to add to their well-being. A unisex beauty salon is conveniently nearby.

The Palace Theatre, a 550-seat room, has musical theater and headliner entertainment on the third floor, near the Pavilion restaurant. Other restaurants are on the second floor, as well as an electronic games arcade.

There's only valet parking at the Claridge. If you prefer to park yourself, you'll find lots on Pacific Avenue and nearby side streets.

Sports is of more than passing interest at the Claridge. Mickey Mantle, the all-time great Yankee Hall of Fame outfielder, is the hotel's director of sports promotions, and Sparky Lyle, Cy Young Award-winning relief pitcher, is also on hand.

Restaurants

The restaurants at the Claridge, like those at the other hotel-casinos, have a setting to match your every mood, from a quiet, intimate dinner by candlelight to just a quick bite before you get back to the casino.

For an elegant repast served on Lenox china, the **Pavilion** is the place to go. You'll find yourself in a sophisticated, softly lit room, with crystal chandeliers and comfortable traditional dining chairs. You may have your appetizer hot or cold, and it's not easy to decide between choices like Maryland backfin lump crabmeat with cocktail sauce ($10) or marinated phaesant ($8.50). Salads are also quite special: I liked the house salad. Entrees range from lobster tail to veal, with chicken, and beef. Selections from the pastry cart are super-rich and calorie-laden, especially the creamy cheesecake. Your dinner will be no less than $40, and could be more.

The Pavilion (tel. 340-3400) is open every night for dinner from 6 p.m. to 11 p.m.

The **Garden Room,** open 24 hours on the third floor, has expansive ocean views and will get you through the day with standard coffeeshop fare for breakfast, lunch, dinner, and snacks.

The **Great American Buffet's** menu changes daily, covering a full panoply of American cuisine—appetizers, salads, hot and cold entrees, vegetables, desserts, and coffee and tea. Lunch from 11 a.m. to 4:30 p.m. costs $8.95; dinner from 4:30 p.m. is $9.95.

Wally's Snack Bar is a fast-food emporium, dispensing hot dogs, burgers, fries, soft drinks, and coffee. A bite here shouldn't set you back any more than $5 for a sandwich and a drink.

The **Stadium Deli,** across from the video games arcade, rounds out the hotel's dining facilities. It's an informal spot: black and white tile floors, red-topped tables, and photos of sports greats fill the space. The deli is open 11 a.m. to 11 p.m. weekdays, till 2 a.m. on weekends.

SANDS HOTEL & CASINO: **Sands Hotel & Casino, Indiana Avenue and Brighton Park, Atlantic City, NJ 08401 (tel. toll free 800/257-8580, or 609/441-4444).**

The Sands, formerly the Brighton, is prospering the second time around. Together with the Claridge and Bally's Park Place, it shares the outdoor mall at Brighton Park. Although the Brighton was the first hotel-casino to be built completely from the ground up, in 1980, the Sands was treated to a more recent $30-million transformation that added an additional guest floor of seven luxurious suites, a three-story glass-enclosed escalator leading from a new park entrance, and an atrium-style food court on the third and fourth floors of the complex.

The escalator goes directly to the two-story Food Court, where café tables on a brick floor, street lamps, and a city street-scape are the setting for dining on the provisions purchased from a number of famous establishments' branches.

Entertainment is provided by headliners and revue shows in the Sands' Copa Room. An enormous gold lamé Austrian puff curtain covers the proscenium. There are red plush banquettes, with seating for 850. Headliners who have appeared here include such superstars as Raquel Welch, Robin Williams, Eddie Murphy, and David Brenner. The Copa Room is also the site of nationally televised boxing matches, including world-class bouts. The Punch Bowl on the second floor and the Players Lounge, near the casino floor, have continuous live music.

The 50,000-square-foot casino is decorated in shades of red. The opulent baccarat "salon" is set off by a gleaming brass railing. There are 88 table games—58 blackjack, 16 craps, 10 roulette, 2 big-six, and 2 baccarat—and over 1,000 slot machines. Variations on the basic slots are nonprogressive million-coin jackpot; video blackjack, poker, and dice; and a Big Bertha.

The Sands has good sports and fitness facilities. A glass-enclosed, heated indoor/outdoor pool is available year round. A Nautilus center, sauna, and Jacuzzi complete the on-premises facilities. Owned by the same company, the Greate Bay Country

Club nearby is considered part of the Sands sports program. It has a par-72 championship golf course, professional-caliber tennis courts, and a swimming pool. The Sands will provide guests with transportation to the country club.

From the pink and beige marble lobby to all its 501 guest rooms, the Sands has a sleek, contemporary presence. Beige, black, and burgundy with polished-brass trim is one of several soothing color schemes. The standard rooms have two double beds or one king-size. Typically a guest room has a beige rug and draperies, and a burgundy, beige, and black striped bedspread. Burgundy arm-chairs, beige walls, and brass lamps complement the warm wood tones of the dresser and night table. Cable color TV with HBO is standard. Suites on the higher floors have Jacuzzi tubs and luxurious appointments. Some are duplex suites with a spiral staircase.

Rates change four times a year, and you can request a city, partial ocean, or full ocean view. Summer prices are $99 to $149, fall and spring are $95 to $139, and winter is $80 to $130. Prices depend on the view, time of year, and weekend versus midweek occupancy.

Several midweek packages are available at considerable savings. A one-nighter, the Sands Choice, is $98 per person, based on double occupancy. Also included in the package are dinner for two at the Brighton Steakhouse or Mes Amis and club breakfast for two. For $220, double occupancy, you can sink into a Total Indulgence one-night package, which features tickets for two to the Copa Room revue, dinner for two in the Brighton Steakhouse, club breakfast for two, a massage, two cocktails, free parking, and health-club privileges.

Restaurants

The Sands gourmet dining room with a French accent is **Mes Amis.** It's romantically candlelit by a long, white taper set in a silver candleholder in the center of each table. Moire-covered French provincial armchairs and banquettes and white-lace-covered peach tablecloths are gracefully elegant. Blue napkins, gold-rimmed china, and cut flowers set a fine table. Polished wood panels and an occasional vase of flowers enhance the setting.

Start your meal with a consultation about the wine—the cellar has a selection of fine domestic and imported wines—and then proceed to cold or hot appetizers, like oysters Florentine, fried brie cheese, or fresh sturgeon caviar; then perhaps on to a rich beef consommé with sherry and a Belgian endive salad. Appetizers are $6 to $9 each (the caviar is $28). Soups and salads run $3 to $4. Now for the entrees, which average about $15 to $22. Highlights are blackened redfish and roast duck. Should you possibly have room for dessert, the pastry cart will be able to please. Dinner will range from $45 upward.

Mes Amis (tel. 441-4200) is open for dinner from 6 p.m. to midnight seven days a week. Reservations are advised.

The blue ribbon with Prime stamped on it that's affixed to the front of the menu is a sure giveaway to the offerings at the **Brighton Steakhouse.** A clubby, English atmosphere prevails here. There are various kinds of seating: comfortable banquettes, plush armchairs, and upholstered wing chairs. The warm glow of wood paneling frames the pretty floral arrangements, peach-colored tablecloths, and napkins and glass candleholders that adorn the tables.

The food is simple American fare, but the ingredients are of the best quality. All sirloin is USDA prime. Delicious appetizers include snails baked in herb butter ($6.95) or a crabmeat cocktail ($8.50). You can order such main dishes as roast beef with horseradish sauce, broiled sirloin and sautéed mushrooms, and thick-cut broiled veal chops, T-bone steak, broiled to order, served with a duchess potato border, grilled tomato, and vegetables, is the house specialty. Entrees are $15 to $35. A smooth finish is the chocolate mousse. For a full dinner, you can expect to pay in the $40 to $50 range.

The Brighton Steakhouse is open for lunch, noon to 3 p.m. Monday to Friday. The fare is somewhat lighter, featuring sandwiches as well as hot entrees. Dinner is served 6 p.m. till midnight seven days a week. A bounteous Sunday brunch, from 11 a.m. to 3 p.m. is $17.95 per person.

Rossi's, adjacent to the Food Court on the third floor, has a smashing Italian-style buffet. The menu is not a set one, but you're bound to find your favorites among the 25 or so items featured nightly for $19.95. Set out in the buffet are the likes of antipasto, lasagne, manicotti, sausage and peppers, chicken cacciatore, veal parmigiana, and calamari; several entrees are prepared to order, including scampi, steak pizzaiola, and veal marsala. Desserts feature Italian pastries, pies, cakes, and ice cream. Open nightly 6 to 11 p.m., later on weekends.

The **Food Court** on the third and fourth levels consists of a pleasant old-fashioned streetscape setting with intimate tables and chairs that you can occupy after choosing your snack or meal from the likes of Nathan's hot dogs, Pat's Philly cheese steaks,

Bookbinder's seafood, Sly Stallone's burgers, a pizza franchise, and Mary Elizabeth cakes.

The **Carnegie Deli** on the fourth level of the Food Court is the Sands' 24-hour deli/coffeeshop, and goes the route from bagels with lox and cream cheese to overstuffed deli sandwiches to hot entrees.

TRUMP'S CASTLE HOTEL & CASINO: Trump's Castle Hotel & Casino, Huron Avenue and Brigantine Boulevard, Atlantic City, NJ 08401 (tel. toll free 800/441-5551, or 609/441-2000).

Truth to tell, Trump's Castle is a high-rise modern structure with a rainbow 67 feet high affixed near the roofline. It has neither ramparts nor a tower, but for those who find the Boardwalk a nice place to visit, but a little too hectic to stay at, the Castle offers an interesting alternative.

Located right across the street from the Farley State Marina, the hotel is designed to take advantage of its marina location and to offer the high standard of sophistication that its owners, the Trump Organization, set in New York City with its elegant Fifth Avenue Trump Tower complex.

A key element that contributes greatly to the hotel's popularity is its nine-story parking garage, connected directly to the hotel, which provides complimentary parking for 3,000 vehicles. Separate bus and auto entrances to the hotel add another element of convenience. There is also jitney service to the Boardwalk.

At the heart of the hotel is a six-story-high glass-enclosed atrium. A three-story escalator ride from ground level brings guests to the lobby reception area, which is sheathed with rose marble and trimmed with brass and strands of tivoli lights. The atrium is capped by a skylight dome and two enormous chandeliers.

The casino, also on the third floor, has lots of rainbows flashing, no doubt to wish you good luck at the 117 table games (24 craps, 74 blackjack, 13 roulette, 3 baccarat, and 3 big-six) and 1684 slot machines.

Two lounges on the third level, Viva and the Casino Lounge, offer musical entertainment. The King's Court Theatre has a permanent ice rink where such performers as skating star Peggy Fleming have appeared.

Sports and the health club reign on the fifth floor 3½-acre recreation deck. A jogging track, tennis courts, pool, kiddie pool, and shuffleboard courts provide for the sports-minded. The fitness buffs will head for the health club and its Universal weight training equipment, steam room, sauna, Jacuzzi, and massage tables. A poolside café provides light snacks from May through September, and it's a lovely place to come watch the sunset and the sailboats in the bay.

All of the hotel's 605 rooms offer great views of the city skyline and the marina below. The standard guest rooms, with either two double or one king- or queen-sized bed, are decorated in restful tones of aqua, beige, or brown, with light wood furnishings and marble bath vanities. Rates (single or double occupancy) are $105 to $175 in summer, $75 to $125 in winter, and $85 to $135 in spring or fall. There are some 76 suite combinations (studio, one bedroom plus parlor, etc.); rates on request. The Casino Royale one-night package offers a deluxe room, $10 in food coupons per person, a T-shirt, and other bonuses, for $45.50 per person, double occupancy.

Restaurants

With some of the top cooking talent in town, Trump's Castle's five restaurants offer some tasty options.

Delfino's will transport you to the Italian countryside in a colorful setting of tile, ceramics, stucco, plants, and flowers. The imaginative menu might offer you soft-shell crab soup for starters or a salad of tenderloin of duck, asparagus tips, tomatoes, and lettuces. You might choose a poached combination of sole and salmon for your main course. The pastry cart offers a selection of good things. Expect to pay from $45 and up for your meal. Open daily from 6 p.m. to midnight; reservations are suggested (tel. 441-2000).

At the **Beef Barron** the Old West lives again, from the two Remington sculptures at the entrance to the buffalo tusk hurricane lamp chandeliers in the dining room. Beige leather tabletops and chair coverings, solid oak furniture, and shelves of pottery carry out the southwest theme, as does the hearty steakhouse fare. Pecos bean soup ($2.95) would be a suitable appetizer, and whether you choose a steak, lamb, or seafood entree you'll get some sweet corn pudding as garnish. Bourbon chocolate pie and a cup of strong coffee will put you back in the saddle in good order. Dinner will be in the $40 and up range, lunch about half that. The Beef Barron is open for lunch from 11:30 a.m. to 3 p.m. and dinner from 5:30 on. Reservations suggested (tel. 441-2000).

The **Food Fantasy Buffet** offers lunch (11 a.m. to 5 p.m., $8.95) and dinner (5 to 11 p.m., $11.95) daily in a pastel setting of pink, white, and green, with blond wood furniture. Bring a strong appetite to the spread—salads, pastas, vegetables, hot and cold en-

trees, fresh fruit, cakes, puddings, and pies. C
brunch is $8.95.

The **Coffee Shop** adjoins the buffet on the third floor a
ries along the same subtle color scheme. Open 24 hours, it features the full complement of coffeeshop fare.

The fourth-floor Deli has corned beef, pastrami, or roast beef
sandwiches, salads, and soft drinks for a set price of $5.94. Open
daily from 11 a.m. to 10 p.m.

SHOWBOAT HOTEL CASINO: Showboat Hotel Casino, Delaware and
States Avenues at the Boardwalk, Atlantic City, NJ 08404 (tel.
609/343-4000).

Scheduled to open early in 1987, the Showboat brings a new
element to the varied offerings of the casino/hotels. Positioning
itself toward a family crowd, Showboat will have a 60-lane Bowling Center on the second level that will feature automatic scor-
ing, below surface ball return, a pro shop, and a bar and
beverage/snack bar. On the same level as the bowling alleys a
youth care center and a video games center have been designed
for family recreation.

The hotel's gleaming white cruise ship-like exterior encompasses some 10½ acres, including 516 guest rooms, 40 suites, and
a 60,000-square-foot casino. Adjoining the casino, appetites can
be appeased in some seven restaurants—the gourmet Mr. Kel-
ley's, the seafood Ocean Inn, Italian Casa di Napoli, deli Star-
board, Polynesian Outrigger, and two snackbars. On the second
level the Captain's Buffet, an ice-cream parlor, and two snackbars will keep the munchies at bay. The principal entertainment
room, the Mardi Gras Lounge, will be supplemented by three
cocktail lounges in the first and second levels.

The recreation center on the second level will include a pool
and two Jacuzzis along with the Bowling Center. The parking garage is attached to the main building with an enclosed walkway.

Other Hotels and Motels

For rooms in the moderate price category, most lower rollers
stay at one of the welter of motels along Pacific Avenue. Some of
the major chain operations in the moderate and lower price
brackets are opening in Atlantic City and on Routes 30 and 40,
just five or ten minutes from the center of the action.

Other changes are in store to bring more hotel and motel
rooms to town, among them the Boardwalk Marketplace development project that will encompass several beach blocks. One

motel that we've recommended in the past, the Acapulco, is on one of those blocks and has already had a refurbishing that includes a name change (it's now the Westminster).

In general, you'll find that motels do try to meet the needs of the fantastic summer invasion of visitors. Most stick to their published rates and will provide you with reasonably priced accommodations.

Unfortunately, some motels don't have rate sheets, and these will try to extort whatever the traffic will bear when rooms are tight. If you have an advance reservation, with a deposit paid and written confirmation, you'll be saving yourself from this kind of costly situation.

The noncasino-hotel accommodations are listed below in descending order of price bracket and also by location. First are the "downtown" accommodations, this is to say the most centrally located, closest to Brighton Park and the Sands, Claridge, and Bally casinos. Next I've grouped together the motels near Resorts International, toward the north part of town. The third group is, roughly, between the Tropicana and Golden Nugget casinos. Next are some listings on the way into town, along Routes 30 and 40. And finally, for those interested in longer stays, some deluxe hotel/condos and a real budget alternative, a campground.

DOWNTOWN: The **Best Western Inn,** in the center of town at Indiana and Pacific Avenues (P.O. Box 5309), Atlantic City, NJ 08404 (tel. toll free 800/528-1234, or 609/348-9175), is now owned by Bally Manufacturing of Chicago, but affiliated with Best Western. The guest rooms have fine lighting and a handsome color scheme of plum and rose for the rugs, bedspreads, and accessories. The rooms have two double beds, a sitting area, color TV, good closet space, a dressing room/vanity area, and a full tile bath in pretty pastel colors. Many rooms have a balcony.

The mezzanine holds a small game room, and the garage has direct access to the hotel. Parking is free for one car per room (although if it's used during the day, there's a valet charge). An outdoor pool is on the fifth floor, available free to hotel guests, as is the Finnish sauna bath.

Rates at the Best Western range from $80 in winter to $98 and up in summer, single or double occupancy. Add $10 for each additional person or a crib. Children 12 and under may use the same facilities as their parents with no charge.

The **Midtown-Bala Motor Inn,** two motels rolled into one at Indiana and Pacific Avenues, P.O. Box 267, Atlantic City, NJ

08404 (tel. 609/348-3031 for Midtown, 609/348-0151 for Bala), provides 300 rooms at reasonable rates. The excellent management has instituted a toll-free number for reservations (tel. toll free 800/932-0534 for the East Coast, in New Jersey 800/624-0986).

The Bala, with an entrance on Illinois Avenue, has been redone in natural fibers and earth tones; the corridors have jute to waist level, and bamboo laid horizontally above that. The 108 rooms are very, very clean, with bamboo motifs in blue and brown. All rooms come with two double beds, color television, AM/FM radio, and overlook the "oasis"—a pool surrounded by potted trees, miniature golf, and fountains. The Sands has built right up to the edge of the property, which gives it a dollhouse feeling in certain lights.

In season guests at the Bala can use the pool featured at the Midtown which is being completely redone.

Rates at either establishment can be as low as $55 a night in winter. The rates rise along with the thermometer, though, and you can expect $95 to $110 on weekends in summer. In the Midtown is a 24-hour restaurant, Chips, a spacious room with standard American fare at moderate prices.

The **Westminster (formerly Acapulco) Motel,** 117 S. Kentucky Ave., Atlantic City, NJ 08401 (tel. toll free 800/257-6223, or 609/344-9093), says that reservations are mandatory, since hotel occupancy is 100% May through October. Most rooms have two double beds; rooms with one double are a bit cheaper. Midweek winter rates are about $55 a night, $65 on weekends. In summer it's $85 to $95. For pleasant rooms in a convenient location, you couldn't do much better.

The rooms have balconies and small tables suitable for summer snacks. All rooms have Zenith color TV, AM/FM radio, and full bath. Six of the 60 rooms form master suites, perfect for a family with two children who can use the sofa bed. There is limited self-parking.

The **Mt. Royal,** Park Place near the Boardwalk, Atlantic City, NJ 08404 (tel. toll free 800/257-8579, or 609/344-7021), is a serviceable, central, and reasonable motel in the heart of town. Its red, white, and blue tile entrance is also the patriotic color scheme in the lobby, where a tile maple-leaf inset at the elevator harks back to the French Canadian source of the motel's name.

There are 150 air-conditioned rooms, all with two double beds, and a low-key color scheme in shades of brown. The Mt. Royal provides a modest but comfortable accommodation. The view varies, but only from Pacific Avenue's traffic to the massive granite wall of nearby Bally's Park Place, which surveys the inner court and pool, used in summer only.

The Mt. Royal has quite a decent coffeeshop at the Pacific Avenue entrance (see Chapter III). Although the free-standing staircase in the motel's lobby looks like a pile of checkers about to fall down, the rooms are fine by local standards. Winter rates are $38 to $44 midweek, $50 to $65 on weekends. In summer, rooms cost $65 to $70 midweek, $80 to $90 on weekends. Rooms fill up quickly, especially on summer weekends, so reservations are recommended. Parking is free.

The Mt. Royal recently offered a European Plan daily special for $19.95 per person, double occupancy, in the winter.

Jack Hochberg and Tony Bove took over the **Trinidad Motel** in 1977, taking a chance that casino gambling would create a need for a low-budget but respectable motel in the heart of Atlantic City. The Trinidad, at Tennessee Avenue near the Boardwalk, Atlantic City, NJ 08404 (tel. 609/344-8956), fulfills the requirements beautifully, and they've upgraded the 71 rooms with carpeting and lots of counter space. Many of the rooms have kitchenettes, and family rooms have sofa beds along with two doubles, which translates into $115 for six people.

All motel rooms are very clean, with color TV and sliding doors from an outdoor corridor. The Tennessee Avenue rooms have a diamond brick wall pattern, full-size refrigerator, and durable carpeting. Those with ocean views have a double bed with a curtain divider for the sofa bed. Fluorescent lights with chain pulls go the length of the headboards, and the cool rust and white interiors give lots of luggage room. The tile kitchenette areas in the 1½- and 2½-room efficiencies provide oven, electric range, stainless-steel sink, and garbage disposal. The court outside holds a small swimming pool and free parking for registered guests.

Summer rates for the bedrooms range from $55 to $75; those units with the kitchenettes cost $80 a day. Since this is one of the best motel values in the city, reservations are imperative.

At the **Continental Motel,** Illinois Avenue and the Boardwalk, Atlantic City, NJ 08404 (tel. 609/345-5141), all rooms have balconies or terraces overlooking the pool, in a typical U-shaped motel configuration. Some of the rooms have ocean views. Two double beds are standard throughout the motel. A restful setting in tones of beige, good light, phone, TV, dressing area, full tile bath, and year-round temperature control provide a cheerful, well-appointed accommodation. Elevator service supplements foot power to all three levels.

The price for guest rooms in winter ranges from $45 on weekdays to $66 on weekends. In July and August weekday rates are $72 per room; weekends $82. There is an additional charge of $10 for the third or fourth occupant of the same room.

The **Fiesta Motel,** at Tennessee and Pacific Avenues, Atlantic City, NJ 08401 (tel. toll free 800/341-2279, 609/344-4193), is within easy access of the Boardwalk, Resorts, and the Sands and Claridge casinos. It offers a swimming pool, plus comfortable rooms with two double beds, equipped with phone, full tub/shower bath, and color TV. The Fiesta is owner-managed and appears well kept. Summer rates are $70 to $74 in midweek, $90 to $120 on weekends. Winter rates are about $50 and $65, respectively. Rooms with kitchenettes are also available.

Atlantic City used to be full of places like the **Endicott Hotel,** 209 S. Tennessee Ave., Atlantic City, NJ 08401 (tel. 609/345-2653)—not 10 or 20 years ago, but 40 years ago—uncommercialized rooming houses with personal management and bungalow taste in interior decoration. Mrs. Lewis Gatti still runs the Endicott that way, and the prices haven't escalated much since those times either. You'll have to decide how responsible you can be to the ground rules of the hostelry, which include keeping visitors at the ground-floor level, quiet evenings on the awning porch, and a baleful eye on unruly behavior. But the Endicott has a solid clientele, charging $25 to $40 in winter and $35 to $45 in summer per double-bedded room, and it could be a good choice for a family you'd rather insulate from the casinos.

The Endicott has 45 rooms on five floors, each of which is painted each winter. The chambers, entered through solid wood doors, display prints of flowers and birds near the twin beds. Two easy chairs recline near the hot-water radiator, and most rooms have matching sets of nice maple furniture. Blue, pink, turquoise, and white are the predominant colors. The baths are done in pink and blue tile. The reading room on the first floor is everything you'd expect from a livable resort rec room of the 1940s. Some of Mrs. Gatti's best customers are used to this, but almost everyone responds positively to the delicate charm of the place—a real find, if you're in the mood.

NEAR RESORTS INTERNATIONAL: The 11-story brick and limestone **World International,** 110 S. Pennsylvania Ave. (P.O. Box 899), Atlantic City, NJ 08404 (tel. 609/347-8000, or toll free 800/257-8522; for the toll-free number in your area, call toll-free information, 800/555-1212) opened in 1927 as the Colton Manor. One of the employees who's been there over 20 years told me that bit of hotel lore, and you'll find long-term loyalty among the guests as well as the employees at this well-run establishment. A two-story motel with a rooftop pool was added to the hotel's Pennsylvania Avenue front, stretching toward the beach. The hotel's facilities include a dining room, the Thirsty Pilgrim Lounge, and a 14th-floor solarium overlooking the ocean. You'll be just a few steps from the Resorts casino here, and the Boardwalk is just down the block.

The lobby is traditionally furnished, pleasant and businesslike. There's no reason to linger, but comfortable chairs are there if you do. Most rooms are equipped with one or two double beds or two twin beds; a few rooms have a double and a single bed. In the hotel section, a traditionally furnished guest room will be comfortably outfitted with TV, phone, a sitting area, and full tile bath. Motel rooms facing Pennsylvania Avenue have colonial-style furnishings; those with a pool view have white-painted French provincial pieces.

The rates range in winter from $55 (hotel) and $65 (motel) in midweek to $65 and $75 respectively on weekends. Summer rates start at $90 and $95 in midweek; on weekends the cost is $100 and $115. A Modified American Plan is also available. For $21 per person per day additional you'll get a full breakfast and dinner (see below).

If you definitely want to see casino shows, the World's getaway packages are good value; otherwise I'd stick with the standard room rate and just add on the two meals for $21 per person. A winter weekend getaway package, Friday to Sunday, is $119 per person, double occupancy, for two nights and three days. You'll get one full-course dinner, two full breakfasts, tickets to a casino show, a welcome cocktail, and a box of saltwater taffy. A summer weekend package with similar offerings is $179 per person, double occupancy.

The traditionally furnished Colonial lounge outside the dining room entrance is a well-upholstered and spacious room to relax in before or after your meal. The dining room is open for breakfast from 8 a.m. to 11 a.m.; dinner is 5 to 8 p.m.

The breakfast menu features juice, fruit, hot cereal, eggs, home fries, choice of breakfast meats, toast, danish pastries, and beverages. Full-course dinners consist of appetizer or soup, entree, salad, vegetable, potato, dessert, and coffee. For an appetizer you might choose prosciutto with melon, a small mixed salad, or the soup of the day. Entrees run a three-flag gamut (American, Italian, and French) with the likes of fried shrimp,

shrimp scampi, and broiled fish almondine. There are also veal, beef, and chicken entrees. A coconut snowball with chocolate sauce is an inspired conclusion. A glass of wine with dinner is $1.75.

Owned by the same management as the World, the **World Tower Hotel,** on the beach block of North Carolina Avenue, Atlantic City, NJ 08404 (tel. toll free outside New Jersey 800/257-8522, or 609/347-8000), is strategically located just down the block from Resorts International. There are about 200 rooms and five suites, a rooftop pool, and the Gazebo restaurant. Whether your room has one or two double beds, it will be outfitted with individually controlled heat and air conditioning, color TV, bedside phones, and cedar closets. Rates are the same as at the World International.

The **Barclay,** 121 S. North Carolina Ave., Atlantic City, NJ 08404 (tel. 609/348-1156), has 75 rooms, all with two double beds, on its five floors. Summer rates are $80 at midweek, $90 on weekends. There's a swimming pool, and valet parking is free for registered guests.

Across the street are the Barbizon-Catalina and Burgundy Motels. The **Barbizon-Catalina,** on the ocean block of South North Carolina Avenue (P.O. Box 1257), Atlantic City, NJ 08404 (tel. toll free 800/257-8610, or 609/348-3137), has nicely appointed rooms with a contemporary-motel look. Floral spreads, matching drapes, and wall-to-wall carpeting harmonize nicely. Bedside reading lamps and phones, color TV, a refrigerator, and individually controlled heat and air conditioning are standard equipment throughout. In summer the midweek rates are reasonable—a room with one double bed is $64; larger rooms with two double beds are $72 or $84. Efficiencies, with a kitchenette right in the room, are $10 more (than the $72 or $84 rooms). You can eat in the room or on the terrace overlooking the pool. Free on-site parking is offered to guests. Children under 14 are free if they share room facilities with adults. In the winter, ask for their special rate—$18 per person, double occupancy. If there's a convention in town the rate won't be offered, but it's worth asking about.

Next door is the **Burgundy Motel,** 116 S. North Carolina Ave., Atlantic City, NJ 08404 (tel. 609/345-7514), also a few steps from Resorts casino. All rooms have two double beds, and are equipped with color TV, individually controlled heat and air conditioning, and room phones. Summer rates are $65 to $80 on weekdays, $75 to $85 on weekends. Each additional person in a room is $8; a roll-away bed is $5. Winter rates are $45 to $50 on weekdays, $60 to $70 on weekends.

NEAR THE TROPICANA AND GOLDEN NUGGET: On the southern reaches of Pacific Avenue are a number of moderately priced choices. The **Ascot,** at South Iowa and Pacific Avenues, Atlantic City, NJ 08401 (tel. toll free outside New Jersey 800/225-1476, or 609/344-5163), faces the Tropicana. Its 75 two-double-bedded rooms have terraces facing the pool. Color TVs and phones are in all the rooms, which are nicely turned out with orange tweed rugs and blue spreads. A free continental breakfast is an extra treat. Winter midweek rates are $45 to $60; in summer, rates go up to $75 and $85.

The **Flamingo Motel,** 3101 Pacific Ave., Atlantic City, NJ 08401 (tel. 609/344-3061), strikes a colorful note with its big orange panels. It's well situated between the Golden Nugget and the Tropicana and there's ample free parking. Color TV and air conditioning are in all of the nicely kept rooms. A 24-hour restaurant is a real convenience; you can get a good breakfast for less than $5. In winter rates start at $35 midweek, $65 on weekends. Summer rates range from $65 a night during the week, and $150 on weekends.

Comfortable, upholstered couches in the chandeliered lobby set off the Dunes, 2819 Pacific Ave., Atlantic City, NJ 08401 (tel. 609/344-5271), from the usual motel decor. Each of the rooms is pleasantly styled in brown tones with floral bedspreads and beige lacquered furniture. The service is attentive here, and the rooms are spick-and-span clean. Winter rates start at $30 midweek to $75 on weekends; in summer rates start at $85.

The **Baronet** (tel. 609/344-2925) and **Castle Roc** (tel. 609/345-9121) face each other across Pacific Avenue at Morris, Atlantic City, NJ 08401. The rooms are pleasantly furnished in tones of brown and white. There's a choice of one queen-size or two double beds. Both of these motels are two-story yellow brick structures, with parking just steps from your door. Both motels request a deposit with advance reservations. Lowest winter rates are $32 a night; in summer the lowest is $75, the maximum $125.

The **International Motel,** at South Chelsea and Pacific Avenues, Atlantic City, NJ 08401 (tel. toll free 800/257-8612, or 609/344-7071), is rather large (120 rooms) and offers kosher dining facilities (see the Restaurant chapter) on a Modified American Plan as well as room-only rates. Newly refurbished rooms offer clean, modern accommodations in this five-story motel. A swimming pool, sauna, and exercise room complete the facilities.

Summer rates for a room for two are $94 and up at midweek, $124 and up on weekends. Winter rates are about $30 less. With two full-course meals daily, the summer rates are $144 per day at midweek, $164 and up per day on weekends.

HIGHWAY HOTELS: Close to town on Route 40 (the Black Horse Pike), the **Airport Inn,** 500 N. Albany Ave., Atlantic City, NJ 08401 (tel. 609/344-9085), has 80 rooms, all air-conditioned, two-double-bed units. You'll be right across the highway from Bader Field, and only five blocks from the Boardwalk. There's a children's wading pool as well as a regular swimming pool. Winter rates are $38 at midweek, $58 on weekends. In summer it's $68 at midweek, $90 to $100 on weekends. Rates are higher on holiday weekends.

Part of the new generation of motor inns on the Atlantic City scene, two Comfort Inns along Route 40 provide first-class accommodations as well as free shuttle service to the casinos. The **Comfort Inn West,** U.S. 40 at Dover Place, West Atlantic City, NJ 08232 (tel. toll free 800/228-5150, or 609/645-1818), has lots of space to spread out along Lakes Bay. The rooms are in tip-top shape, decorated in shades of a pleasing dusty rose color, and have all the modern conveniences plus Bay views. A lobby coffeeshop also has those water views. Winter rates are $65 to $80 a room; in summer rates go up to $70 to $85. Extra person charge is $10.

The **Comfort Inn Victorian,** 1175 Route 40 (P.O. Box 739), Pleasantville, NJ 08232 (tel. toll free 800/228-5150, or 609/646-8880), is farther away from Atlantic City than its sister hostelry but its rates are a bit more affordable and they do advertise discounts for seniors and family plans. In a parklike setting, this two-story clapboard townhouse-style motel has rooms furnished in a very appealing, contemporary country look. Midweek rates in summer are $70, $80 on weekends; winter rates drop substantially.

The **Lido Motel,** Absecon Boulevard (Route 30) at Indiana Avenue, Atlantic City, NJ 08401 (tel. 609/344-1975), is a convenient overnight stop, within easy distance of Harrah's Marina. It has 27 rooms altogether, all with floral-print spreads and pink tile bathrooms; two are two-bedroom units. The rooms rent for $40 to $70 per night. A reservation deposit is required.

The **Comfort Inn,** 405 E. Absecon Blvd. (Route 30), Absecon, NJ 08201 (tel. toll free 800/228-5150, or 609/646-5000), has a bright modern presence set back from the White Horse Pike. The cream-colored concrete five-story structure is colorfully highlighted by red/orange/yellow banded awnings and an orange marquee. The rooms are soothingly outfitted in tones of beige, rose, and a soft blue. In winter rates are $32.50 per person, double occupancy. Bay-view rooms are $5 more per night. In summer rates escalate to $75 and $80 per night. Parlor suites are available. All rooms have full baths, HBO TV, and phones. Shuttle service to the casinos is available, as are discount coupons for food and/or shows at some of the casinos.

Near the Route 9 intersection is the two-story red-brick **Starlite Motor Inn,** 461 White Horse Pike, Absecon, NJ 08201 (tel. 609/645-7499), offering simple clean rooms, furnished in tones of brown and tan. Color TVs and tile baths throughout. Winter rates start at $35 a night, $50 in summer.

A bit farther away from town, the **Atlantic City Econo Lodge,** 328 White Horse Pike, Absecon, NJ 08330 (tel. toll free 800/446-6900, or 609/652-3300), upholds the motto of this budget chain, "Spend a night, not a fortune." All 22 units at this one-story, red brick, typically U-shaped motel cost $30 or $35 a night in winter, going up to $40 in summer. Summer holiday weekends you'll pay more. Free coffee is available in each room, along with remote control cable color TV.

For Longer Stays

HOTEL/CONDOMINIUMS: Offering accommodations for purchase or rental on a nightly, weekly, monthly, or seasonal basis, hotel/condos offer a luxurious way to go. Two are right in town on the Boardwalk: **The Enclave,** 3851 Boardwalk, Atlantic City, NJ 08401 (tel. toll free 800/ENCLAVE, or 609/347-0400), and the **Ocean Club,** 3100 Boardwalk, Atlantic City, NJ 08401 (tel. 609/345-3100). Call for rates. At the **Admiral's Quarters** at Marina Club, 655 Absecon Blvd., Atlantic City, NJ 08401 (tel. toll free 800/833-3242, or 609/344-2201), rates range from $70 a night (winter) to $150 a night (summer).

CAMPGROUNDS: The **Atlantic City KOA Campground,** 1997 Black Horse Pike (Route 40) Pleasantville, NJ 08232 (tel. 609/641-3085), has 175 sites for campers of every persuasion, from RVs to tenters. Sites are $14.75 a night; with electric and water hookups, they're $16.75 for two people. Each additional person over 3 years of age pays $2.50 per night. There are a swimming pool, grocery store, cable TV, and laundromat on the camp grounds. You can also stay at the KOA motel, with full motel service at rates that are comparable to any moderately priced motel in the vicinity. If you don't want to drive the eight miles into Atlantic City, a casino package for $10 will buy a round trip from the camp. There's usually a bonus in cash and/or food credit that will reimburse your $10 expenditure. Sites go quickly in summer, so be sure to reserve. From September 24 to April 30 they have a "Super Casino Package" with campsites for $5 and motel rooms for $15, including free transportation to Atlantic City.

Chapter III

ATLANTIC CITY RESTAURANTS

DINING OUT IN ATLANTIC CITY can be a lot of fun—whether you're biting into an enormous, onion-scented submarine sandwich at the White House Sub Shop, lunching al fresco at the Flying Cloud Café overlooking the marina, or discussing the right wine to accompany your exquisitely prepared pheasant at Johan's.

There's been a restaurant revolution in this town where less than a dozen years ago restaurant fare offered three (albeit delicious) alternatives—Jewish, Italian, and for lack of a better name, South Jersey seafood. Nothing to sneer about, certainly. Atlantic City's seasonal visitors had a happy choice of spicy deli delights, hearty pasta dinners, and the fresh clams and oysters and the fried shore dinners that spelled summertime for millions of vacationers. All that's still here, but now there's much, much more.

A variety of classy and interesting restaurants with a dazzling range of ethnic diversity has made Atlantic City a world-class eating town, all year round. At the hotel-casinos alone, continental European, Chinese, and Japanese specialties are everyday fare, plus there are the all-you-can-eat buffets that are outstanding values for the money.

Why venture outside the casino-hotels for dining? There are lots of possible answers: for fun, for a refreshing change of pace from the glittering casino atmosphere to a more relaxed setting, for a chance to see what the rest of the town is like. And most mysterious and potent of all—as Sir Edmund Hilary said when asked why he had climbed Mount Everest—"Because it's there." Outside the casino-hotels, sometimes on back streets that at night you'll feel safer driving or taking a cab to, there are some really fine restaurants that are trustworthy and take pride in their quality and service.

Atlantic City restaurants are pretty casual. A jacket and tie are needed only in the most elegant spots, and even there the maître d' has a jacket or two on hand to loan you. At most moderately priced restaurants in the area, the keynote for dress is casual.

Wherever you eat, you'll soon notice the high quality of the produce, the fruits and vegetables right off neighboring New Jersey farms, and the fresh seafood, traditionally the stuff of a New Jersey feast. The food is top-quality, and prices are right up there too. In general, Atlantic City restaurants have à la carte menus.

The restaurants I've previewed below offer good food, ambience, and overall enjoyable dining—at all price ranges and in various ethnic categories. I've divided the listings by type of food (more or less), and then by price, the most expensive first. Most of the restaurants are in the medium-priced category; a couple are deluxe. The low-cost restaurants are, of course, important for those who must keep their costs down. But many of them are worth a visit even if you aren't trying to save money.

Note that restaurants in the hotel-casinos have not been included here, but were described along with the hotels in Chapter II.

SEAFOOD: The **Knife and Fork Inn** is without question one of the finest seafood restaurants anywhere, and has been a standard of excellence at the corner of Albany and Pacific Avenues for over half a century. Mack and Andrew Latz preside over the Flemish structure with genial watchfulness. The atmosphere, simple and unpretentious, lets you concentrate on the uniformly marvelous meal, although the open Belgian fireplace and copper fixtures can be appreciated in their own right. Service is quick and attentive from the polite waitresses, dressed in black skirts and white aprons.

It's best to make reservations (tel. 344-1133) unless you're arriving early in the evening, and the coat-check lobby lets you walk in unburdened. Some prefer the intimate, darker dining rooms, particularly upstairs; others, a glassed-in terrace with plenty of greenery and yellow-and-green canopy.

You might begin with an appetizer of Maryland crab fingers ($5.25). They are perfectly fresh, and served on a bed of ice. The accompanying mild sauce of sugar, egg, and mustard is semi-sweet, and tasty enough to make you want more crab fingers as an excuse for sampling more. A green salad with bleu cheese

($3.75) mixes peak curly, romaine, and iceberg lettuce with cherry tomatoes. The shrimp ($16) and crabmeat ($18.50) salads use chunks of fresh meat, and make superb cold entrees. Most entrees fall in this price range, although lobster prices rise to $21 (for an extraordinary lobster Newburg laced with sherry). The bay scallops are most tender and bouncy, without a hint of rubberiness. They're served in a clam shell, and the best accompaniment (in season) is fresh buttered asparagus ($4.50). The fried zucchini ($2) is a house specialty. The fried fish dishes have no taste of oil, and retain delicacy; the stuffings for shrimp and lobster are prepared on the premises. Presentation is fairly unassuming—Knife and Fork Inn feels that the best preparations for seafood are usually the simplest, and no monkeying around with inferiority taints the raw material. For dessert with the excellent coffee, try the strawberry sundae with just-whipped cream or the mousse au chocolat. All in all, expect to pay $30 per person.

The wine list, divided equally between whites and reds, starts at $14 the bottle, and due to some fortunate investments, the prices of superior French vintages remains reasonable. Rhine and California wines round out the lower priced end of the list.

The Knife and Fork Inn serves dinner from 5:30 to 10:30 p.m. year round. Closed Monday except for major convention dates. Cash or American Express only, and free parking nightly (except Saturday, when it's $5). Reservations are taken except on Saturday, when no reservations are accepted for after 6:30 p.m.

Dock's Oyster House, 2405 Atlantic Ave. (tel. 345-0092), has seen Atlantic City grow since 1897, under three generations of Doughertys. Now it's a fish house that manages to look both contemporary and nautical. Maybe it's the oak tables, maybe the glass etched in scallop and rope patterns and set in the booth dividers. Maybe it's the Scandinavian slatted ceiling, or the mirrors framed with crustacean antics. Dock's is not the cheapest seafood spot in town—but it is one of the best.

A piano under the painted glass panels by the entrance foyer provides live music. There's a bar, but more service than lounge trade. Various boat models and a lobster tank under the whaling harpoons in the back of the room complete the decor. Service is relaxed but efficient, like the handsome menu.

Dock's gets a lot of trade from the Convention Hall, two blocks west, and most of its clientele starts with the enormous oyster stew ($8), prepared with six fresh oysters, butter, milk, cream, and seasonings. It comes with a fine pepper hash and crackers. Many proceed to order one of the lobsters ($22 broiled or steamed, $25 stuffed with pure unbreaded crab imperial), or one of the broiled or sautéed delicacies, which average $13. Sautéed scallops are done to your liking—you can ask for more (or less) garlic on many entrees. All dinners include pepper hash and bread. Vegetables and potatoes are à la carte. The cheese pie ($3.50) is a dessert favorite. A carafe of wine is $10.

Dock Dougherty might not recognize Dock's today, but he'd surely enjoy the food. Dock's is open Tuesday through Saturday from 5 p.m. until the wee hours.

Strictly speaking, the **Flying Cloud Café,** on North New Hampshire Avenue (tel. 348-3290), isn't totally a seafood restaurant, although the menu is weighted on the fishy side. However, the setting, at Historic Gardner's Basin, is delightfully nautical. The rambling, weathered-gray clapboard building is trimmed in a bright sea blue and surrounded by wooden decking where in summer picnic tables are set out for al fresco dining or lunching.

You can come out here by jitney, or if you're driving, there's lots of free parking. The nautical theme is quite evident inside too, in the sturdy captain's chairs, rough-hewn wooden tables, ship's-wheel chandeliers, the hurricane lamps on each table, and of course, the water views. It's a very relaxed, informal atmosphere, far away (in spirit) from the casinos' bustle and the Boardwalk's crowds.

For lunch a basket filled with "Lotsa Munchies" is better than the name implies. It's filled with potato skins, fried cheese, zucchini, fried chicken strips, and fried mushrooms with dipping sauce. A seafood salad—shrimp, crabmeat, lobster, or tuna—is served on a bed of lettuce with potato salad and coleslaw. Customers find a sandwich en croissant is a meal in itself. It's a flaky croissant filled with a number of good things; for example, gruyère, cucumber, bacon, and alfalfa sprouts, and is served with french fries or potato salad and coleslaw.

Dinner entrees feature a delicious crab sautéed in butter and garlic, and there are many other traditional seafood combinations. Entree prices include salad, potato, roll and butter, and coffee. If you don't want to go near the water for your entree, a tasty combination of barbecued chicken and baby back ribs with a special secret sauce will be a satisfying choice. Order the mousse of the day for dessert—it's good. Cocktails, beer, and wine are available. Lunch will be in the $10 range, dinner about $15 to $20.

Open only for the traditional Memorial Day to Labor Day season, **Abe's Oyster House,** 2031 Atlantic Ave. (tel. 344-7701), was so strongly recommended to me that I'm including it here, though it was closed when I stopped by. It's a local landmark, purveying the fruits of the sea. Highest accolades from local fans go to the steamed clams. Prices are in the medium range, with entrees between $7 and $12. If it doesn't live up to its reputation, let me know!

CONTINENTAL, WITH A FRENCH ACCENT: Far and away the most original and authentically European restaurant in the vicinity, **Johan's Zelande** is tucked away in a modest frame house at 3209 Fairmount Ave., at Sovereign Avenue (tel. 344-5733). Don't be put off by the location, as Johan's is in the classic European tradition of small, chef-owned restaurants. Occupying the first floor of the house, the restaurant has a small foyer, two intimate dining rooms, and in the back, Johan's domain, the kitchen. The flowered wallpaper, undistinguished paintings, and the heavy white tablecloths set with china and crystal are the most notable features of the rooms. At Johan's the food is definitely more important than the decor.

In fact, the food is superior. It's all prepared by Johan himself, a tall, blond Zeelander, using the best of local produce and provisions he has flown in from Europe. There are two sittings a night of the prix fixe, seven-course dinner, at 6:30 and 9 p.m. The cost is $47.50, plus tax, tip, and liquor.

You'll have a choice of five entrees, plus an appetizer, soup, fish, salad, cheese, and dessert each evening. Veal with crabmeat sauce, lamb with morels, filet mignon with truffles, pheasant with bacon and sauerkraut, and duckling formed one recent entree offering. Preceding the entree were a velvety fresh salmon mousse, a soup of imported fresh white asparagus, and sautéed shrimp. After the entree came a red-leaf-lettuce salad and assorted imported cheeses, and for dessert a hazelnut mousse and fresh berries with liqueur. The wine list is exceptional.

In summer Johan's is open seven days a week; in winter it's closed on Sunday. Reservations are essential.

One Flew Over, 5214 Atlantic Ave., Ventnor (tel. 823-4411), is the place to go when you want something a bit different. This tiny (12 tables) restaurant has paintings on its whitewashed walls, and its menu and ambience are reminiscent of a New York Soho–style restaurant. They serve fresh orange and carrot juice. For lunch a smoked turkey and brie omelet ($4.75) strikes the right nouvelle note. There are a number of other unusual omelet variations and soups—a crabmeat bisque ($2.75) is one possibility. At dinner fresh fish, stir fries, and charbroiled specialties highlight the fare. Lunch is 11 a.m. to 3 p.m. Monday to Saturday. Dinner is Sunday to Friday 5:30 to 10 p.m., Saturday 5:30 to 11 p.m. Sunday brunch is served 10 a.m. to 3 p.m. It's a pleasant five-minute drive to Ventnor, you'll enjoy a reasonably priced meal, and have a chance to see a pleasant community.

At the Central Square shopping mall, south of Atlantic City on Route 9, in Linwood, two country French-style restaurants make the ride worthwhile. **The Umbrella** (tel. 927-1699) is run by a young husband-and-wife team, Kathy and Claude Ayme. Diners sit on pretty bentwood chairs amid blooming plants in pots set near the many-paned windows. The à la carte menu features nicely sauced entrees, most of them under $10. You can expect to spend about $15 for dinner here.

Lunch or gourmet take-out dinner from **La Petit Café** (tel. 653-0292) has more elegance than the prices would lead you to expect. It's like a country café, with pretty provincial wallpaper, cut flowers on your table, and very thoughtful service. Seafood quiches, fresh salads, omelets are all just fine. Open 11:30 a.m. to 3:30 p.m. Monday through Saturday, 5 to 9 p.m. on Friday and Saturday. In winter open for dinner by reservation only.

AMERICAN INTERNATIONAL: Aubrey's, at the corner of Pacific and Arkansas Avenues (tel. 344-1632), is especially popular in the summer with its enclosed patio. Year round it's an appealing spot, open till very late, where both tourists and casino employees stop in for a drink and late-night snack of clams casino or a croissant sandwich of ham and Swiss or turkey. Outfitted in simple contemporary style with light-wood and etched-glass panels, its fare includes hamburgers, served with french fries, for $5.25, eggs, omelets, and quiches ($5.25), and those croissant sandwiches. More substantial entrees—jumbo shrimp, steaks, or lobster—range from $12.95 to $18.75. Open for dinner, seven days, from 5 p.m.

McGee's, 1615 Pacific Ave. (tel. 344-7521), is in the heart of town, under the same owner since 1959. Not its decor, but its reputation for dependably good food brings locals here year round.

The surroundings are quite pleasant—yellow stucco walls, dark-wood tables covered at night with chocolate-brown cloths and cream-colored napkins, and a kerosene lamp on each table. Oyster crackers and horseradish are a hospitable nibble compliments of the house. The lunch menu is predictable, but enjoyable. Seafood soups and salads, eggs, cold and hot sandwiches, and house specials, served with a side dish of slaw or potato salad. A fried fish platter—filet, oyster, clam, and shrimp—is $5.50. Weekdays there's also a blackboard lunch special.

Recommendable entrees at dinner are the crab imperial at

$13.75 and the sirloin steak with french-fried onion rings at $16.75. All entrees include rolls and butter, salad or coleslaw, and baked stuffed or french-fried potatoes or rice pilaf. Platters for children under 12 are $6.75. Open 11 a.m. to about 10 p.m. weekdays in winter, later on weekends and in season.

Twelve South, 12 S. Indiana Ave. (tel. 344-1112), is open for lunch, dinner, and late-night snacks from 11 a.m. to 8 a.m. It has an inviting decor: pressed-tin and wood-paneled walls, polished wood tables with bentwood chairs in the front room, booths with café curtains on brass rods for a look of privacy in the back room, where the walls are covered with old newspapers. An eclectic assortment of decorative objects hang from the ceiling; watch out for the old French horn.

Daily lunch and dinner specials are on the blackboard. For lunch, the daily special is $2.95 and always includes a mug of beer. Spaghetti with clam sauce (red or white), salad, and garlic bread is a popular lunch offering.

Their "munchies," defined as substantial starters or significant snacks, are sparked by tangy dips—avocado, onion and sherry, and spinach and garlic. The "crudités colossal" is a basket full of fresh vegetables with dips; at $3.95 it's a good value. Dinner entrees feature a 16-ounce steak and prime ribs.

THE BEST ITALIAN RESTAURANTS: Finding an Italian restaurant in Atlantic City is not much of a challenge. There must be at least two dozen that could keep you happily eating pizza (often home-made), scampi, and sausages for weeks. But since most visitors don't have that much time to sort out their favorites, I've chosen what I consider the top nine to preview for you. *Buon appetito!*

Scannicchio's, on the beach block at 119 S. California Ave. (tel. 348-6378), is the current favorite of the locals (and visiting entertainers as well). Behind an unprepossessing exterior, you'll find an equally modest, dimly lit, rather large room, where you'll just about be able to discern some pleasant oil paintings and hanging plants decorating the walls. Luckily the menu is printed in bold, large type, so you won't be deterred by the dim light from a good look at the offerings.

Scannicchio's makes good use of local Jersey seafood (appetizers include clams—steamed, casino, oreganata, and posillippo, all in the $6 range), and a favorite main dish is seafood alla Scannicchio—lobster, shrimp, scallops, clams, and mussels, for $19.50. There are also freshly made manicotti, lasagne, and gnocchi for starters. Veal specialties are on the entree list. Veal parmigiana ($10.95) and saltimbocca ($14.95) are delicious choices. Homemade rum cake ($2.50) or ricotta pie ($2.25) are worth the calorie splurge.

As you can see, there's good reason for Scannicchio's popularity. Dinner is served from 5 p.m. till about midnight; the bar is open later.

Since 1964 **Culmone's,** 2435 Atlantic Ave. (tel. 348-5170), has been serving hearty Italian specialties along with continental seafood and beef entrees, in this medium-sized, attractive room. Sparkling chandeliers, crisp white tablecloths, and wall mirrors set an elegant but informal atmosphere. The service is careful and efficient, but since food is cooked to order, a little patience is required.

Clams stuffed with shrimp, lobster, and crabmeat in a cream sauce ($7.50) makes a great start; homemade manicotti ($7) is a more traditional appetizer. Italian specialties and regular menu items include chicken cacciatore or pizzaiola ($11), veal scaloppine ($12), and lobster française. All entrees are served with vegetable and a side order of linguine or a baked potato. Chianti makes a fine accompaniment. Homemade pastries are the grand finale—if you've got room. A full dinner will range from $15 to $20. Culmone's is open for dinner from about 4 to 11 p.m. Closed Tuesday.

A long-established restaurant recently taken over by new management, **Mama Mott's,** 151 S. New York Ave. (tel. 345-8218), upstairs dining room is elegantly Victorian, with rich reds, glass candles, fresh flowers, and gold draperies. The downstairs dining room shares the same menu, but it's a bit noisier.

If you're with a party of four, Mama Mott's has a special "Trip Around Italy" dinner that has salad, pasta, meat, fowl, homemade specialties, dessert, a carafe of house wine, and coffee, all for $70. Homemade pasta and gnocchi and veal piccante are among the house specialties. Another delectable house specialty is the seafood ristorante for two. It's a combination of lobster, clams, scallops, and jumbo shrimp prepared in a special sauce and served on linguine, plus a salad and coffee. Chocolate mousse amaretto is a light, fluffy dessert; the traditional Italian spumoni and tortoni are also at hand. Mama Mott's is open 5 to 10 p.m. weekdays, till midnight on Friday and Saturday.

Ristorante Alberto, 2303 Pacific Ave. (tel. 344-7000), features northern Italian cuisine in a very convenient location, across the street from Convention Hall. There are appetizers like clams on the half shell ($6) and spinach salad ($4.25), but it's worth going Italian and trying traditional dishes like trenette filetto, thin noodles in tomato sauce; or vitello fiorentino, veal with spinach and white wine ($18.50). A savory osso buco in brown sauce is served with rice milanese. Open from 5 p.m. till late evening for dinner.

Angelo's Fairmount Tavern, 2300 Fairmount at Mississippi Avenue (tel. 344-2439), is a tan brick, two-story structure that looks like a neighborhood bar from the outside. It is that, but it's also *the* local restaurant for Atlantic City's Italian population. The bar and rear dining room are unpretentious, with café curtains, Formica-topped tables, and photos of sports heroes over the bar, where the stools are usually filled with customers having a meatball sandwich ($2.75) and a glass of house wine or draft beer. Angelo's meatballs have the aroma of Italy; they're made by the owner himself and I give them my highest recommendation. If it's lunch you're here for, a steaming bowl of minestrone is hearty and nourishing with lots of pasta and vegetables ($1.60).

At dinner, well, I'd recommend the spaghetti and meatballs, but you already know how I feel about Angelo's meatballs. Shrimp fra diavolo is served on linguine and accompanied by salad, as are shrimp and mussels marinara. Excellent, too, are the other spaghetti dishes—with oil and garlic, clam sauce, or sausages. Entrees run from about $6 to $10. For dessert, spumoni is a fitting conclusion. Lunch is served from 11:30 a.m. to 2 p.m., dinner until 10:30 p.m.

Angeloni's II, at Georgia and Arctic Avenues (tel. 344-7875), has a baronial air, imparted by its coats-of-arms on the walls, black leather chairs, and subdued lighting. You'll find the likes of veal florentine, chicken marsala, and zuppe di pesce on the impressive entree list. Dinner will be in the $15 to $20 range. It's served seven nights, from 5 p.m. till midnight.

At **Sabatini's,** 2210 Pacific Ave. (tel. 345-4816), the owner-chef dishes up an in-depth pasta selection of nine different spaghetti dishes, six ravioli variations, baked manicotti, and gnocchi. It's solid Italian cooking. If you want a meat entree, I understand the jumbo pork chops are satisfying. Spaghetti dishes are $7.50 to $11, ravioli is $8.50 to $10.50, and entrees run $10.50 to $16.95. Sabatini's is open from noon to 8 a.m. for lunch and dinner (served till about midnight).

The **Lido,** 3006 Atlantic Ave. (tel. 345-1211), is much frequented by both locals and visitors to Atlantic City. This atmospheric spot has a beamed ceiling, stucco walls, comfortable captain's chairs, and yellow glass lamps on each table. There's a deejay nightly, except Tuesday, from about 11 p.m. Entree specials like chicken marsala ($10.95) or shrimp parmigiana ($11.95) are offered nightly. Dinner is served from 5 to 11 p.m.

The **Brajole Café** for a delicious, moderately priced lunch or dinner, the **Savoia** for a good Italian dinner, and **Club Ancoppa** for disco dancing have made this tripartite establishment one of Atlantic City's hot locales—all at 2233 Atlantic Ave. (tel. 348-5080).

CHINESE: The **Jade Beach** is at Iowa Avenue and the Boardwalk, in the Tropicana (tel. 345-8132), and has lunch specials as well as a complete dinner menu. At lunchtime the price of the main course ($6.95 to $8.95) will also bring you rice and a choice of three soups. Entrees include hot-and-spicy shredded pork with garlic sauce and sweet-and-sour shrimp. If you like hot food, you might try scallops with garlic sauce for a dinner entree ($14.95), or Hunan chicken—sliced with broccoli and mushrooms in hot Hunan sauce ($9.95). Less spicy, but also tasty are steak kew ($16.95), lemon chicken ($10.95), and steamed fish Cantonese style ($19.75).

The decor is simple, light and airy, and the ocean view is the main feature. Try to get a window seat. It's very busy here at mealtime, so don't be surprised if there's a line. The Jade Beach is open from noon to midnight weekdays, till 2 a.m. on Friday and Saturday.

The **Peking Duck House,** at Iowa and Atlantic Avenues (tel. 344-9090), is one of the prettiest rooms in town, so don't be put off by the green tile front or the golden duck that looms over the front door. Inside it's all cool and sophisticated, with subtle lighting and three lovely archways between the foyer and the dining room that frame very handsome floral arrangements.

You have to call in advance for the house specialty. The ducks are cooked to order in a special oven so that excess fat is drained and the skin becomes crisp. The whole duck is carved at your table and served with rice crêpes, green scallions, and cucumber juliennes, with a special sauce. A whole Peking duck is $30.

Lunches are inexpensive—entrees are $4.95 and $5.95 and come with soup, salad, rice, tea, and a fortune cookie. The dinner menu has lots of interesting entrees besides the duck, chicken with black-bean sauce ($9.50) among them—plus 15 special gourmet favorites ($10.95 to $14.95). Open for lunch and dinner.

KOSHER: In the **International Motel,** Chelsea and Pacific Avenues, there are two restaurants, one for meat and one for dairy (tel. 344-7071), run strictly according to kosher tradition. The dairy restaurant, a sparkling place with bright green leather booths and white Formica tabletops, offers such fare as smoked fish platters, cheese blintzes, and vegetable cutlets. Entree prices range from $4.95 to $8.95. Open for breakfast, lunch, and dinner, 8 a.m. to 8 p.m. The meat dining room offers three-course dinners with a choice of four or five entrees for $14.95 ($16.95 for steak).

MEXICAN: Stucco walls, red tile floors, and a gaily painted ceiling create a festive, south-of-the-border ambience at **Los Amigos,** 1926 Atlantic Ave. (tel. 344-2293). Completing the decor are the sombreros and Indian rugs on the wall and the hand-inlaid wood bar. At this popular and inexpensive restaurant, open from 11:30 a.m. to 7 a.m., you can have a drink, a snack, lunch, or ample dinner fare. Mexican pizza, a tortilla with spicy toppings and garnishes, is $5.25. The menu features Mexican favorites like chicken mole ($7.85), chile rellenos ($6.75), and flauta, a tortilla filled with chicken and spices and topped with guacamole and sauce ($7.25). For a vegetarian meal, there are meatless platters like one of fresh greens, vegetables, cheese, and salsa. There's even gringo food—burgers (seven ounces) with pickle and french fries for $3.95 to $4.75, depending on the fixings. In this informal spot, nothing on the menu exceeds $8.95.

INFORMAL AND INEXPENSIVE: Something of an institution in Atlantic City, this narrow little sandwich shop at Mississippi and Arctic Avenues (tel. 345-8599) numbers among its customers New Jersey's governor, Dean Martin, Tony Orlando, Burt Lancaster, Susan Sarandon, and Jerry Lewis—and they've got the autographed photos to prove it. The **White House Sub Shop** is a straight-from-the-shoulder restaurant: orange leather booths, beige Formica tables, a take-a-number ticket machine, and those celebrity photos are what you'll see as you wait in line for your submarine sandwich, if you're taking it out. There's table service at the booths, or you can sit at the five-stool front counter. The house staple is the regular sub—$2.50 for half a loaf of Italian bread, $4.90 for a full loaf—a many-layered thing of salami, cappicola, cotechine, provolone, lettuce, tomatoes, hot peppers, oil, and vinegar. There are other choices: tunafish, ham, Philly cheese steak, sausage, hamburger—they're all cheerfully slapped on the bread to make sandwiches by a staff of six that stands behind the back counter, feverishly trying to keep up with the flow of customers who queue up daily for these tempting jawbreakers. Over 11 million sold, says the sign outside, and you can come in and add to the total daily from 10 a.m. to midnight.

Margie's is a cozy restaurant near Convention Hall, at 2309 Pacific Ave. (tel. 345-4533). Flower-sprigged tablecloths add a cheerful touch to the tables (there are just six) and five booths. The menu lists the usual breakfast fare: juice, eggs, omelets, muffins, pancakes, and danish pastry. Sandwiches from grilled cheese ($2.50) to roast beef ($3.50), and salads round out the menu. Margie's is open from 6 a.m. to 4 p.m. daily.

The **Mt. Royal's coffeeshop,** off the motel lobby at Park Place and Pacific Avenue (there's an entrance on Pacific), has break-fast, lunch, and dinner at prices that are sure to please. The food is wholesome and hearty, the kind you'd get in any Main Street restaurant across America. Sandwiches of tuna or chicken salad, and bacon, lettuce, and tomato are $2.79. Hamburgers are $1.99 to $2.99 (which includes french fries and salad). Dinner platters include soup, salad, vegetable, potato, and roll and butter. The chopped steak, southern fried chicken, or flounder filet platters each cost $5.99. There's an attractive display of layer cakes and cheesecake for dessert fanciers. Hanging plants add a touch of green. If you're pressed for time, you can eat at the counter in-stead of at a booth or table.

While it may not have occurred to you to have breakfast in a bar, the **Silver Dollar Saloon,** 1719 Pacific Ave. (tel. 344-2202), provides a low-cost, creditable one. A wood-paneled back room with Tiffany-style lamps, ceiling fans, old sheet music, and beer ads on the wall, and red-checked oilcloth on the tables, provides a pleasantly funky setting for 24-hour eats. Two eggs with ham, bacon, or sausage, plus potatoes and toast, are $2.95. Sandwiches—corned beef, roast beef, baked ham—are $3.50, and there are lots of others, plus submarine sandwiches ($2.75). It's one of the best deals in town.

A popcorn machine at the front bar dispenses snacks for bar patrons. To wash down the popcorn, how about a "boot" full of beer? It's $2.75, and you can keep the mug; refills are $1.25 each. You can buy a Silver Dollar souvenir in the shape of a cap ($4), sweatshirt ($8.50), or cigarette lighter ($1.50).

Completely different in character from the Silver Dollar is the **Copenhagen Danish Pastry & Coffee Shop,** 3205 Atlantic Ave. (tel. 348-3394). Danish pastry and cinnamon buns still warm from the oven are two of the treats in store if you stop for a cup of coffee or tea, or a more substantial breakfast or lunch. To reach the yellow leather booths at the back of this cozy shop, you walk past an appetizing display of napoleons, eclairs, tarts, hazelnut squares, cannolli, and assorted cookies—all baked on the prem-ises. Paintings of scenes from Hans Christian Andersen's tales adorn the walls. The breakfast menu will start you off with a pleasant morning. A typical meal of eggs, home fries, coffee, and danish will bring you back change from a $5 bill. A club sandwich for lunch with a filling of turkey, bacon, lettuce, and tomato is $3.75; a roast beef sandwich, $3.95 (they're the most expensive). Sodas, coffee, or tea are the beverages. You can, of course, buy bakery items to take out. In summer the Copenhagen is open seven days a week from 7:30 a.m. to 5 p.m.; in the winter it's 7:30 a.m. to 2 p.m., and they're closed on Monday.

The friendly folks at **Tony's Baltimore Grill,** 2800 Atlantic Ave. (tel. 345-5766), will be glad to pack your pizza to go, or you can stay and play your jukebox favorites in this relaxed spot. Tony's special pizza is a juicy pie with cheese, mushrooms, and sausage. There are antipasto ($2.25) and spaghetti platters ($2.20 and $3.75) to eat in or take out. Sandwiches and fried seafood platters are decent, but it's the pizza that keeps the locals and visitors coming to Tony's. The kitchen is open 11 a.m. to 3 a.m.; the bar, 24 hours.

A profusion of fast-food outlets, from national franchises like Burger King to the indigenous delights of Dip-Stix, saltwater taffy, Taylor pork roll, pizzas, plus the sparkling cafés and ice-cream parlors in the casino-hotels line the Boardwalk. There's a full preview of these eateries in the section on the Boardwalk in Chapter VI.

AT OCEAN ONE: This red and white pier in the shape of a 900-foot ocean liner docked at the Boardwalk, right across from Caesars, is a combination of shopping mall, exhibition center, fast-food dining areas, and sit-down restaurants (for details on shopping in Ocean One, see Chapter VI).

Diversity is king at the **Food Court,** on the second level, where a potpourri of fast-food stalls encircles the deck. Although some of the food stands are shut in winter, you won't go hungry with the bewildering variety: an oyster bar, barbecued chicken and ribs, Pasta Plus, Japanese specialties, Philly cheese steaks, beer-steamed franks, burgers, Pick-a-Pocket pita bread falafel and salad sandwiches, Taco Don's, Hillside Farms ice cream, Belgian waffles, hero sandwiches, Greek shish kebab and stuffed grape leaves, Boston Brownies, a Strudel Factory—the list seems endless. My only advice here is to walk around and weigh the possibilities before taking the plunge.

Don't worry about having to balance your purchases as you walk around eating. There's a wonderful mezzanine picnic area one flight up from the Food Court, with long tables and comfortable chairs, and wrap-around windows that give you a fantastic ocean view. Here's where you really do feel as though you're at sea on an ocean liner.

Here at Atlantic City's answer to the suburban shopping mall are an international array of dining options on the third level.

The cold sausages, hams, and jars of sauerkraut displayed in the delicatessen counter at the entrance to the **Black Forest** restaurant (tel. 348-0700) will give you a good idea of what's in store for you inside. Würst mit kraut is the traditional German street snack, but here you can savor it sitting down, with a great ocean view in a contemporary setting of light wood and ceramic tile. The würst platter, served with weinkraut and German potato salad is $7.29. If you're really starving, you may be able to do justice to weiner schnitzel for $9.95. There's an exceptional selection of imported beers, bottled and draft, to enjoy with your meal. Soups, salads, and double-decker sandwiches are also at the ready. Hot apple strudel with whipped cream and, of course, Black Forest chocolate cake ($2.50 for either) are in the right spirit for dessert. The Black Forest is open for lunch and dinner from 11 a.m.

The **Spaghetti House** (tel. 345-8799) provides a comfortable setting for some hearty fare. Lunch specials are mainly in the sandwich line—hoagies, meatball, and such, and range from $2.75 to $4.75. At dinner pasta is king with tortellini, cannelloni, and gnocchi among the possibilities. Most entrees have an Italian accent and range from $6.75 (manicotti) to $15.75 (crab diavolo). Meat and fish entrees come with soup, salad, pasta, and garlic bread. Open from 11 a.m. to 10 p.m. in winter; closing hours are later in summer.

Starr's Delicatessen (no phone) is light, airy, and has views of the ocean and Boardwalk. Originally a New York–style deli, it's added some entrees in the barbecued chicken and ribs theme. Deli sandwiches, eggs, omelets, and salads are always on hand, too. Sandwiches range from $4 to $7; the barbecued chicken and ribs combo platter is $8.95. Carrot, cheese, and layer cakes are $2.50 a slice. Open daily from 11 a.m.

H. I. Rib & Co. (tel. 347-7066) is famous for tender, juicy barbecued baby back ribs—a full order is $10.95; a half order, $7.95. If you're having trouble deciding between the barbecued chicken and ribs, you can have some of each for $9.95. A hefty onion ring loaf is $2.95. There are tossed green salads to enjoy with your entree, and char-broiled hamburgers for die-hard traditionalists. Lunch specials from 11 a.m. to 4 p.m. feature such sandwiches as beef or pork barbecue with french fries and coleslaw ($4.95). H. I. Rib & Co. is open from 9 a.m. to midnight seven days.

Beefsteak Charlie's (tel. 348-1122) unlimited shrimp and salad bar is for lovers of those specialties who never get enough. They will here. You can have the shrimp and salad as your complete dinner ($9.99) or as part of a dinner with entrees like New York sirloin ($13.99), or chicken teriyaki ($10.99). Entrees alone, without the unlimited bars, are $3 cheaper. The burgers here are justly renowned—nine ounces (before cooking) of ground sirloin makes a meaty burger ($6.49; with unlimited shrimp and salad, add $3.50). Soups and sides, sautéed mushrooms or french fries ($1.99) will help fill up the empty spaces. There's a menu for children under 12. The restaurant is open noon to 10 p.m. weekdays, till 11 p.m. on Friday and Saturday.

FARTHER AFIELD: The **Ram's Head Inn** is not hard to find, and it's definitely worth the trip on Route 30 (9 West White Horse Pike; tel. 652-1700), just west of the Garden State Parkway intersection. This elegant colonial-style inn is among the most picturesque in the state. It's a rambling white clapboard building with several different dining rooms, including an outside courtyard and patio, and lots of free parking space. The front room, where you can check your coat, has an outsize brick fireplace, Windsor chairs, and polished round table. The gallery is a long, plant-filled room with cocktail tables overlooking a pretty brick patio; there's piano music in the gallery in the evening. In the bar, a white-manteled fireplace has a glass firescreen in place when the fire is lit. Fresh flowers, wall sconces, and gleaming china and silver on the carefully appointed tables welcome guests in all the dining rooms. So charming is this spacious and serene establishment that it's become a popular wedding site as well.

The American and continental cuisine at the Ram's Head have been awarded four stars by the Mobil travel guides. Though the food is rather pricey, it's not exorbitant. For a first course you might order a cold appetizer of assorted shellfish ($6.95) or a hot one of baked clams casino ($4.95). House salads are offered if you wish. Breast of chicken stuffed with Vermont ham and mushroom duxelles ($13.75) is a specialty, or you could have the roast beef with Yorkshire popover ($18.25). Vegetables, like fried zucchini ($1.95) or broccoli hollandaise ($2.95), are à la carte. Pastries from the dessert cart or ice cream completes the meal. There's a fine wine list. The Ram's Head is open for dinner from 5 to 10 p.m. Monday to Saturday, from 3:30 to 9 p.m. on Sunday. Lunch is served 11:30 a.m. to 2:30 p.m. Monday to Friday. The lunch menu features soups, salads, sandwich platters, and main courses. Quiche of the day with a side dish of fruits is $6.50. Chicken with dumplings is $6.95.

You don't have to speak in hushed tones at **Library III,** on the Black Horse Pike (tel. 645-7655), even though the walls are lined with books. It's a very popular restaurant, multiroomed and softly lit, with a devoted following, many of whom like to sit in the front lounge in comfortable leather chairs and listen to the live music. Among the books, old movie posters, and an old ice box (surprisingly decorative) is a salad bar, which is complimentary with dinner. Prime ribs are a fine entree ($12.50) and so is the T-bone steak ($13.75). Nightly specials, like broiled scallops with rice, are even more reasonable ($8.95). The Library is open Monday to Saturday from 4 p.m. to 2 a.m., serving dinner till 1 a.m., on Sunday from 3 p.m. to 1 a.m., serving dinner from 3:30 p.m. to midnight.

Remember **Tull's,** 1503 Black Horse Pike (Route 40; tel. 641-6014), for some of the freshest seafood in the area. You can buy it raw at their fish market, or eat it, cooked to order, in their unpretentious dining room next door. There's an early-bird dinner special from 4 to 6 p.m., lunch from 11 a.m. to 4 p.m., and dinner until about 10 p.m. The catch of the day is the feature here—caught in Tull's own boats—plus a full range of seafood entrees. Lots of free parking.

Chapter IV

NOTES ON GAMBLING

MOST PEOPLE WHO GAMBLE think they might make a fortune gambling if only luck stays with them. This elusive dream keeps people coming back, trying out elaborate systems, reading books on how to beat the odds, betting excitedly with the house when a craps table gets hot, or casually dropping spare change into slot machines as they pass by.

From relatively small beginnings in 1978, gambling in New Jersey has grown to be an enormous industry with gross revenue in 1984 totaling $1.95 billion. The take in 1985 is expected to pass $2 billion. For an operation that didn't even exist ten years ago, these are impressive numbers.

According to casino managers and pit bosses, all systems are bunk. Which is not to say that somebody who, say consistently backs the same number at roulette, or who always stands pat with two cards at blackjack, won't occasionally strike it lucky. But systems as such just don't work, and the only one that gives the casino cause for alarm is some gamblers' habit of doubling their stake each time they lose. This, however, is countered very simply by imposing a limit on the amount of stake, usually $1000 or less.

Of course, some people's idea of a system is to cheat, and by now Atlantic City dealers feel they've seen almost everything. In fact, any casino that hired amateur dealers would probably be out of business within months. The most common dodge is for a player to try to slip a little extra onto his stake when the dealer's attention is diverted (sometimes a gambler's confederate will deliberately create a diversion). Specially marked cards with identifying lettering that can be read through tinted spectacles have occasionally been slipped into blackjack games, and shaved or weighted dice can be substituted for the original ones by a smooth crook.

Dealers, naturally, are always under supervision, not only by the pit boss in their immediate area and various plainclothes security men wandering randomly through the casino, but by strategically placed television cameras or overhead mirrors. For anyone who appreciates style, watching an old-hand blackjack dealer, seemingly bored but actually always alert, is a study in professionalism. Flipping each player a card, noting his own, scooping up lost stakes, paying the winners, and filing the used cards without a wasted motion or change of expression is a graceful exhibition of manual dexterity that bears absolutely no relationship to the outcome of the game itself.

Dealers at any Atlantic City casino are not permitted to gamble anywhere in town. If they're caught at it, the penalties are stiff, ranging from suspension without pay to losing their dealer's license. Overseeing the casinos, the New Jersey Casino Control Commission has authority over all employees and is the license-issuing body. Uniformed commission representatives are at every casino, and if you have complaints about gaming procedures, they're the ones to see.

Serious gamblers, or those who are trying to be, can save themselves considerable strain and can learn a lot by buying booklets in the *Facts of Gambling* series, which sell for about $2 each. Among them are *The Facts of Craps, The Facts of Blackjack . . . Roulette . . . Slots . . . Baccarat.* They cover history of the games, winning percentages, how to play, and procedures to follow to reduce the casinos' advantage. You can order these booklets by mail from the publisher, Gambler's Book Club, 630 South 11th St., Las Vegas, NV 89101, or request a free catalog (tel. toll free 800/634-6243, Monday to Saturday, 9 a.m. to 5 p.m. Las Vegas time).

The **Gambler's Emporium,** 2517 Pacific Ave., Atlantic City, NJ 08401 (tel. 609/344-8767), has a complete selection of gaming books (including the *Facts of Gambling* series) and gaming tapes, and even runs seminars for beginners. **Connie's News,** 1118 Atlantic Ave. (tel. 344-9813), is open 24 hours; it's a complete newsstand but it has a large gambling section of books and magazines.

Never be too timid at the tables to ask questions of dealers. They're advised to be pleasant, helpful, and instructive to all players. If you should encounter an unhelpful dealer, move to a more congenial table—or take your business to another casino. Gambling should be fun. And all the experts will tell you to indulge in gambling only as a pleasant pastime.

Casino Hours and Age Limits
    Casinos in Atlantic City open at 10 a.m. and close at 4 a.m. on weekdays, at 6 a.m. on weekends and holidays.
    The minimum age for gambling in Atlantic City is 21.

The Rules of the Games

All gambling experts agree on four basic rules: (1) don't play games you can't understand; (2) set a daily limit and keep to it (a small bettor can't win big, but he can lose big); (3) play your hunches; and (4) don't fail to walk away from a game when you're ahead. After all that—if you're lucky—you'll come out having a good time, and perhaps even some money ahead.

Now that you're ready, here's how the games are played.

SLOT MACHINES: At all the casinos, colored lights at the top of each machine indicate which coin denomination the machine accepts. Usually a red light is for 5¢, yellow is 25¢, orange is 50¢, and blue is $1.

Also, there are various models of machines. On a multiplier machine you can play more than one coin. Each additional coin will increase the amount of payoff, but all awards are on the basis of the center line.

You can put in more than one coin in the multiline machines. This gives you the chance to win on the line above and below the center line. On some of the machines additional coins give you the chance to win on diagonal lines also.

Progressive slot machines have a jackpot that increases as the machine is played. Another recent variation of the basic slots theme are the video blackjack machines. These new machines simulate a TV screen that displays cards and you play blackjack according to the instructions on the front of the machine.

The latest models print out electronic messages everytime you pull the handle: "Good Luck," "Easy Come, Easy Go," "Happy Days Are Here Again," "Columbus Took a Chance," etc.

Atlantic City slot machines are fixed to pay back 83% of what they ingest.

CRAPS: This game is played with dice. The craps table is divided into marked areas (Pass, Come, Field, Big 6, Big 8, etc.), where you place your chips to bet. Here are a few simple directions:

Pass Line: A "Pass Line" bet pays even money. If the first roll of the dice adds up to 7 or 11, you win your bet; if the first roll adds up to 2, 3, or 12, you lose your bet. If any other number comes up, it's your "point." If you roll your point again you win, but if a 7 comes up again before your point is rolled, you lose. Once the point is established, Pass bets cannot be removed or reduced.

Don't Pass Line: Betting on the "Don't Pass" is just the opposite of betting on the Pass Line. This time, you lose if a 7 or 11 is thrown on the first roll, and you win even money if a 2 or a 3 is thrown on the first roll. If the first roll is 12, though, it's a stand-off and nobody wins. If none of these numbers is thrown and you have a point instead, in order to win, a 7 will have to be thrown before the point comes up again. A Don't Pass bet also pays even money.

Come: Betting on "Come" is just the same as betting on the Pass Line, but you must bet *after* the first roll, or on any following roll. Again, you'll win on 7 or 11 and lose on 2, 3, or 12. Any other number is your point, and you win if your point comes up again before a 7.

Don't Come: This is the opposite of a Come bet. Again, you wait until after the first roll to bet. A 7 or 11 means you lose; a 2 or 3 means you win even money; 12 is a stand-off and nobody wins. You win if 7 comes up before the point (the point, you'll recall, was the first number rolled if it was none of the above).

Field: This is a bet for one roll only. The "Field" consists of seven numbers: 2, 3, 4, 9, 10, 11, and 12. If any of these numbers is thrown on the next roll, you win even money, except on 2 and 12 which pay two to one.

"Hard Way" Bets: In the middle of a craps table are pictures of several possible dice combinations together with the odds the bank will pay you if you bet on any of those combinations being thrown. For example, if 8 is thrown by having a 4 appear on each die, and you bet on it, the bank will pay eight for one; if 4 is thrown by having a 2 appear on each die, and you bet on it, the bank will pay eight for one; if 3 is thrown, the bank pays fifteen for one, etc., etc. You win at the odds quoted if the *exact* combination of numbers you bet on comes up. But you lose if either a 7 is rolled, or if the number you bet on was rolled any other way than the "Hard Way" shown on the table. In-the-know gamblers tend to avoid "hard way" bets as an easy way to lose your money.

Any Craps: Here you're lucky if the dice "crap-out," that is, if they show 2, 3, or 12 on the first roll after you bet. If this happens, the bank pays eight to one. Any other number is a loser.

Place Bets: You can make a "Place Bet" on any of the following numbers: 4, 5, 6, 8, 9, and 10. You're betting that the number you choose will be thrown before a 7 is thrown. If you win, the payoff is as follows: 4 or 10 pay at the rate of nine to five; 5 or 9 pay at the rate of seven to five; 6 or 8 pay at the rate of seven to six. Place bets can be removed at any time before a roll.

Some Probabilities: Because each die has six sides numbered from 1 to 6—and craps is played with a pair of dice—the probability of throwing certain numbers has been studied carefully. Professionals have employed complex mathematical formulae in searching for the answers. And computers have data-processed curves of probability.

Simplified, however, suffice it to say that 7 (a crucial number in craps) will be thrown more frequently than any other number over the long run, for there are six possible combinations that make 7, when you break down the 1 to 6 possibilities on each separate die. As to the total possible number of combinations on the dice, there are 36. Comparing the six possible combinations that add up to 7, other numbers—or point combinations—run as follows:

> *2 and 12* may be thrown in *1 way only*
> *3 and 11* may be thrown in *2 ways*
> *4 and 10* may be thrown in *3 ways*
> *5 and 9* may be thrown in *4 ways*
> *6 and 8* may be thrown in *5 ways*

So 7 has an advantage over all other combinations, which over the long run, is in favor of the casino. You can't beat the law of averages. Players, however, often have winning streaks—a proven fact in ESP studies, etc.—and that's when the experts advise that it's wise to increase the size of bets. But when a losing streak sets in, stop playing!

Craps Payout Odds

Wager	Payout Odds
Pass Line	1 to 1
Don't Pass Line	1 to 1
Come	1 to 1
Don't Come	1 to 1
Field Bets	
3, 4, 9, 10, or 11	1 to 1
2 or 12	2 to 1

Hard Ways
    Hard 6 or 8   9 to 1
    Hard 4 or 10   7 to 1

Place Bets to Win
    Points of 4 or 10   9 to 5
    Points of 5 or 9   7 to 5
    Points of 6 or 8   7 to 6

BLACKJACK OR "21": The dealer starts the game by dealing each player two cards, face up, and himself one card up and one card down. Everybody plays against the dealer. The object is to get a total of 21, or as close to it as possible. All face cards count as 10, all other number cards except aces count as their number value An ace may be counted as 1 or 11, whichever you choose it to be.

Starting at his left, the dealer gives additional cards to the players who wish to draw (be "hit"), or none to a player who wishes to "stand" or "hold." If your count is nearer to 21 than the dealer's, you win. If it's under the dealer's, you lose. Ties are a "stand-off" and nobody wins. After each player is satisfied with his count, the dealer exposes his face-down card. If his two cards total 16 or less, he must be "hit" (draw an additional card) until he reaches 17 or over. If the dealer's total goes over 21, he must pay all the players' hands that have not gone "bust" before him. It is important to note here that the blackjack dealer has no choice as to whether he should stay or draw. His decisions are predetermined and known to all the players at the table.

How to Play

1. Place the amount of money you want to bet on the table.

2. Look at the first two cards the dealer starts you with. If you elect to draw an additional card, you tell the dealer to "hit" you by making a scratching motion with your fingers (watch your fellow players). If you decide to stand, indicate that with a wave of your hand. *Never* touch the cards. The dealer is the only person allowed to handle, remove, or alter the location of the cards.

3. If your count goes over 21, you go "bust" and lose, even if the dealer also goes "bust" afterward.

4. If you make 21 in your first two cards (any picture or 10 with an ace), that's blackjack. You collect 1½ times your bet, unless the dealer has blackjack too, in which case it's a stand-off and nobody wins.

5. If you find a "pair" in your first two cards (two 4s or two 8s, etc.), you may "split" the pair into two hands and treat each card as the first card dealt in two separate hands. Indicate your decision to split verbally to the dealer and place another bet the size of your original bet alongside the first. Only after you play out the first hand, do you act on the second hand. A split hand may not be split again if another pair of cards with the same value is formed. If the split pair are aces, you are limited to a one-card draw on each hand. Where the dealer subsequently gets a blackjack, you lose the money wagered on the first bet only.

6. If your first two cards total 11 or under, you may, if you choose, double your original bet and make a one-card draw. If the dealer gets a blackjack, you lose only the amount of the original bet.

7. Any time the dealer deals himself an ace for his "up" card, you may insure your hand against the possibility that his hole card is a face card, which would give him an automatic blackjack. To insure, you place an amount not greater than one-half of your bet on the "Insurance" line. If the dealer does have a blackjack, you do not lose, even though he has your hand beat, and you keep your bet and your insurance money. If he does not have a blackjack, he takes your insurance money and play continues in the normal fashion.

8. *Remember!* The dealer *must* stand on 17 or more, and *must* hit a hand of 16 or less.

Professional Tips

Advice of the experts in playing blackjack is as follows:

1. *Do not* ask for an extra card if you have 17, 18, 19, 20, or 21 counts in your cards, no matter what the dealer has showing in his "up" card.

2. *Do not* ask for an extra card when you have 13, 14, 15, 16, or more . . . *if* the dealer has a 2, 3, 4, 5, or 6 showing in his "up" card.

3. *Do* ask for an extra card or more when you have a count of 13 through 16 in your hand . . . if the dealer's "up" card is a 7, 8, 9, 10, or ace.

There's a lot more to blackjack-playing strategy than the above, of course. So consider this merely as the bare bones of the game.

A Tip From Me

One more point: Avoid Insurance Bets; they're sucker bait!

ROULETTE: Roulette is an extremely easy game to play, and it's

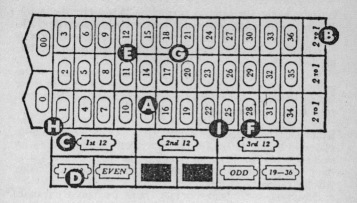

Roulette Chart Key	Odds	Type of Bet
		Straight Bets
A	35 to 1	*Straight-up:* All numbers, plus 0 and 00.
B	2 to 1	*Column Bet:* Pays off on any number in that horizontal column.
C	2 to 1	*First Dozen:* Pays off on any numbers 1 through 12. Same for second and third dozen.
D	Even money	
		Combination Bets
E	17 to 1	*Split:* Pays off on 11 or 12.
F	11 to 1	Pays off on 28, 29, or 30.
G	8 to 1	*Corner:* Pays off on 17, 18, 20, or 21.
H	6 to 1	Pays off on 0, 00, 1, 2, or 3.
I	5 to 1	Pays off on 22, 23, 24, 25, 26, or 27.

really very colorful and exciting to watch. The wheel spins and the little ball bounces around, finally dropping into one of the slots, numbered 1 to 36, plus 0 and 00. You can bet on a single number, a combination of numbers, or red or black, odd or even.

If you're lucky, you can win as much as 35 to 1 (see the table). The method of placing single-number bets, column bets, and others is fairly obvious. The dealer will be happy to show you how to "straddle" two or more numbers and make many other interesting betting combinations.

A number of typical bets is indicated by means of letters on the adjoining roulette layout. The winning odds for each of these sample bets are listed below. These bets can be made on any corresponding combinations of numbers.

BACCARAT: The ancient game of baccarat—or chemin-de-fer—is played with eight decks of cards. Firm rules apply and there is no skill involved. Any beginner can play. The cards are shuffled by the players, reshuffled by the croupier, and then placed in a box which is called the "Shoe."

Players may act as banker or play against the bank at any time. Two cards are dealt from the Shoe to the player who has the largest wager against the bank, and two cards are dealt to the person who is acting as banker. The player acts first. If the rule calls for a third card (see rules on chart below), the player or banker, or both, must take the third card.

The object of the game is to come as close as possible to the number 9. To score the hands, the cards of each hand are totaled and the *last digit* is used. All cards have face value. For example: 10 plus 5 equals 15 (score is 5); 10 plus 4 plus 9 equals 23 (score is 3); 4 plus 3 plus 2 equals 9 (score is 9); etc. The closest hand to 9 wins, and is paid one to one. If the two hands tie, the bettor on that outcome wins eight to one.

Each player gets a chance to deal the cards. The Shoe passes to the player on the right each time the bank loses. If the player wishes, he may pass the Shoe at any time.

Player's Hand

Having	
0-1-2-3-4-5	Must draw a third card
6-7	*Must stand*
8-9	Natural. Banker cannot draw

Banker's Hand

Having	Draws When giving Player 3rd card of:	Does Not Draw When giving Player 3rd card of:
3	1-2-3-4-5-6-7-8-9-10	8
4	2-3-4-5-6-7	1-8-9-10

5	4-5-6-7	1-2-3-8-9-10
6	6-7	1-2-3-4-5-8-9-10
7	*Must stand*	
8-9	Natural. Player cannot draw	

If the player takes no third card, the banker must stand on six. No one draws against a natural eight or nine.

BIG-SIX WHEEL: There's an Old West frontier look to the big-six wheel that stands upright above a table layout. It's a simple game to play.

The bettor just chooses a number or symbol. The dealer spins the wheel, and the winning number is indicated when the wheel stops by the pointer at the top. You can bet more than one number if you wish.

All bets must be made before the dealer spins.

If you bet on	A win pays
$1	1 to 1
$2	2 to 1
$5	5 to 1
$10	10 to 1
$20	20 to 1
Joker	45 to 1
House Insignia	45 to 1

Chapter V

ATLANTIC CITY AT NIGHT

WHEN THE SUN GOES DOWN, a brilliant light show of orange and purple, blue, yellow, and red illuminates the skyscrapers along the Boardwalk. Inside the casinos the action continues, day into night (from 10 a.m. to 4 a.m. on weekdays, till 6 a.m. on weekends). Casino activities are the same at all the hotels: banks of slot machines, accepting coins of various denominations or tokens worth $1 each, ring and whirr. The table games are loosely linked together to form an enclosure where a pit boss can keep the dealers under scrutiny. The baccarat salon or pit is elegantly withdrawn with velvet ropes or polished brass rail from the rest of the casino floor. Change people and cocktail servers move around the room. Although beverages are complimentary, the servers aren't permitted to approach you. Ask for a drink, though, and it will be served. Don't take out your camera, whatever you do. Photographs are forbidden on the casino floor, and the rule is enforced.

In the Casinos

Superstar entertainers in the big casino-hotels attract huge crowds, and the showrooms are packed to the gills on nights when Sammy Davis, Jr., Dom de Luise, or Joan Rivers are performing. The nighttime hotel scene has three kinds of entertainment. Right off the casino floor, and sometimes on other levels as well, the cocktail lounges feature live entertainment, ranging from a single-person act to a small band with a singer. Entertainment in the casino lounges starts as early as 1 p.m. and continues till near casino closing, with breaks. There's no admittance charge to the lounge, but a one- or two-drink minimum (around $2.50) is the rule for a table. The lounges are not closed off, and nearby gamblers can play the slots and watch the performance at the same time. At Harrah's Marina Atrium, the two-level setting lets you stand above the lounge and see and hear the show gratis.

Lavish productions, either original musical revues or reruns of Broadway extravaganzas, occupy the casino-hotels' showrooms. At Bally that's the main event; there are no headliners on weekends. At Resorts, which is committed to top-flight entertainment in a big way, a nightly revue is supplemented on weekends by headline acts. Dinner shows are largely a thing of the past. One casino-hotel entertainment director told me that they can't do justice to a fine dinner, which must be hustled along, and set up a show to their satisfaction.

This next tidbit seems a little obvious to me, but that same entertainment director assured me he gets asked about it all the time. You do not have to be a guest at a particular hotel to see the show. All the shows are open to the general public. Tickets are sold on a first-come, first-served basis, and as I noted earlier, big names draw big crowds. You can't expect to waltz in for a ticket for a same-night performance by a major star.

There's an exciting nightlife scene outside the casino hotels too, and it goes even later. Twenty-four-hour bar licenses keep a lot of places open around the clock. When the late shift of casino employees leaves work in the wee hours of the morning, it sometimes seems as if none of them go home, but instead they head for nearby nightspots to unwind, and the music goes on till dawn.

After a preview of the theater nightclubs and other entertainment facilities at the famous casino-hotels, I'll deal with the clubs and lounges that complement the casino night scene.

RESORTS INTERNATIONAL: When Luciano Pavarotti's "Voice of the Century" boomed throughout a specially constructed tent in 1983, Resorts definitely clinched first place in Atlantic City's entertainment industry. Its claim to frontrunner in entertainment is bolstered by a full schedule of events.

The biggest names in show business perform regularly at the 1,700-seat **Superstar Theater**—Johnny Mathis, Liberace, Tom Jones, Alan King, Donna Summer, Engelbert Humperdinck, to name a few—as well as ballet companies and concert orchestras such as the New York Philharmonic. Nationally televised boxing matches are held in the theater once or twice a month. Showtimes and prices vary. Call 340-6830 for information.

In the **Carousel Cabaret** a Las Vegas-style revue, *Wild,* has been running for some time. Showtimes are Sunday through

Thursday at 7 and 9 p.m. and Saturday at 8 and 11 p.m. Tickets are $10. Call 340-6830 for reservations.

The **Rendezvous Lounge** on the lobby level, and **Casino Royale,** near the Pennsylvania Avenue entrance to the casino, have nightly entertainment.

HARRAH'S MARINA: Harrah's state-of-the-art, 850-seat **Broadway-by-the-Sea** theater, decorated in vibrant tones of purple and red, hosts headliner entertainment 37 weeks of the year. Everything from an extravagant revue to championship boxing has been featured. Roberta Flack, Bill Cosby, the Temptations, Andy Williams, and Crystal Gayle have been at Harrah's. Showtimes in winter are usually just on weekends. In summer the schedules are 8 and 11:30 p.m. Tuesday to Saturday, on Sunday at 6 and 9:30 p.m. Prices are about $17 during the week, $22 on Saturday. Tickets are on sale 30 days prior to performance. For reservations, call 800/242-7724.

The **Atrium Lounge** has a lovely indoor garden setting with 20-foot trees, a three-tiered waterfall, and its two-story skylight ceiling. The bar is open 24 hours, with waitress service from noon until 4 a.m. on weekdays. Live entertainment seven days a week is provided by small groups.

High-energy sounds spill onto the casino floor from the **Bay Cabaret,** at the northwest corner of the room. A diverse lineup of performers, from country to contemporary to disco, keeps the beat going from 3 p.m. until closing six days a week, from noon on Sunday.

Wide-screen TV viewing attracts sports fans to the **Winner's Circle.** This cocktail lounge is close to the action, at the northeast corner of the casino.

GOLDEN NUGGET: The **Opera House** theater features such headliner talent as Frank Sinatra, Diana Ross, Liza Minelli, Paul Anka, Harry Belafonte, and a host of other fine performers. Call 340-7200 for ticket information.

Also on the first floor, but adjoining the casino, the **Rangoon Saloon** is tropical Victorian in decor. Along with **Elaine's** on the second floor, it offers entertainment nightly.

TROPICANA: The Tropicana's 1700-seat, plush burgundy **Showroom** is the setting for such headliners as Frankie Valli, Sha-NaNa, Glen Campbell, Patti LaBelle, and Pat Cooper. Ticket prices range from $12.50 to $17. Call 340-4020 for schedules.

Most Tuesday nights there's boxing in the Showroom. The doors open at 7 p.m. and the first bout is at 7:30. Tickets are $12.

Located on the 21st floor of the Tropicana, the **Top of the Trop** dazzles patrons with a magnificent view of the ocean and the city, which you can take in with some outstanding jazz music till 3 a.m. nightly.

The **Wild Swan Lounge** is open 24 hours a day. Exotic plants, a circular stage, and mirrored walls and ceiling are a sophisticated setting for "top 40" music and comedy stars.

Grapes, Grapes, Grapes is the most informal of the lounges. It's got a TV for die-hard sports fans, comfortable chairs, and small cocktail tables for a drink and a view of the passing parade between the casino and the restaurants. Grapes is open daily from noon to 4 a.m.

Every Wednesday through Sunday night the **"Comedy Stop at the Trop"** showcases young comedy talent on the first floor. Admission is $8.50. In winter showtimes are 9 p.m. on Wednesday, Thursday, and Sunday. Friday and Saturday shows are at 9 and 11:30 p.m., and 1:15 a.m. In summer there are shows daily; check for show times.

ATLANTIS: The **Cabaret Theater** has featured both cabaret revues and headliner performers. Since their theater schedule was not yet in place as we went to press, Atlantis suggests that you call 344-4000 for information on shows and reservations.

There's music nightly at **Le Club** in the salon on the third floor and in the **Shangri-la** lounge.

TRUMP PLAZA: Headliner attractions appear weekly in the 750-seat purple and orange hotel theater. Superstars like Sammy Davis, Jr., Mitzi Gaynor, Rich Little, and Suzanne Somers are some of them. Call 441-6000 for up-to-the-minute information on tickets and performers.

This establishment abounds in lounges—among them are **Swizzle's,** which offers you a choice of looking at the casino floor or a TV set; **Jezebel's,** a plush spot with etched-glass decorative accents and live entertainment; and **Trump's,** outfitted in bright colors and lively with musical entertainment. Actually, my favorite is still another lounge, the glass-enclosed **Skyway** overlooking the sea. All are open from early afternoon through the wee hours of the morning.

CAESARS: The 1100-seat **Circus Maximus Theater** hosts headliners and variety shows as well as sports exhibitions. Lola Falana, the Pointer Sisters, Buddy Hackett, or Joan Rivers may be on the bill when you're in town, so call 348-4411 for ticket information.

Open during casino hours, the **Arena lounge** has continuous music on stage. It is also home to a 17-foot-tall replica of Michelangelo's statue of *David*. The **Forum** is a glass-enclosed cocktail lounge, open nightly, with live entertainment and a fine ocean view.

BALLY'S PARK PLACE: In the **Park Place Cabaret** the revue *An Evening at La Cage* has been pulling in the customers for some time. You can see for yourself why the show has been so successful every night but Tuesday. There are two shows on Monday, Wednesday, and Thursday (8 and 10 p.m.), Friday (9 and 11 p.m.), and Sunday (7 and 9 p.m.). Admission those nights is $14. There are three shows on Saturday (7:30, 9:30, and 11:30), and admission is $17. There is a one-drink minimum. Call 340-2709 for reservations.

Bally's near-the-casino lounge is **Billy's Pub,** with nightly entertainment from about 4 p.m.

Upstairs in the Park bar, on the restaurant level, has music too.

There's no bar in the **Dennis Lounge,** a survivor of the old Dennis Hotel that functions as a restful spot to hang out or meet friends. It's a handsome room with a great ocean view.

CLARIDGE: The Claridge has been presenting Broadway shows with name stars in the Palace Theater. *Hello, Dolly*, starring Lainie Kazan, and *No, No, Nanette* were recent productions. Show tickets are $12.50; a dinner show package is $17.50. Call 340-3700 for particulars. When weekend entertainers are on hand the shows are dark.

In the **Celebrity Lounge** up-and-coming entertainers are on view. There's no admission charge, but a one-drink minimum is required.

THE SANDS: In the Sands' glittering **Copa** room (tel. 441-4000), you could have seen Robin Williams, Gregory Hines, Billy Crystal, David Brenner, or Linda Ronstadt on past weekends.

The **Punch Bowl Lounge** and the **Players Lounge** both feature live entertainment.

TRUMP'S CASTLE: The **King's Court Theatre** presents a 90-minute ice, dancing, and musical mélange called City Lites every night but Wednesday. There are two shows nightly and tickets cost

$12.50 per person; there is also a one-drink minimum. For schedules and reservations call 441-8300.

On the third floor two lounges will entertain you: The **Casino Lounge** features name cabaret performers Sunday through Thursday till 6 a.m., till 8 a.m. Friday and Saturday. Contemporary musical groups perform in the **Viva Lounge.**

Nightlife Outside the Casinos

With the casinos attracting the country's major entertainers and planning more than enough entertainment to keep you inside their doors, you may not have the time or inclination to look further for nighttime diversions. A dance floor is the only thing lacking at any one of the casinos, so if that's your idea of evening's fun, you definitely will have to look elsewhere. I do hear, though, that the Sands is putting in a late-night dance spot, the **Club Copa,** which may be open by the time you read this. It's a sure bet that if the Club Copa draws in a crowd, the other casinos won't be slow in setting aside some space for dancing, too.

Above the Brajole Café, the **Club Ancoppa,** at Mississippi and Atlantic Avenues (tel. 344-1733), is a two-tiered disco that makes clever use of its space. On one floor a deejay booth sends out the disco beat from 10 p.m. to 8 a.m. to patrons of the futuristic round bar and dancers, some of whom are on a suspended floor overlooking the booth. Upstairs there's also a glassed-in piano lounge that seems to attract a slightly older crowd than downstairs, and a fascinating-to-stare-at 18-foot-long fish tank with fresh and salt water tropical fish. (It's actually two separate tanks.)

The **Melody Lounge,** 22 S. South Carolina Ave. (tel. 348-9746), has parties at the slightest excuse every Wednesday night, plus disco Wednesday to Saturday from 10 p.m. to 5 a.m.

Duke Mack's, at California Avenue and the Boardwalk (tel. 345-2719), claims to have the best parties in town, with dance music spinning seven nights from around midnight to 8 a.m. Dinner is served at Duke Mack's from 5 to 11 p.m. They push back the tables when it's time for dancing.

Further afield, **Copsey's,** a fine restaurant at Mill Road and White Horse Pike in Absecon on the mainland (tel. 641-0654), also features dancing in their lounge on Wednesday, Friday, and Saturday nights until 2 a.m. Back on the island, but downbeach in Margate is another current hot favorite, **Red's,** 9217 Atlantic Ave. (tel. 822-1539), where, I'm told, you'll hear the rock of the '80s.

Atlantic City is no stranger to bar and lounge activity, especially very late night, for casino employees whose schedules have them seeking after-work relaxation in the predawn hours more traditionally associated with the milkman's rounds. One of the favorites of off-duty casino employees is **12 South,** 12 S. Indiana Ave. (tel. 344-1112), which has a laid-back, relaxing charm.

The **Irish Pub,** 164 S. St. James Place (tel. 345-9613), is another fine Gaelic grog dispenser that few tourists frequent. It's never closed, and you can always pick up a frosted mug of Harp Lager or Guinness Stout, along with moderately priced lunches and dinners. Entertainment from the Old Country, too.

In Gordon's Alley, the **Express Lounge** (no phone) has snacks till late, and there may be dancing as well. For a swank, understated lounge, **Grabel's** (tel. 344-9263) at Harrisburg and Atlantic Avenues is popular.

Other Evening Entertainment

Many people don't associate cultural pursuits with Atlantic City, but they're in for a surprise. Theater, ballet, films, and musical programs are regularly scheduled in the area. Local and national performing arts groups also appear at the casinos.

The **Little Art Theater,** Harbor Village Square Shopping Mall, Zion Road and Ocean Heights Avenue, Egg Harbor Township (tel. 653-1626), features fine arts, foreign, and first-run special motion pictures.

The **Stockton State College Performing Arts Center,** Pomona (tel. 652-1776), is a hub for public cultural events. Among their regular activities are lectures by distinguished authors and artists, and concerts by various musical organizations such as Jury's Irish Cabaret of Dublin, the Connecticut State Opera Company, and jazz great Dave Brubeck. The Stockton Chamber Players recently staged a production of *Brigadoon.*

At the Atlantic Community College's **theater,** Black Horse Pike, Mays Landing (tel. 625-1111), a cultural series includes films, dramatic productions, and concerts featuring the New Jersey Composers Guild.

A full theatrical season is offered by the South Jersey Regional Theater at the **Gateway Playhouse,** at Bay and Higbee Avenues, Somers Point (tel. 653-0553).

SEEING THE SIGHTS
OF ATLANTIC CITY

ONCE IN ATLANTIC CITY your activity schedule will take care of itself. The casinos are the main attraction year round, but in summer the beaches are crowded too. For variety, the city and environs offer good sports facilities (especially fishing), shopping at specialty boutiques in Ocean One and Gordon's Alley, museums, and historic sites. Nearby is the fascinating wine-growing area of South Jersey; the Brigantine National Wildlife Refuge; a re-creation of a mid-19th-century New Jersey town at Smithville, complete with restaurants and shops; the old iron village of Batsto; and the Pine Barrens. I'll preview all that for you in this chapter, and more, including the barrier island north of Atlantic City, Long Beach Island, the home of Barnegat State Park and the Barnegat Light.

Most excursions can be done in a day or less, but take your time. Ramble at a leisurely pace, poking in country stores and flea markets or taking pot luck at a roadside restaurant.

The Boardwalk

Most people coming to Atlantic City are there for the casino games, which is a far cry from the days when the source of the good times and entertainment was the Boardwalk.

What were the Boardwalk's celebrated amusements? There were the mechanical rides—the Ferris wheel (an Atlantic City first), rollercoasters, merry-go-rounds—whose motion, up, down, or around gave passengers an exciting thrill. The Haunted Swing was a macabre attraction in the 1890s. Riders thought they were turning topsy-turvy, when actually the room was going back and forth—the swing was stationary! Freak shows exhibited the likes of two-headed Millie Christine. Vaudeville and variety shows drew in the crowds that later repaired to the beer gardens and dancing pavilions to trip the light fantastic. The intrepid could ascend in balloon rides, the daredevils float down in parachutes.

On Easter Sunday throngs of paraders in springtime finery crowded the Boardwalk for a promenade, borrowed from New York's Fifth Avenue by the city fathers to bring visitors to the resort before Memorial Day. The traditional **Easter Parade on the Boardwalk** is still a big event in Atlantic City. The great American sport of flagpole sitting had its heyday in Atlantic City in 1930, when "Shipwreck" Kelly broke his own record (49 days). Oohs and aahs of amazement and thousands of spectators came to the world's largest tire (Goodyear), a giant typewriter (Underwood), and of course, the gigantic Lucy the Elephant still in Margate.

Alas, the glory days of the Boardwalk have passed. Still thronged by gamblers hastening from one casino to another, or stopping for a moment's respite and a breath of fresh air, the Boardwalk is most beautiful in the early morning hours, when the joggers, bicyclers, or early strollers have it to themselves, to enjoy the crisp, tang of the salt breeze, the sun's brilliant white light reflected off the gentle swell of the sea, and watch the beachsweepers getting ready for another day's bathers.

But there are still some vivid reminders of the old Boardwalk, some tastes and smells and sights that evoke the old Atlantic City between the shining glass-and-concrete towers of the new.

Fralinger's Salt Water Taffy has been in demand since Joseph Fralinger first decided to box the sweets in the 1880s; the candy was first sold by the piece. Why it's called saltwater taffy is not at all certain. One version, probably apocryphal, has it that a storm hit a Boardwalk taffy stand so severely that the owner sadly dubbed his offerings "saltwater" taffy. Today's Fralinger's, a one-pound box for $3.25, is sold at three or four Boardwalk locations in a rainbow of hues with flavors like molasses, chocolate, vanilla, licorice, orange, lemon, peanut butter, cherry, strawberry, and coconut. Fralinger's wares now include crystallized ginger, chocolate-covered pretzels, seafoam fudge, cashew patties, nonpareils, almond macaroons, and twice-dipped mints. **James'** and **Steel's** are two more oldtime taffy merchants on the Boardwalk.

Dip-Stix have the flavor of the old Boardwalk days and nostalgic visitors look for the giant lemon atop the gaudily painted yellow-and-green stands. What are Dip-Stix? They're juicy, garlic-scented hot dogs, dipped in corn meal batter and deep-fried. Fresh lemonade is the classic accompaniment.

Taylor Pork Roll is sold in supermarkets nowadays, but old-timers know it's a Jersey shore treat. There's been a shop on the Boardwalk since 1939, selling Taylor Pork Roll sandwiches. In case you're not an old aficionado—it's a ground ham concoction in a sausage casing, great on a sandwich or fried with eggs. The shop is near Kentucky Avenue.

There must be at least ten pizza stands along the Boardwalk, most open 24 hours a day in summer, till around 10 p.m. in winter. **Tony's Little Italy** and **3 Brothers from Italy** vie for honors here; they both tasted swell to me. And the price was right—$1.50 a slice.

Mr. Peanut was a dapper walking advertisement for Planter's. He doesn't greet visitors to the Boardwalk anymore, but the store's still selling America's favorite snack.

Peanuts, pizza, and pork roll, soda, candy, and ice cream! It's a junk-food maven's heaven, the old Boardwalk. And then there are the signs of the new—a Burger King, a Roy Rogers for the low-scale diner, the casinos' flossy ice-cream shoppes and cafés for the upscale snacker.

There are other relics of bygone days. The old **Food & Brew** building stands near Caesars; a Moorish-looking little stucco confection, painted in soft pastel colors with turned columns and swoops and swirls of decoration that have inspired local preservationists to fight for its survival (we wish them well; it's worth the fight).

There are souvenir stores all along the Boardwalk, between Resorts and the Golden Nugget. It's staggering to think of all the different objects that can bear the magic name—"Souvenir of Atlantic City": the sunshades, key rings, mugs, shoelaces, pennants, purses, address books, spoons, cups and saucers, red life-size lobsters, boxes, paddles, and of course T-shirts. Wood and wicker, plastic or china, it all ends up as a souvenir of Atlantic City. Little seashells are glued together to form boxes, planters, anchors—everything but a large seashell.

Souvenirs of another kind are sold at **Elliot's**, 1329 Boardwalk. Japanese netsuke, ivory and jade carvings, embroidered linens, lace, handmade Oriental rugs, and beautifully lacquered Japanese screens invite the gambler to dispose of the winnings. Next door to Elliot's, an art glass shop that might be doing business in Venice has hand-blown glass in the shape of a carousel, different animals, beads, candlesticks, plates and cups.

Electronic game and pinball arcades add to the Boardwalk's honky tonk.

To Atlantic City and nearby communities, the Boardwalk is a

daytime community center and arts forum. A spring arts festival brings jazz, mimes, brass, dance, paintings, sculpture, and pop music together for a day in Brighton Park at Park Place in the middle of May.

Shopping

OCEAN ONE: It's a red, white, and star-sequinned blue, three-decker shopping center, international food court, and exhibition space, with strolling magicians, musicians, and other entertainers to keep the crowd amused. The components are typically suburban shopping mall, but leave it to Atlantic City to come up with all that—in the shape of a gleaming white ocean liner that juts into the water at the Boardwalk and Arkansas Avenue, facing Caesars. Ocean One's 170 shops and restaurants are open 11 a.m. to 8 p.m. Sunday through Friday, 11 a.m. to 9 p.m. on Saturday.

Casual Corner has the latest in women's sportswear. The **Newsstand** on the first level has all the newspapers, major magazines, and special-interest periodicals you'd expect. Such renowned shops as Benetton sportswear, Hoffritz cutlery, Crabtree & Evelyn soaps, and even Frederick's of Hollywood lingerie offer their wares, along with the many giftshops purveying souvenirs, scented candles, cards, stationery, and mugs. There's also a health-food store on the premises.

The **Food Court** on the second level (there are escalators) is a tantalizing roll call of nations—tacos, bagels, sushi, Philly cheese steaks, egg rolls, barbecue . . . (see Chapter III). On the top deck is the picnic seating area for Food Court customers (or anyone else). Expansive ocean views are featured up here. The sit-down restaurants are also on the third floor—the Black Forest, Spaghetti House, Starr Delicatessen, H. I. Ribs & Co., and Beefsteak Charlie's (all described in Chapter III).

GORDON'S ALLEY: Following the pattern of San Francisco's Ghirardelli Square and Denver's Larimer Street, Gordon's Alley is Atlantic City's first pedestrian mall. It's between Virginia and Pennsylvania Avenues (where there's a parking lot) and Pacific and Atlantic Avenues (tel. 344-5000). This picturesque collection of row houses converted into small shops and restaurants is paved with cobblestones and has such attractive touches as gas lamps, pretty floral paintings, and benches. Ralph Lauren sportswear, a children's shop, Caswell & Massey scents and soaps, and Coach leather products are the quality merchandise here. **Alley Books** has both adult and children's books that you can take upstairs to read (after you've bought them) to an informal salad and sandwich café. The **Alley Deli** is at street level. The **Fromage Express** has drinks in the Express Lounge. Gourmet cookware, office supplies, flowers, and jewelry are all sold in the alley. Wherever you shop, Gordon's will give you free gift wrapping for your purchases.

Sights in Town

CONVENTION HALL: The Boardwalk widens in the colonnaded arc of Kennedy Plaza, where a bronze bust of John F. Kennedy, dedicated in 1964, names the arcade. Facing Kennedy Arcade, Atlantic City's famed Convention Hall stands, somewhat over shadowed by the Atlantis casino and Trump Casino on either side.

Home of the Miss America Pageant and the world's largest pipe organ, the hall has been the site of huge rock concerts, professional ice hockey and basketball games, midget auto races, and horse, dog, boat, and flower shows. It was completed in 1929 and has since been considerably expanded. A further expansion and renovation has been completed. There are two fine organs in the hall. One is in the ballroom, itself of gigantic size—181 feet long, 120 feet wide, and 75 feet high. It's larger than Radio City Music Hall, and is considered its superior acoustically. The really big organ in the auditorium stands alone in size and power. Its inspiring proportions and glorious tone keep a maintenance man busy walking the length of many city blocks surveying its parts.

ATLANTIC CITY ART CENTER/HISTORICAL MUSEUM: Sharing a building at the Garden Pier, Boardwalk at New Jersey Avenue (tel. 347-5844), both institutions are open daily from 9 a.m. to 4 p.m., admission free. The art center has changing exhibits of painting, sculpture, and photography. In the historical museum you'll hear the strains of old-time Atlantic City tunes as you view a fascinating collection of memorabilia—Miss America Pageant trophies and photos, souvenir china and glassware, and old postcards among them. A special exhibit honors Atlantic City photographer Al Gold; his daughter, Vicki Gold Levi, who established the exhibit, wrote *Atlantic City, 125 Years of Ocean Madness,* a delightful compendium of photos and anecdotes about the resort.

ABSECON LIGHTHOUSE: Visit Old Ab, set in a small park at Rhode Island and Pacific Avenues (tel. 345-6328). First lighted in 1857, the 150-foot-high landmark now houses a small marine museum. It's open daily except Wednesday from 10 a.m. to 5 p.m. in summer; weekends only in winter.

HISTORIC GARDNER'S BASIN: A trip to Atlantic City's maritime past is the experience you'll capture at the open-air museum called Historic Gardner's Basin at North New Hampshire Avenue and the Inlet (tel. 348-2880). It's a public park, and except for the restaurant, it's all free. You can get there by jitney, or if you're driving, there's lots of free parking on site.

Other Adventures

LUCY THE MARGATE ELEPHANT: Everybody loves Lucy today. She's a National Historic Landmark, a treasured relic of Victorian America who has survived a century of abuse from wind and weather, salt air and neglect.

She was built as a pachydermian promotion to stimulate real estate sales in Margate, south of Atlantic City, by James V. Lafferty, a developer from Philadelphia. She was a great success, and prospective buyers loved to climb the stairs in Lucy's back leg to the howdah (basket) on her back to view the surrounding land. Having served the purpose for which she was built, she was sold in 1887 to a local family, who fixed up her inside and charged admission for entrance. Lucy was the only elephant you could walk through and come out alive. But the novelty wore off and Lucy was left to the mercies of time. By the 1960s she was an old hulk, deteriorated almost beyond repair. The land she was sitting on was valuable, and another real estate developer appeared who wanted to destroy the old elephant and build an apartment house there. When news of the impending demolition was known, the local citizenry was aroused. A Save the Lucy Committee was formed and headed by a local housewife, Josephine Harron.

In order for Lucy to be saved, she had to be moved. Funds were raised (by a white elephant sale!), and with great fanfare, in 1970, the 90-ton metal-sheathed wood structure that was Lucy was put on wheels and rolled two blocks away to her present site, at Decatur and Atlantic Avenues in Margate. Handsomely restored, Lucy is open to the public again on weekends from April 1 to June 15, and September and October from 10 a.m. to 4 p.m., daily from June 16 to the end of August till 8:30 p.m. Admission is $1.50 for adults, $1 for children. Free parking is available. Inside this now-cherished relic there is a Lucy exhibit with old photos and elephant memorabilia.

STORYBOOK LAND: This low-keyed fantasy land has pretty painted buildings and displays depicting famous children's stories like Sleeping Beauty, Snow White and the Seven Dwarfs, the Old Woman Who Lived in a Shoe, Cinderella's Pumpkin Coach, the Crooked House, and Mistress Mary's Garden. There are live animals to see, a picnic area, snackbars, and rides—Happy Train, Merry-Go-Round, Tin Lizzie cars, and Flying Jumbo, among them. During the Christmas and Thanksgiving holiday season, over 70,000 lights turn Storybook Land into a winter wonderland with Mr. and Mrs. Claus on hand to visit with the children.

One admission charge—$5.50 for each adult or child—includes all attractions and rides. Open weekends March to mid-June and mid-September through mid-November from 11 a.m. to 5 p.m., and daily mid-June to mid-September from 10 a.m. to 5:30 p.m. From Thanksgiving to December 30, the Christmas Fantasy with lights at dusk is open Monday to Friday from 5:30 to 8:30 p.m., on Saturday and Sunday from 2 to 8:30 p.m. Closed December 24 and 25. Storybook Land is ten miles west of Atlantic City on the Black Horse Pike, Route 40 (tel. 641-7847).

NOYES MUSEUM: Traveling just a few miles north of Atlantic City along Route 9 will give you quite a different perspective on the area. If you go too fast, you might miss the turn-off on the right to Lily Lake Road, and the Noyes Museum, in Oceanville, (tel. 652-8848).

The museum is beautifully situated on the sloping shore of Lily Lake across from the Brigantine Wildlife Refuge. On entering the museum, which is a contemporary gray frame structure that harks back to the regional buildings from the 18th and 19th centuries, you can see the lake through the glass end wall of the center gallery.

Incorporated in the museum is the rare antique duck decoy room from Fred Noyes' collection; some date back to the Civil War era. A decoy carver demonstrates the craft daily at 2 p.m. in a portion of the gallery designed to resemble a carver's studio at the turn of the century.

The museum features rotating exhibitions of contemporary

American paintings and sculpture in addition to a permanent collection of American art and the antique duck decoys. In the permanent collection are works by such renowned New Jersey artists as Richard Anuszkiewicz, Walter Darby Bannard, and Jacob Landau.

The museum is closed on major holidays and from Christmas until March 1. Admission is $1.50 for adults, $1 for senior citizens, and 50¢ for students. If you're with a group of six or more, you can call ahead to reserve a free gallery tour.

BRIGANTINE NATIONAL WILDLIFE REFUGE: Whether you choose the self-guiding, eight-mile auto tour or one of the shorter walking trails, a visit to the Brigantine Division of the Edwin B. Forsythe National Wildlife Refuge, in Oceanville (tel. 652-1665), will bring you in touch with the flat open spaces of pristine salt marsh and barrier beach, tidal bays and channels. The 20,229 acres of the refuge were set aside for the protection of the waterfowl that traverse the Atlantic Flyway: they nest in Canada and then winter south into Florida and along the Gulf of Mexico. At the peak of the fall migration, in late November, over 150,000 waterfowl, geese, and swans can be seen. Many waterfowl, such as the Canada goose, pintail, gadwall, and shoveler, which used to bypass this vicinity, now stop for varying lengths of time.

Dedicated bird-watchers can get a calendar of seasonal wildlife events that details the best time to come. You're most likely to see a bald eagle in December; the northbound waterfowl migration peaks between March 20 and April 15; ducks hatch from about June 15 to July 15; and the wading birds gather in August.

The refuge is open to the public from a half hour before sunrise to a half hour after sunset every day. There is no admission fee. At the headquarters building, where you can pick up the calendar and the auto- and walking-tour booklets, there's an interesting exhibit explaining the ecology of the area. The building is open from 8:30 a.m. to 4 p.m. weekdays, and some weekends, generally in the spring and fall.

If you're coming from the Noyes Museum, the refuge is about a quarter of a mile, or even less, north along Route 9; it's a right turn that is marked with a sign. You're about ten miles from Atlantic City here, and on a clear day you can see the skyline.

SMITHVILLE: As much fun to browse through as to shop at, the **Towne of Historic Smithville** recaptures the flavor of a mid-18th-century New Jersey town with its brick and slate sidewalks, colonial-style buildings and gardens, and beautiful Lake Meone.

Thirty-two little shops, three fine restaurants, arts and crafts demonstrations, and plenty of ducks to feed are the main attractions.

Many of the buildings are re-creations and some were moved here from other locations, but the historic **Smithville Inn,** which serves lunch and dinner, has been on this site since 1757. An early stagecoach stop, it's now a rambling white clapboard building with two hospitable-looking settles at the front door. A huge stone fireplace dominates the front room. Windsor chairs, plank floors, costumed waitresses, candles or hurricane lamps on the tables, a flagstone terrace overlooking the lake, and big fireplaces in many of the rooms contribute to the ambience of a classic country inn.

Have a Smithville punch to begin your meal with a glow—it's a mixture of orange juice, rum, grenadine, and lemon juice ($2.95). On Sunday you can have a bounteous brunch from 10 a.m. to 2 p.m., from 2 till 9 p.m. it's dinnertime. On weekdays the restaurant is open for lunch (11:30 a.m. to 2:30 p.m. except on Monday and Tuesday in January and February, when the inn is closed) and dinner (from 4 p.m. Monday through Saturday).

New England clam chowder ($2.95), or if you're really hungry, a bucket of steamed clams with drawn butter ($5.95), makes a fine appetizer. Seafood entrees include crab imperial ($15.50), and fried shrimp ($13.95). Meaty main dishes are beef kabobs ($14.50) and prime ribs ($16.95). All the bread and baked desserts are made on the premises and are for sale at the Village Bakery.

The **Quail Hill Inn** is a weathered gray, shingle-roofed reconstruction of an old barn building. It's extraordinarily spacious, with a number of large dining rooms. A huge stone fireplace in one dining room and in another a wall-length primitive mural of country life in south Jersey are in keeping with the large-scale rooms. Throughout there are paintings, ship models, old hutches, and other antique pieces. The restaurant here is called **Prima's** (tel. 652-8814), and it's got a distinctly Italian accent. An antipasto salad bar, soups, and breads are included with all entrees. Pasta is featured—lasagne, spaghetti, fettuccine—all prepared differently, but costing $9.95 each. Traditional Italian entrees, such as veal parmigiana ($12.95) and chicken with white wine ($11.95), are made well and well worth the price. The chef's specials go into the realm of lobster fra diavolo ($16.95), scampi ($12.95), and steak Nicole ($14.95). Frozen zabaglione is an outstanding dessert ($2).

Walk into **Joe's Place** (tel. 652-8819) around the bend from the

Smithville Inn, for delicious baby back ribs ($11.95) or a tostado grande ($5.45) topped with cheddar cheese and a square of corn bread. Go past the gleaming copper bar into the main room, which is really a window-enclosed terrace with small trees, ceiling fans, Tiffany–style lamps, and two unicycles decorating the one brick wall. Omelets, salads, sandwiches, barbecued chicken and ribs, and entrees like steak and seafood are served with informal style in this attractive, relaxed setting. The prices are moderate.

Having partaken of some sustenance in one of the foregoing Smithville restaurants, it's time for a walk around the quaint, harmoniously painted shops. Little girls will love the dolls and dollhouse furniture in the **Village Craft Shop.** Their parents will admire the pretty colonial-print pillows, brass stencils, stuffed animals, and other whimsical gift items. The **Gourmet Food Shop** specializes in Smithville goods, especially the unusual selection of cheese spreads—with horseradish, pink champagne, port, bacon, etc.—at $2.49 a half pound. Vintage accessories, old movie-star stills, porcelain dolls, old jewelry, and other relics are in **Collectibles Corner.** Bordering the lake, **Grist Mill Antiques** has an 18-foot waterwheel at the side of the building and an assortment of glass, brass, china, and wooden objects. An **ice-cream parlor** provides some sustenance for hungry browsers. The **Christmas Shop** keeps the spirit alive year round with ceramic wreaths, cups and saucers, table and tree ornaments, bags, stockings, aprons, and doodads of every sort, all in the cheery red and green of everybody's favorite season. **Cramer's General Store** was moved here from New Gretna in 1957. Of mid-19th-century vintage, it's got a cracker barrel, pot-bellied stove, penny candy, and reproductions of kitchenware for sale.

In winter Smithville's shops are closed on Monday and Tuesday; otherwise open 11 a.m. to 6 p.m. on weekdays, to 9 p.m. on Saturday, and to 7 p.m. on Sunday. In summer they're open 11 a.m. to 9 p.m. daily. In May the town sponsors a Mayfest with music, arts-and-crafts demonstrations, and other goings-on. An Oktoberfest has a German band, carnival booths, and entertainments.

Restaurant hours and times are subject to change, so it's a good idea to call ahead for exact hours (tel. 609/652-7777). The Towne of Historic Smithville is on Route 9, about two miles north of the Brigantine Wildlife Refuge. If you're coming from New York on the Garden State Parkway, take exit 48 to Route 9 south.

BATSTO VILLAGE—IRON IN THE PINES: Once upon a time New Jersey had an iron industry. It was one of the main sources of ammunition for Washington's Revolutionary War army, and the British even sent a force to destroy the furnaces (they were unsuccessful). What the British were unable to accomplish by force became a reality a century later, when the industry declined rapidly, due to a combination of economic factors and technological advances. One of the ghost towns left in the wake of this once-flourishing industry was acquired by the state and has been restored.

To reach Batsto Village, take exit 52 on the Garden State Parkway southbound to N.J. 542 west to Batsto. Start your visit at the visitors center at the parking lot, where you can sign up for a tour of the mansard-roofed mansion on the hill. Across the river are the workers' houses, occupied by craft demonstrations of weaving, spinning, candlemaking, pottery, and chair caning and rushing. In between the mansion and the workers' houses are the industries—the furnaces, the gristmill, the sawmill, and a brick yard.

Batsto Village is open Memorial Day to Labor Day from 10 a.m. to 6 p.m., Labor Day to Memorial Day from 11 a.m. to 5 p.m. There's a $2 parking fee on weekends and holidays from Memorial Day to Labor Day. In the wintertime many of the craft demonstrations are closed; if that's your particular interest, be sure to call beforehand (tel. 609/561-3262). The village is closed on Thanksgiving, Christmas, and New Years Days.

PINE BARRENS: Less than a hundred miles from New York City there's a vast stand of pine trees, white sandy soil, cranberry bogs and blueberry bushes, swamps and ponds in a primeval wilderness that stretches as far as the eye can see. This deep pine land lays over a great reservoir of water, a resource that caused the financier Joseph Wharton to purchase great tracts of land here, which he ultimately planned to use to sell water to nearby cities. State law prohibited Wharton from carrying out his money-making scheme, and eventually the state bought the land.

It's now a state-owned forest, and if you really want to get away from the worry and strain of urban life, **Wharton State Forest** offers rental cabins for a real back-to-nature experience. The cabins are on Atsion Lake, off Route 206; each has a screened porch, electricity, bunks with mattresses, a fireplace, sink, refrigerator, and hot and cold running water. Bedding, cooking, and eating utensils are not provided. Rentals are $20 per night for a cabin that sleeps four, $40 for one that sleeps eight. Reservations are essential. Write to Wharton State Forest, Batsto, R.D. 4, Hammonton, NJ 08037, or call 609/561-0024.

Renting a canoe for a day is another way to experience the primitive beauty of the pine barrens. This is not a hazardous "white water" adventure. The pine barrens streams are lazy waters and any excitement on your ride will come from counting the pretty bog flowers along the banks or sighting a pine barrens' tree frog. Paradise Lake Campground, on Route 206 (P.O. Box 46), Hammonton, NJ 08037 (tel. 609/561-7095), rents canoes for $13 a day, including life jackets. If you're a camper, this is a pleasant private camp; sites rent for $11.50 a day for a family of four. Electricity and water hookups are also available.

NEW JERSEY GRAPES: The story of New Jersey's wineries begins in Rheims, France. Master vintner Louis Renault came from there in 1855 to the U.S. to establish a vineyard free of the disease that was ruining Western European vines. After failing in his mission in California, Renault heard of a native American grape, known as the Labrusca, that was resistant to the disease. When he came to southern New Jersey where it thrived, Renault found a climate and soil similar to what he had left in France. In 1864 he purchased land to establish his own vineyard in the Egg Harbor area. By 1870 he was producing traditional French champagne from American grapes. Although ownership of the winery has changed hands twice since Renault died in 1919, it has been in continuous operation.

During the 14 years of Prohibition, Renault Wine Tonic (for medicinal purposes) was sold in drugstores throughout the U.S. After repeal, Renault sparkling wines were sold nationwide. Today the winery's products include several sparkling wines, a blueberry champagne, pink champagne, and red, white, and rosé dinner wines, and other blends. The present owner, Joseph Milza, has introduced wine tours and Saturday buffets, and most recently has opened the restaurant atop the winery.

To reach the winery tour's starting point in the retail store, you enter the grounds via a little footbridge that crosses a stream well populated with ducks and geese, and cross the front courtyard past the picnic tables and benches. The tour takes you through the entire winemaking process, and includes wine tasting. One of the most fascinating rooms is the museum that holds a fine collection of antique glass. Nicely lighted display cases show off to best advantage such curiosities as a 14th-century green glass champagne coupe with gold leaf, medieval crystal goblets, and unusually shaped wine cups. In the Burgundy Room the Saturday night buffets ($9.50) are held with a selection of six to eight wines tasted, plus a full dinner. A pretty natural-light courtyard reminiscent of a French country house leads into the antique equipment room, where champagne is fermenting. In the aging room, 300,000 gallons of wine are held in white oak and redwood casks. Red wine stands for three to four years, white wine for less. The tour ends back in the retail shop, where a full panoply of wine paraphernalia—goblets, flasks, corkscrews—is sold along with Renault products.

The **Restaurant Renault** is above the winery and it's entered via a passageway constructed of old wine barrels. The restaurant's booths are formed from barrel staves. Wine riddling racks stacked one above the other comprise the bar, and the green glass ceiling over the bar is made of shattered glass from champagne bottles set in polyurethane. All the drinks are made from Renault wine, including the delicious strawberry daiquiris, a creamy blend of strawberries, ice milk, May wine, and whipped cream.

The restaurant has a prix-fixe dinner, ranging from $17.50 to $22.50, which includes a five-course meal and a choice of wines or dessert. The menu changes weekly. One recent dinner started with spinach balls with mustard sauce, followed by corn chowder with pimiento purée garnish. Tortellini with pistachio sauce preceded a choice of entrees: chicken breast palimitana, seafood Newburg, steak, lamb chops, or roast beef—accompanied by broccoli, potatoes, and a salad. The restaurant is open only on weekends; on Friday and Saturday from 5 p.m., on Sunday from 3 p.m. Reservations are recommended (tel. 965-2111). The **Garden Café**, serving lunch and snacks, is open Monday to Saturday, noon to 4 p.m.

Winery tours are held Monday through Saturday from 10 a.m. to 5 p.m., on Sunday from noon to 5 p.m. Tour admission is $1. The candlelight buffets, on Saturday evening only, are by reservation.

You can get to the Renault vineyard and winery (tel. 965-2111) from Atlantic City via Route 30 east to Bremen Avenue. From the Garden State Parkway south, exit 44 (northbound take exit 36) to Route 563, and follow Egg Harbor City signs.

Other wineries have also prospered in the hospitable south Jersey soil. The **Bernard D'arcy Wine Cellars** in Absecon (tel. 652-1187) welcomes visitors to explore the winery and sample its over 20 varieties of dinner, dessert, and sparkling wines. If you're coming south on the Garden State Parkway, take exit 40 to Route 30 east. Go left at Sixth Avenue to the winery. Northbound on the parkway, use the Absecon/Atlantic City service plaza exit ramp to Jim Leeds Road and turn right to the winery. Open Monday to Saturday from 10 a.m. to 6 p.m.

BARNEGAT LIGHT: If you've been to see the lighthouse in Atlantic City, you may have noticed that the color schemes of Absecon and Barnegat lighthouses are different. The Barnegat Light is white with a red top; Old Ab has three bands of color—white, red, and white. In the daytime, vessels at sea could identify the lighthouse from the colors and so could determine their positions.

Although lighthouses seem rather romantic to us nowadays, they served a very important function in their era. Before the advent of steam, ships could not estimate with any accuracy their time of arrival at a port. Windless days, storms, the flow of the tides could delay a ship for hours or days. Therefore it was not uncommon for a vessel to arrive near a port at night, and have to wait till daybreak before it could board a harbor pilot to guide the ship into port.

The danger of cruising all night off an unfamiliar coast, when poor visibility made it impossible to tell the difference between sand, rocks, and sea, was obvious. With a lighthouse, not only could the danger be marked, but the safe passages as well. How did the lighthouse convey its message? Each lighthouse had its own characteristic light, with an individual color, type of flash, and time lapse between flashes. New Jersey, strategically situated between the ports of Philadelphia and New York, was often the first land sighted by transatlantic sailing vessels.

Both the Absecon and Barnegat lighthouses were designed by Gordon Meade, who in later years was a general in the Union Army and commander at the Battle of Gettysburg.

Historic Barnegat Lighthouse has stood on the northern tip of Long Beach Island since 1858. Its light, which flashed every ten seconds at each point of the compass, no longer warns away ocean vessels from the "graveyard of the Atlantic." In 1927 a lightship anchored off Barnegat took over the lighthouse's work, and it's now the **Barnegat Light Historical Museum,** open on weekends in June and September from 2 to 5 p.m., in July and August daily from 2 to 5 p.m. The magnificent view from the top of the tower brings visitors up its 217 steps.

Don't forget to bring your bathing suit. The state park in which the lighthouse now stands has bathing under a lifeguard's protection. Picnic tables along the Barnegat Inlet are well placed to give you a good view of the boats using the waterway. Fishing is permitted along the stone jetty and the inlet bulkhead, and there's surf casting from the beach. Route 72, which crosses both the Garden State Parkway and Route 9 north of Atlantic City, connects the mainland with Long Beach Island. Barnegat Lighthouse State Park, P.O. Box 167, Barnegat Light, NJ 08006 (tel. 494-2016), is open all year.

The 18-mile length of Long Beach Island is a vacation area of wide sandy beaches and small resort communities. Boating, swimming, fishing, and relaxing in the sun are main attractions. Bathers will need to purchase beach passes, about $2 for a week's use. Free outdoor concerts in **Beach Haven Bicentennial Park,** flea markets, and the **Long Beach Historical Museum** (tel. 492-0700) provide other diversions for vacationers.

Sports

There's a sport for everyone in Atlantic City, either right in town or within a short drive. So if your idea of physical activity extends beyond pushing a stack of chips across a blackjack table, you'll find a great many ways to occupy your time—swimming, fishing, boating, surfing, running, biking, tennis, racquetball, golf, bowling, horseback riding, and canoeing among them. Also, there's horse racing at the Atlantic City Race Course and professional boxing matches at the casinos if you'd rather watch than participate.

Here's a rundown on the major sports activities, starting with the one that first put Atlantic City on the map:

SWIMMING: The best things in life are free in Atlantic City, unlike most other communities along the Jersey Shore. You don't need to buy a beach pass or have resident's credentials to enjoy the summer sun or the ocean surf on the sandy beach. The water here is exceptionally gentle also, due to the slope of the ocean floor, I'm told, so there's almost no undertow here compared to other East Coast beaches. Atlantic City beaches are protected in summer by lifeguards, from about 9 a.m. to 6 p.m. The oceanfront casinos have brightly colored cabañas on the beach and lounge chairs for rent. Beware: there are no parking facilities at the beach. Staying within walking distance of the surf pays off, or else you'll have to leave the car at a lot a block or two back from the beach.

Most motels have swimming pools that are exclusively for their guests' use, which also is the case for the casino-hotels.

Surfing is only permitted at city beaches after regular bathing hours.

FISHING: Tuna, sea bass, mako shark, weakfish, bluefish, fluke, striped bass, and flounder abound in New Jersey's salt waters. Party and charter boats at the **Farley State Marina** (tel. 441-3600), at the northern tip of the island, offer novices or experienced anglers an extensive fleet. On a party boat you pay individually, as you board, on a first-come, first-served basis, until the boat is full. Charter boats are reserved in advance, usually with a deposit.

Party boats sail daily for a specific species. Rods, reels, tackle, and bait are on board. Capt. Applegate's party boats (tel. 345-4077 or 652-8184) offer four-hour half-day trips, costing adults $13 and children $8, leaving at 8:15 a.m. and 1 p.m. The all-day fishing trips leave at 8 a.m. daily, and the fare is $20 for adults, $12 for children. Night sailings, Wednesday through Saturday, at 7:30 p.m. for blues cost $25. Capt. Applegate's boats are at Pier 1, Farley State Marina, South Carolina Avenue and Brigantine Boulevard, just before the Brigantine bridge.

Farley State Marina has 400 docking berths and full facilities for boaters: gasoline, diesel fuel, water, showers, and rest rooms. Harrah's Marina has 100 or so slips ready for rental. Call 441-5315 for particulars.

BIKING: Morning bike rides along the Boardwalk are a wonderful way to get around, breathe in some exhilarating fresh air, and enjoy healthy exercise as you see the sights. You can rent a bike year round at **H. Longo,** Boardwalk and North Carolina Avenue (tel. 344-8288), next to Resorts. Rentals are $3 per bike. Biking on the Boardwalk is permitted only from 6 to 10 a.m.

BOWLING: **Verona Lanes,** on the Black Horse Pike in West Atlantic City (tel. 641-5117), is open 24 hours. If you like to bowl late at night, this is the place for you.

GOLF: Several area golf courses are open to the public. The closest to Atlantic City is the **Brigantine Country Club** (tel. 266-1388), on the bay side of the island on East Shore Drive.

TENNIS AND RACQUETBALL: Guests at Harrah's Marina, Trump Castle, or at Trump Plaza (tennis), Resorts (racquetball), or the Tropicana (tennis), have on-site facilities just an elevator ride away. If you're staying at the Sands, the facilities of the Great

Bay Country Club in Somers Point are available; transportation is provided by the Sands.

Golf & Tennis World, on the Black Horse Pike in West Atlantic City (tel. 641-3546), has both outdoor and indoor tennis courts, a driving range, and instruction in both sports.

Public tennis courts are on Albany Avenue at **Bader Field** (tel. 347-5348).

HORSEBACK RIDING: A guide will accompany you, if you wish, along the 60 miles of trails behind **Bill's Lazy B Stables,** on Route 9 in Oceanville (tel. 652-1973). It's $6 an hour from 10 a.m. to 5 p.m. for a pleasant trek through the wooded countryside.

ATLANTIC CITY RACE COURSE: Watch those thoroughbred horses racing from the gate-opening bell to the thundering stretches and photo finishes! You'll have an evening to remember, and get a run for your money, at the Atlantic City Race Course, 14 miles west of the city on the Black Horse Pike, Route 322 (tel. 641-2190). From the beginning of June through August post time is 7:30 p.m. (closed Sunday). The track is park-like, with attractive greenery and flower gardens. The race course boasts top horses and jockeys, and hosts the prestigious Grade I Invitational United Nations Handicap. Simulcasting or inter-track wagering keeps the excitement hot with virtually year-round racing. Two dining rooms are open in the clubhouse. Admission is $2 for grandstand seats, $3 for the clubhouse.

Atlantic City with Children

It's not only possible, but it's great fun, as it always has been. The gently sloping ocean floor makes the Atlantic City surf safer and smoother than the rough waters at some East Coast beaches. The **beach** is cleaned daily, and it's exceptionally well guarded too, by the city's Beach Patrol and by lifeguards who are employed at the beachfront casino-hotels.

If you're a guest at Caesars, you can leave the youngsters with other kids in a **supervised play area** right on the beach. Harrah's Marina has the best facilities for taking care of kids indoors. The **teen fun center** is well outfitted to keep older kids amused, and next door to it, a supervised playroom for younger ones is open daily from 10 a.m. to 6 p.m. Trump Casino has a supervised nursery for ages 3 to 8.

For **babysitters** the best thing to do is consult with the good people at your hotel's guest services desk. They're equipped with a list of reliable sitters. Most of the hotels will let you do the calling (the fee is generally $5 an hour or so) and make the detailed arrangements. Some of the hotels will do all the legwork, and you just have to let them know what time you'd like the sitter to come.

The Boardwalk's **electronic games arcades,** saltwater taffy shops, and motorized trams will not go unnoticed by your children. In fact, I'd say it's positively unearthly how they manage to find the arcades without a word of direction from a parent. As a change of pace, you might take the family over to **Ocean City,** about nine miles south on Route 9 or take the Garden State Parkway to the Ocean City exit. Check out the Ocean City boardwalk, its amusements (from about 6th Street to 11th Street), and compare the quality of its saltwater taffy. If you go via Margate, a stop at **Lucy the Elephant** will please everyone, and a walk-through will be a memorable first for all (when did you last see the inside of an elephant?).

A late-morning or early-afternoon jitney ride to **Historic Gardner's Basin** is an excellent choice for an outing. There's plenty of room for the younger family members to run around and stretch their legs, and middle-age children (around 8 and up) will find the maritime exhibits interesting. A bite to eat (lunch, or dinner too) at the Flying Cloud Café is easy to handle at the outdoor picnic tables. Inside it's also comfortable, lots of room between tables and highchairs for the youngest.

Storybook Land, a ten-minute ride away on Route 40, may be more intriguing for the under-7s, but siblings a year or two older will be drawn into the fun.

Although I've included **Wheaton Village** under the Cape May section, it's also within an hour's ride of Atlantic City, and it's a really delightful day trip. You can picnic on the grounds or have lunch at the cafeteria. To get there, take the Atlantic City Expressway west to exit 12 (Racetrack) then Route 40 west to Mays Landing. One mile west of Mays Landing, bear left to Route 552 to Millville. In Bridgeton, just a 15-minute ride past Millville on Route 49, the **Cohansic Zoo** is part of a lovely park along the Cohansic River.

Budget at least half a day for the interesting places to see along Route 9 north of Atlantic City. Try to schedule the day so that you'll be able to watch the duck decoy-carving demonstration at the **Noyes Museum** at 2 p.m. (Wednesday to Sunday only). The **Brigantine Wildlife Refuge** is less than a mile farther north. The trails or auto-drive tour can be a wonderful way to introduce children to the pleasures of birdwatching. A pair of binoculars will add greatly to the fun. **Smithville** has something for all ages. Feeding the ducks or the little train ride is fun for little ones. Teens (and you too) will enjoy browsing through the quaint shops after lunch or dinner at one of Smithville's fine restaurants.

Chapter VII

ATLANTIC CITY ABC'S

THE BITS OF PRACTICAL INFORMATION about your home city that you have at your fingertips can sometimes be difficult to track down in a new place. In Chapter I I've tried to present all the practicalities of transportation for getting to and around Atlantic City, but there are a host of other everyday situations—like getting your shoes repaired, for example—that I know from my own experience can be frustrating and time-consuming to take care of when you're away from home. While I can't promise to provide answers to all your needs, I hope you'll be well armed with this alphabetical listing of services in Atlantic City that can smooth the way for any visitor.

Another good source of information is the Guest Services desk, to be found in the lobby of every casino-hotel. I've found the men and women behind these desks to be unfailingly cheerful and willing to help. They'll always try to answer your queries and, if you're a guest at their hotel, will make reservations for dinner or show tickets, secure car rentals, make arrangements for a babysitter, etc.

AREA CODE: For all shore points from Atlantic City south to Cape May Point, the area code is 609.

CALENDAR OF EVENTS: The folks at the **Atlantic City Convention & Visitors Bureau,** 2314 Pacific Ave., Atlantic City, NJ 08401 (tel. 609/348-7100), have a complete list of annual events designed to attract tourists the year round.

Highlights of the year include the **Atlantic City Easter Parade,** which starts shortly after noon on Easter Sunday at Virginia Avenue, goes down the Boardwalk to the Golden Nugget, and then returns to Convention Hall. All participants have a chance to be considered for prizes for the prettiest bonnet, best outfit for a couple, etc. The summer season is "officially" open with the **Opening of the Beach** ceremonies at the Beach Patrol Headquarters (South Carolina Avenue and the beach) on the Friday of Memorial Day weekend. Every Father's Day weekend the **Boardwalk National Art Show** brings outdoors the annual fine arts display that is one of the two major arts festivals of the summer. At the end of June, the annual **Maxima 8-Pound Test Line Fishing Tournament** is held. In July you can count on seeing a fireworks extravaganza along the beach in celebration of the Fourth; location varies from year to year depending on which casino-hotel is the sponsor. For a quieter kind of event, although the color displays can be just as breathtaking, follow the **Hydrangea Trail,** all the way from Atlantic City to Cape May. The mild sea air is particularly conducive to hydrangeas' growth, and it's really a spectacular show.

The annual **Greater Atlantic City Inshore Boat Fishing Tournament** comes at the end of July. The **Blessing of the Sea** is the culmination of a procession from St. Michael's Church, 10 North Mississippi Ave., on August 15 (Assumption Day in the Catholic calendar). The city's other major arts festival, the **National Indian Summer Art Show,** on the Boardwalk the week following Labor Day, emphasizes crafts as well as fine arts displays.

Recently moved to the week *following* Labor Day week, the **Miss America Pageant Competition** is a four-night event—second Tuesday after Labor Day is the parade, then Wednesday to Friday nights are the three public competitions (evening dress, swimsuit, and talent) in Convention Hall, where the crowning of Miss America takes place on Saturday evening, as those of us not packed into the hall sit glued to our TV sets and watch the contestants vie for the title.

Throughout the summer months there are also a number of free concerts, ranging from military bands to classics concerts to local rock groups in front of casino-hotels or in Brighton Park.

CLIMATE: Thanks to the prevailing ocean breezes, Atlantic City enjoys a pleasant, temperate climate, and you won't suffer the extremes of heat or cold experienced in nearby New York, Philadelphia, or Washington. Since ocean temperatures lag behind air temperatures, you'll find that the air remains refreshingly cool until well into the summer, and the weather will be quite mild into late autumn. Ocean temperature ranges from an August high of 78°F. to a January low of 37°F. Average monthly air temperatures are:

January	32	July	75
February	32	August	78
March	45	September	77
April	49	October	57
May	53	November	57
June	68	December	35

A word of warning here to sun worshippers: moderation is the key word. No matter how delightfully warm the sun may feel your first days at the beach, remember that you can get sunburned even if the air does seem just springtime warm. Be prepared with suntan oil or, if you're very fair, a good sun block, and come to the beach with a protective coverup and a beach hat. Once you've gotten too much sun, there's really no cure except sympathy and possibly some aloe plant oil for your tender skin.

CLOTHES: Once upon a time Atlantic City had a stiff bathing-suit code that included long pants and a top for the gents and ankle-length stockings and a bathing dress for ladies. For better or worse those days are long gone, and today's visitors dress with relaxed informality—comfort and convenience are today's code words. Sportswear—shorts, slacks, blue jeans, sun dresses, skirts—is fine for summertime garb. If you're staying in a casino-hotel, I'd recommend that you have a bathing suit coverup if you're going through the lobby. In the evening only the more elegant restaurants request that men wear jackets. (Should you appear without one, I've noticed that restaurants have a supply of jackets on hand to loan to customers.)

Even in summer you'll be glad to have taken along a light sweater or jacket for an evening stroll on the Boardwalk or inside the air-conditioned casinos and restaurants. In spring and fall, suits and woolens are good to have, and an umbrella will come in handy year round. Average annual precipitation for Atlantic City is 47 inches, and in January and February it may be in the form of snow. Warm, heavy coats and waterproof boots will keep you comfortable and dry.

In the casinos, shorts and T-shirts are frowned on at any time of day, and you may not be permitted to enter in your beach garb. Men are requested to wear jackets in the evening.

CREDIT: As one casino credit manager told me, "This is a cash business and we'd like to keep it that way." However all the casino-hotels do permit you to establish credit with a system that is fairly similar to getting a charge account at a department store. You have to fill out an application, give credit references, name your bank, and after about two weeks, you'll have a line of credit. You can also establish credit in advance by writing ahead for the application.

EMERGENCY: Dial 911 for police or fire emergencies.

GAMING: In Chapter IV there's more information about this fascinating topic. Suffice it to say here that casinos are open daily from 10 a.m. to 4 a.m., to 6 a.m. on weekends and holidays. The minimum age for admittance to casinos is 21.

HOUSES OF WORSHIP: The traditional faiths are all represented here in Atlantic City, and this list just names those churches and synagogues closest to downtown. Please consult your telephone directory for other denominations and locations.

    Chelsea Baptist Church, 2908 Atlantic Ave. (tel. 344-1442).

    Church of the Ascension (Episcopal), 30 South Kentucky Ave. (tel. 344-0615).

    Greek Orthodox Church of St. Nicholas, 13 South Mt. Vernon Ave. (tel. 348-3495).

    St. Andrew's Lutheran Church, Pacific and South Michigan Avenues (tel. 345-4407).

    St. Michael's Roman Catholic Church, 10 North Mississippi Ave. (tel. 344-8536).

    Jehovah's Witness, 920 North Illinois Ave. (tel. 344-0781).

    Rodef Sholom Synagogue, Plaza and Atlantic Avenues (tel. 345-4580).

INFORMATION: Take your questions to the **Atlantic City Convention & Visitors Bureau,** 2314 Pacific Ave., Atlantic City, NJ 08401 (tel. 609/348-7100), and they'll do their best to help. Their help can include finding you a place to stay (tel. 609/348-7129 or 7132). You'll also get information from the **Atlantic City Visitors Bureau,** Department of Public Relations, 2310 Pacific Ave., Atlantic City, NJ 08401 (tel. 609/348-7044). For information about the whole south Jersey shore region or the state in general, the place to write is the **New Jersey Division of Travel and Tourism,** CN 826, Trenton, NJ 08625 (tel. 609/292-2470).

MEDICAL: Atlantic City Medical Center, on Pacific Avenue, between Michigan and Ohio Avenues (tel. 344-4081), has 24-hour hospital emergency service and outpatient facilities (neither of which, I hope, will be of concern to vacationers). All the casino-hotels (except the Golden Nugget) have a nurse on duty in an on-premises medical office and a doctor on call.

NEWSPAPERS AND MAGAZINES: In the gift shops of all the casino-hotels (usually a few steps from the front desk), newsstands carry local publications as well as the major out-of-town dailies, and national magazines and newspapers. The *Atlantic City Press* is the local daily; *The Sun* is the area weekly. *Atlantic City Magazine* ($1.95 per monthly copy) has terrific listings of nightlife, restaurants, sports, and almost every other kind of activity you're likely to be interested in. Don't buy a copy, though, until after you've checked into your room, as many casino-hotels will give you a complimentary issue. *WHOOT* is a tabloid-size entertainment weekly and covers the latest events at area discos, nightclubs, restaurants in town and the nearby communities. Free copies are usually available in most hotel and motel lobbies.

PHOTOGRAPHS: Can't wait to see how your pictures turned out? **Atlantic Photo Center** (Fast Foto Corp.), 310 North Albany Ave. (tel. 345-5131), will make your color prints in 24 hours.

POST OFFICE: At the corner of Illinois and Pacific Avenues (tel. 345-4212).

SIGHTSEEING TOURS: Several companies offer sightseeing tours of Atlantic City and nearby points of interest. **Gray Lines of Atlantic City,** at Arkansas and Arctic Avenues, Atlantic City, NJ 08401 (tel. 609/344-3218), has both day and nighttime tours.

Gray Lines offers a three-hour Town and Country trip. The itinerary includes a stop at the Renault Winery and Tomasello Winery and historic Smithville. The fare is $9.

Their 95-mile Southern Shore Circle Tour ($14) takes you south over five different bridges along the scenic Ocean Highway. After visiting Cape May the tour turns north through Cape May County to Cape May Court House, where there is a stop at the Historic Museum, and then back to Atlantic City via the mainland.

Casino and dinner and/or show tours highlight the evening hours.

SHOE REPAIR: You can have your shoes repaired while you wait at **Junior's,** 2325 Atlantic Ave. (tel. 344-2404). They'll also undertake other kinds of leather repair with handbags and jackets.

TIME/WEATHER: Find out the time of day by phoning 976-1616. If you want more weather data than a look out your hotel window provides, give a call to the local weather number: 976-1212.

TRAFFIC: In Atlantic City you may make a right turn at a red light after you've come to a complete stop, unless a sign posted at the intersection says otherwise. State speed limit is 55 m.p.h. on highways, and in town it's 25 m.p.h.

WESTERN UNION: To send a telegram or Mailgram, call toll free 800/325-6000. For other information, the local office of Western Union is at 9 South Tennessee Ave. (tel. 348-0714).

Chapter VIII

THE OCEAN DRIVE

FROM ATLANTIC CITY TO CAPE MAY you have a choice of three routes. Following the impersonal concrete ribbon of the Garden State Parkway, you'll arrive in less than an hour. If time is of the essence, it's the way to go. Paralleling the parkway, Route 9 is a two-lane road for most of the way, as it meanders through the small towns. It will give you a better feel for the countryside. Most appealing is the Ocean Drive, across vast expanses of marshes, sounds, inlets, and islands, over five bridges (40¢ toll at each) with the shrill cries of the shore birds and the ocean breezes to keep you company. It's a 40-mile drive, marked with distinctive gull signs, but you may decide to stop en route and discover the pleasures offered in the resorts along the way.

Ocean City

It's eight short miles south of Atlantic City, but the physical closeness just seems to emphasize the contrast between the two seaside towns.

Ocean City was founded 104 years ago by three Methodist ministers who were looking for a place to hold camp meetings. They found it on an almost-deserted island known as Peck's Beach, a barren waste of sand dunes, meadows, and cedar swamps. The ministers decreed that no alcoholic beverages should be manufactured or sold in the community, and that stipulation is still upheld today.

Despite the restriction on the sale of alcohol, the atmosphere in Ocean City is anything but austere. Its sunny beaches, boardwalk, and amusements draw summer crowds that swell the town population from 14,000 to over 100,000 on weekends. A "Night in Venice" festival in July turns bayfront homes and boats in the bay into a light-strung carnival of color.

The **Ocean City Music Pier,** Boardwalk at Moorlyn Terrace, between 8th and 9th Streets, is the center of entertainment. On

Sunday night there's usually a free concert by the Ocean City "Pops" orchestra; other nights you might hear a string band, brass groups, or a choral concert at the pier. Fourth of July fireworks illuminate the Music Pier, and the whole summer long a succession of craft shows, flea markets, antique shows, dances, and flower exhibits are held there. Ocean City has some highly regarded local contests, such as the Miss Crustacean Contest and the famous Hermit Crab Race (no one has ever had the patience to wait to see who won).

Consult with the **Ocean City Public Relations Department,** Ocean City, NJ 08226 (tel. 609/399-6111), for dates of these annual events and any other information you'd like to have about Ocean City. If you're coming to Ocean City from the Garden State Parkway, you'll be arriving via the causeway from Somers Point. A highway information center on Route 52 has helpful staff and details about places to stay.

WHERE TO STAY: Fine accommodations ranging from a traditional hotel to modern motel to guesthouse are plentiful in Ocean City. But rooms do fill up, especially on weekends, and it's a good idea to arrive with reservations on hand. The ban on sales of alcoholic drinks has produced an extraordinarily safe and crime-free environment that's a big attraction for seniors and families with small children.

It might be said that no hotel in Ocean City has the traditional elegance of the **Flanders,** at 11th Street and the Boardwalk, Ocean City, NJ 08226 (tel. 609/399-1000). Here you'll live very graciously, much as they did in 1924 when the hotel was built. It's a Mediterranean-style, eight-story white villa with a red-tile roof and an Italianate bell tower. The hotel's first-floor lobby (up a short flight of steps) rivals a museum with its collection of handsome antique furniture, porcelain vases, and objects d'art. A gilt clock set in a green marble base, bronze figures on marble pedestals, and a one-of-a-kind carved black walnut desk of heroic proportions decorate the spacious room. In summer a chamber music group plays here in the evening.

The hotel has full resort facilities—an outdoor heated pool, tennis, shuffleboard, miniature golf, an indoor playroom, live entertainment, and a beauty salon. Of course there's a dining room, and in summer rooms are offered only on a Modified American Plan (with two meals, breakfast and dinner). In winter you have a choice of European Plan (no meals) or MAP.

The rooms are all being redecorated and/or remodeled. The

ones I saw were individually furnished in varying color schemes and periods. Contemporary or traditional in style, all were uniformly light in color, many with white walls and bedspreads. The new baths are all in gleaming tile. Summer rates, per person per day, are $68 for a double room with twin beds. Two connecting rooms, for four persons, with a bath between, are $64 to $67 per person. The least expensive accommodation, a single room with half bath, is $68. The hotel has installed the latest in fire-alarm systems. If smoke is present in a room, the alarm will alert not only the occupant but the hotel's operator as well. Off-season rates are $60 MAP, $42 European Plan for the double room with twin beds. The least expensive single room is $55 MAP, $37 European Plan.

For all the comforts of a modern motel on the beach block, try the **Impala**, at 10th Street and Ocean Avenue, Ocean City, NJ 08226 (tel. 609/399-7500). There's a choice of accommodations at the motel or annex across 10th Street, and some rooms have pool or ocean views. Extra-large rooms have sitting areas, and refrigerators are available for daily rental ($5). You may request connecting rooms, and there are one- and two-bedroom apartments. All units have two double beds or one king-size bed, and color TV, plus there's free parking and a heated pool. In the height of the season, July 13 to August 26, rates are from $93 to $102 per room. In September rates drop substantially, to $65 to $75 per room. Apartments can accommodate up to six people; rates are from $145 per day and from $900 to $1075 weekly in midsummer; from September 15 the rates drop to from $80 daily and from $450 weekly. A pleasant restaurant, the Blooming Tulip, has moderately priced meals (dinner entrees from $8 to $15). You can take a limousine to Atlantic City for an evening's entertainment. It costs about $10 per person, and you get the fare back in a casino bonus. The Impala is the last stop before Atlantic City on the limo run, and it's a quick ride.

The Impala offers several off-season packages. Their casino special is a two-night weekend for $140 per person, double occupancy, which includes a dinner and show at Resorts.

There's a very pleasant motel on Great Egg Harbor Bay on the mainland in Somers Point. It's 1½ miles east of the Garden State Parkway; take exit 30 (going south) to the circle where Routes 52 and 559 meet. There you'll find the **Pier 4 Motel**, P.O. Box 215, Somers Point, NJ 08244 (tel. 609/927-9141). Half the rooms overlook the bay and the motel pool; all the rooms have balconies and color TV, and are furnished along clean, modern lines. June 15 to

September 2 is the high season, when bay views are $80 for a single, $92 and up for a double, and $116 for a suite.

You can walk to the Crab Trap Restaurant from the motel and have anything from a snack to a fine dinner. There's a clam bar, and a children's menu too. Prices are moderately high—entrees range from $9.50 to $16.95, and include a salad, two vegetables, and homemade breads.

Ocean City's Guest & Apartment House Association runs a helpful Dial-A-Room service (tel. 609/399-8894) that will assist callers in finding accommodations. By writing them at P.O. Box 356, Ocean City, NJ 08226, you can get a copy of their free booklet.

WHERE TO EAT: Stephen and Carolyn Nicoletti have brought a gourmet touch to Ocean City with their multi-room **Culinary Gardens,** 841 Central Ave. (tel. 399-3713). Their brunch, lunch, and dinner menus have a wide variety of choices. Recommended at lunch are quiche du jour (I had a fine shrimp, tomato, and cheese quiche), a crabmeat omelet, and an Italian tuna antipasto. Lunch entrees are $6 or less.

Dinner is more elaborate, offering a choice of hot or cold appetizers, soups, and salads (stuffed mushrooms with shrimp, crab bisque, or spinach salad are all excellent). Main dishes, which range from $9.25 to $14.25 are expertly prepared—Stephen is a CIA graduate (that's Culinary Institute of America). I can recommend the chicken à la Maryland or pasta Culinary Gardens (with seafood). Sparkling cider is a favorite drink in this "dry" town, and it's a deliciously thirst-quenching beverage.

Watson's, at Ocean Avenue and 9th Street (tel. 399-1065), has been an Ocean City tradition since 1934. They're open in the summer only, from May 1 to the beginning of September for breakfast (8 to 11 a.m.) and dinner (4:30 to 8:30 p.m.). The full-course dinners are reasonably priced, and you'll get with your entree soup or a salad, beverage, and dessert, plus their famous bread basket, for around $7 to $12. Adjacent to the restaurant is Watson's Motor Hotel, which features rooms with kitchen facilities.

On the Boardwalk, in the vicinity of the Music Pier, you can pick up a light lunch from a raw clam bar or other snack stand. Or if you have a room with a refrigerator, it's easy to pick up picnic ingredients and have your sandwich at the beach.

WHAT TO SEE AND DO: Beach tags must be worn between 9:30 a.m.

and 5:30 p.m. during the summer season, mid-June to Labor Day. They're for sale at the Music Pier or the information booth on the causeway. A weekly tag is $3; seasonal is $5 if purchased before June 1, $7 after.

While you're walking on the beach, you'll see the remains of the *Sindia,* a ship that ran aground and sank in 1901. Salvaging the cargo of the *Sindia,* which was returning to New York from Kobe, Japan, has become a local cause célèbre since a diving team began going down to assess the possibilities. Relics from the *Sindia* are in the Ocean City Museum, and rumors of the wealth left aboard have circulated since the night of the shipwreck. It's estimated that about one-quarter of the cargo is still in the hold, buried deep in the sand.

You can fish off the piers in Ocean City or go out on a party or charter fishing boat from marinas on the bayside. **Capt. Joe Zaborowski's Challenger Fleet,** at 3rd Street and Bay Avenue (tel. 399-5011), has four- and six-hour fishing trips, night bluefishing, and sightseeing cruises in the evening at 7 p.m. The four-hour fishing trips cost $12, the six-hour night bluefishing $22. Captain Joe also offers a cruise to Harrah's Marina Hotel/Casino. Although the cruise costs $20, you'll get back $15 in a bonus package from the casino. Call Captain Joe's for the schedule.

Learn to sail on a Sunfish ($30 for three hours rental; lessons are $55 for ten hours) at **Bayview Sailboats,** 312 Bay Ave. (tel. 398-3049). Bayview also rents windsurfers by the day ($40) or the week ($115).

When the weather is not conducive to outdoor activities, a visit to the **Ocean City Historic Museum,** 409 Wesley Ave. (tel. 399-1801), will be rewarding. Antiques buffs will particularly enjoy the Victorian dining room, bedroom, and kitchen furnished with lifelike reality. A fashion room displays dozens of examples of apparel and accessories worn by men, women, and children at the turn of the century. The museum's *Sindia* room has ship models, sailing papers, old photos, and pieces of the cargo. Maps, photos, and documents depict Ocean City's progress since it was founded in 1879. If you're interested in natural history, the seashells, semiprecious stones, and mounted birds native to the seashore are worth seeing.

The museum is open from 10 a.m. to 4 p.m. Monday to Saturday in summer; winter hours are 1 to 4 p.m. Friday and Saturday. Admission is free.

On the mainland, in Somers Point, stands the oldest house (1720–1726) in Atlantic County, the **Somers Mansion,** at Shore Road and Mays Landing (tel. 927-2212). The brick structure was built by Richard Somers, a Quaker whose father had acquired the property in 1695. The house is open Wednesday to Friday from 9 a.m. to noon and 1 to 6 p.m. It opens on Saturday at 10 a.m., and Sunday hours are 1 to 6 p.m.

Stone Harbor

Birdwatchers have a rare treat in store at the **Stone Harbor Bird Sanctuary,** located at the southern end of the town, between 11th and 116th Streets and Second and Third Avenues. The 21-acre sanctuary provides ample feeding grounds for some seven species of heron and the glossy ibis, attracted here by the thickets of holly, cedar, sassafras, and bayberry. At sunrise it's a spectacular sight as thousands of birds fly out of the sanctuary. They return about an hour before sunset, in groups of 20 or 30 or more, and settle into the trees. Some of the many species that have been seen in the sanctuary are loons, grebes, brant, scoters, and the snowy egret. As winter approaches the birds begin to migrate south, and by the end of November practically all the herons have left.

Bring binoculars for a good view of the birds from the Third Avenue side, where there's a parking lot. Pay binoculars are available here too.

A museum, an observation tower, and salt marsh trails are at the **Wetlands Institute,** Stone Harbor Boulevard, Stone Harbor, NJ 08247 (tel. 368-1211), in Middle Township. "When we go down to the low-tide line, we enter a world that is as old as the earth itself—the primeval meeting place of the elements of earth and water, a place of compromise and conflict and change," wrote Rachel Carson in her *Edge of the Sea.* To study this area of land and sea is the aim of the Wetlands Institute, set on a 6,000-acre tract of coastal wetlands. To encourage children's interest, the Wetlandia is a hands-on museum with live animals, games, and microscopes. There are saltwater aquariums, a gallery with arts-and-crafts exhibits, and the Tidepool giftshop featuring a fine selection of natural history books and gift items. Scientific research at the institute has included studies of local fishes and birds and pollution in the marine environment. The Institute is open May to October, Tuesday through Saturday, and October to May on Tuesday, Thursday, and Saturday, 10 a.m. to 4:30 p.m. A $1 donation is requested.

Stone Harbor is on an island, known as Seven Mile Beach, that is about (what else?) seven miles long and only three or four blocks wide. The pleasant resort community of **Avalon** occupies the northern part of the island, Stone Harbor the southern.

You'll get a free booklet describing accommodations, beaches, etc., from the **Stone Harbor Chamber of Commerce,** P.O. Box 422, Stone Harbor, NJ 08247.

The Wildwoods

Continuing south on the Ocean Drive from Stone Harbor, you'll cross the Grassy Sound Bridge to the island that includes North Wildwood, Wildwood, and Wildwood Crest, all popular vacation towns with wide sandy beaches (1,000 feet wide in some places). Stop in the **Hereford Inlet Lighthouse,** a local landmark since 1874, for information about the area.

The central community, Wildwood, is the entertainment hub, with amusement rides, arcades, souvenir shops, nightclubs, and fast-food restaurants. A three-mile-long boardwalk is traversed by a motorized tram ($1) that goes from North Wildwood to Wildwood Crest.

There are motel accommodations to suit every pocketbook. The **Grand, Rochester, and Oceanfront,** Wildwood Crest, NJ 08260, is one of the most luxurious. Formerly the Holiday Inn, the Grand's bedrooms have two double beds, color TV, and a breezy balcony. You'll also find a beautiful pool a few steps from the beach, an outdoor snackbar and grille, and a new indoor pool. Call 609/729-6000 for rates.

WHERE TO EAT: Waterfront dining in the nautical decor of **Urie's Fish Fry,** on Rio Grande Avenue at the foot of the bridge (tel. 522-4947), is a longtime shore tradition. Seafood to take out, to have as a snack, to enjoy in the family-style atmosphere of the dining room, or most formally, up the street at **Urie's Reef & Beef** (tel. 522-7761) are your options.

Campgrounds Between Atlantic City and Cape May

There are 32 great campgrounds to choose from in Cape May County. They're all located on the mainland, many along Route 9. You'll find freshwater lakes, swimming pools, modern bath facilities, camp stores, laundromats, video arcades, and full water, sewer, and electric hookups that you can avail yourself of for a weekend, a week, or the season. And of course the world's finest beaches, boardwalk amusements, fishing, sailing, and boating, not to mention the nearby casinos. These camps offer some of the best bargains around:

Holly Shores Campground, 491 Route 9, Cape May, NJ 08204 (tel. 609/886-1234), only 4½ miles from Cape May, is a Holiday Trav-L-Park. The facilities here are awesome. There is a three-pool complex featuring a heated therapeutic pool as well as adult and kiddie pools. Tennis courts, volleyball, badminton, table tennis, and shuffleboard make this a one-stop resort. The game room is fully equipped with a pool table, video games, and a jukebox. The camp opens the first week in April and closes the last week in September. Rates range from $15 to $25 a day, depending on facilities and number of people on the site. For a family with two children, a site with water and electricity would be $19 a night, $126 a week.

The **Cape Island Campground,** 709 Route 9, Cape May, NJ 08204 (tel. 609/884-5777), also resembles a vacation resort. Convenience is the byword, with a large swimming pool, recreation pavilion, tennis, volleyball, and basketball courts, shuffleboard and horseshoe pitching, mini-golf, and hayrides. All the campsites are equipped with picnic tables and fireplaces. TV and phone hookups, a modern bathhouse, and a camp store bring you all the comforts of home in a lovely setting of over 100 acres of forest and fields. Rates are $18 a night for a family of four, with electricity and water.

North of Cape May Court House, in the Avalon vicinity, the **Blue Dolphin Campground,** on Route 9 (P.O. Box 71), Cape May Court House, NJ 08210 (tel. 609/465-4518), offers the comfort of spacious campsites. In a rustic wooded setting the camp has a large pool, a kiddie pool, a lake, a camp store, rec room, and a playground. No alcoholic beverages are permitted. There are over 600 sites, and the cost is based on the hookups needed (water, electric, etc.) and number of persons; the least expensive site for a family of four would be $19.75.

Chapter IX

ABOUT CAPE MAY

CAPE MAY IS A WORLD unto itself—a gracious island of Victorian charm by the sea—in a country that is often intent on plowing under its past to make room for the new. Cape May is a resort that looks to the future, but it also helps us look back. It bridges the gap between our yesterdays and our tomorrows in a romantic 19th-century setting of beautifully restored little gingerbread houses, adorned with carved bargeboards, dormers, and gables, and magnificent Victorian showplaces with cupolas and captain's walks, wrap-around verandas, and towers crowned with iron cresting.

Explore this charming town, officially designated as a National Historic Landmark city, that has attracted vacationers since the 1700s. Today's visitors come not just for the beaches and ocean breezes but for the relaxing ambience of a more leisured era. Stroll around, rent a bike, or join a walking tour to enjoy the architecture, the sights, and the history of this little community that has been the summer resort for five presidents, famed bandleader and composer John Philip Sousa, and scene of gala balls and the coming-out party of Baltimore belle Wallis Warfield, later the Duchess of Windsor. See where young Henry Ford raced on the beach and visit the surviving old hotels like the Chalfonte. Pause along the quiet, tree-shaded streets to admire the old-fashioned flower gardens in front of these Victorian beauties.

Stay in one of the picture-book Victorian guesthouses, whose beautifully and authentically furnished rooms re-create the era in which they were built and add much pleasure to your visit. Savor the homemade breakfast that the owners of these charming inns provide in an atmosphere so warmly hospitable that you'll really feel like a friend of the family and the other guests who share your meal. There are accommodations choices for every taste and pocketbook. You might prefer to stay at a luxurious, modern beachfront motel or a smaller, family-style motel a block or two behind the ocean promenade. The rambling old hotels provide a simple setting at prices that are also scaled down.

You can dine in a rustic or a sophisticated place, or anything in between, in one of Cape May's many fine restaurants. From an outdoor clam bar overlooking the harbor to a classic French dinner formally served in a Victorian dining room, there are choices to fit your pleasure.

As one of the nation's oldest seashore resorts, Cape May offers the traditional summertime diversions, and more—bathing, boating, fishing, waterskiing, tennis, biking, dancing, antiquing, riding, movies, and concerts. Washington Street, the town's original shopping center, has been turned into a shrubbery-lined mall of little shops, outdoor cafés, and restaurants. You may prefer a spring or fall vacation in Cape May, both are quieter times to come. Even in winter some of the guesthouses are open, especially during the Christmas season (see "When to Come," below), and you can walk on the beach alone except for the sea gulls' company, and return to a cozy fireplace for reading and relaxing.

TOURIST INFORMATION: Whenever you choose to visit, the **Welcome Center**, 405 Lafayette St., Cape May, NJ 08204 (tel. 609/884-3323), will be happy to assist you. It's located across from the bandstand, in a lovely old Colonial-style church building. If you're looking for a room, the free **Touch-a-matic** phone center will connect you with many of the accommodations described below. An information booth in the Washington Street Mall is open all summer long.

A CAPSULE HISTORY: Technically, Cape May is an island, as it was in 1620 when Capt. Cornelius Mey, exploring the Delaware Bay, claimed the shore for the Dutch East India Company and gave the area his name. According to local legend, the Kechemeche Indians had summered on the cape to escape the inland heat. In the mid-1600s whalers moved here from New England; they gradually turned to farming as the whaling industry diminished.

The first stirrings of tourism are noted by local historians in an ad placed in the *Pennsylvania Gazette* in the mid-1700s, soliciting tourists from Philadelphia, then a two-day ($6) ride away. Soon there was a packet picking up passengers in Philadelphia and Delaware and bringing them to Cape May. Visitors from Baltimore and Washington, and as far away as Virginia, came to the blossoming new resort by the mid-1850s. Presidents and presidents-to-be were among them. In 1849 Abraham Lincoln and Mrs. Lincoln came to Cape May, before he took office in 1860. Franklin Pierce, Ulysses S. Grant, Chester A. Arthur, Benjamin Harrison, and James Buchanan resorted in Cape May both during and after their terms as chief executive.

A great fire in 1878 destroyed a 30-acre area of the town. Most of the Victorian buildings we see and admire today were built in the wake of that fire, between 1878 and 1890. Several old buildings, most notably the Chalfonte Hotel on Howard Street, survive from before the fire.

The beach was wider in 1903 when Henry Ford raced along it. He had the outside position in a competition with Louis Chevrolet and Alexander Christy, and nearly won, but a breaking wave brought his car to a standstill. In order to get enough money to return to Detroit, Ford had to leave the car as security.

As the popularity of the automobile increased, the popularity of Cape May declined as people sought out more diverse destinations. It was not until the early 1960s, when the downtown section of town was threatened with abandonment and decay, and the disastrous storm in 1962 destroyed many buildings, did the scattered forces of preservation coalesce to save the unique heritage of Cape May.

ORIENTATION: Cape May lies at the southern tip of New Jersey, at the beginning of the Garden State Parkway. An easy drive from most of the major cities in the eastern half of the U.S., it's a 150-mile drive south of New York City, 120 miles east of Washington, D.C., and 80 miles south and east of Philadelphia. Travelers from the south may choose to come via the Cape May–Lewes, Delaware, ferry, a 70-minute ride that runs year round; auto reservations are not necessary.

Most of the things you'll want to see are in Cape May City, which is what this section's all about (there's also a Cape May County, which goes from the tip of the peninsula north to Avalon). If you're driving, you'll come into town on Lafayette Street, from the Garden State Parkway. Turn left at Ocean Street and you'll cross the heart of the historic district—Washington, Hughes, and Columbia Streets—before coming to Beach Drive, which parallels the length of the beach. Here's where you'll find all the oceanfront motels listed below, Convention Hall, and the seawall promenade.

There's metered parking behind the Washington Street mall. You'll see the lot, on your right, as you're turning from Lafayette Street to Ocean Street.

Public Transportation

New Jersey Transit provides express bus service to Cape May from New York City and Philadelphia. For information call from New York City 201/762-5100, in Philadelphia 215/569-3752; in south Jersey call toll free 800/582-5946.

WHEN TO COME: Summer is a delight in Cape May. There's ocean bathing and the cool breezes of the evening keep the temperature pleasant. There are summer **repertory theater and concerts** at the outdoor stage at the Physick Estate, band concerts behind the Washington Street mall, and a regular weekly schedule of events at Convention Hall, which functions as an oceanfront community center year round. **Walking tours** of the village are held year round, as are the trolly tours; individual Victorian guesthouses have tours of their premises several times a week. Those houses are noted in the descriptions of accommodations, below. If you're strolling around town, you'll find a basket of some sort on the front door, or near it, of many Victorian inns. Brochures inside the baskets are free, and have descriptions of the houses and details on tours.

In the springtime the annual **Tulip Festival** commemorates Captain Mey; whose Anglicized name honors the town's Dutch heritage. Thousands of imported bulbs have been planted in gardens throughout the town, and the flowers are in bloom the last week in April and the first week in May. Highlighting the festival are guided tours of the gardens, Dutch dances performed in costume, a demonstration of street scrubbing (a custom still observed in Holland), and a Cottages at Tuliptime exhibit. Four bed-and-breakfast guesthouses have special tours and exhibits of old porcelain dolls, artworks, decorated eggs, and stained glass.

Cape May's **Victorian Week** is a misnomer, since it lasts for ten days. It's the major festival of the year, celebrating the town's wooden buildings, and it usually includes Columbus Day weekend and the previous weekend as well. There are tours by foot and trolley, lighted stained-glass displays, a Victorian fashion show, and a dinner-dance in a Victorian setting.

Cape May has the second-largest fishing fleet on the East Coast. The **Seafood Festival** in early September is a dual event, celebrating the town's fishing industry and memorializing those fishermen who were lost at sea. Special seafood dishes are served at local restaurants, and an outdoor restaurant festival is a smörgåsbord of local seafood. At the U.S. Coast Guard station helicopter rescues are staged and survival suit races are held. The blessing of the fleet also takes place at the Coast Guard station.

The entire month of December is a festival in Cape May. There are strolling carolers, a candlelight walk on the mall with wine and cheese hospitality in the shops, chiming church bells, twinkling lights on the Victorian houses, and a community tree-lighting ceremony. And that's not all! A **Christmas Bazaar and Crafts Fair** has unique ideas for gifts, there is a series of readings and plays, and a **Christmas Ball** caps off the festivities.

January and February are the quietest months—but some guesthouses are open year round and their hospitality seems even warmer in the winter stillness.

Chapter X

STAYING IN CAPE MAY

STAYING IN ONE OF CAPE MAY'S Victorian guesthouses or Victorian inns is, in my opinion, the best way to enjoy the spirit and fun of a cape vacation. The guesthouses differ, as do their owners, with individual personalities and approaches to running each establishment. Some of the guesthouses are truly museum-like in the quality of their High Victorian furniture and fidelity to precise detail in colors, wallpapers, and room accessories. Other inns have beautiful antiques, too, but the atmosphere seems more homey and comfortable, and a stay is closer to a visit to grandma's house. Still other places seem more like ordinary guesthouses, pleasantly but not spectacularly furnished, some with breakfast, others not.

Most of the very carefully restored houses are near the Main-stay inn, on or near Columbia Avenue a block from the ocean-front. There's another fine group on Jackson Street less than a block from the water, including the Seventh Sister. Others are scattered in the vicinity of the Welcome Center, such as the Barnard-Good House and the Albert Stevens Inn. Almost all the innkeepers would prefer not to have young children, under 12 or so, since the houses are not huge and the strain of keeping children quiet can be difficult, not only for the parents and the children, but for the other guests too. I've noted the few exceptions in the descriptions below.

Don't expect to find TVs or room phones in a Victorian guesthouse—you won't. There's no air conditioning either, but don't feel concerned. The cooling ocean breezes and ceiling fans in the bedrooms provide an energy-efficient and gently cooling ventilation that is quieter and more appropriate to the Victorian decor.

In the summer most guesthouses prefer that you stay a minimum of two or three nights, especially on weekends. A deposit of one night's fee is usually requested to confirm your reservation.

You'll have to send a check or money order, and be prepared to pay for your stay that way also (or in cash), as none of the guest-houses accepts credit cards (most of the restaurants and motels will take credit cards, however).

The bed-and-breakfast guesthouses all charge a flat rate for the room, which they expect will be occupied by two people. For single occupancy, check with the guesthouses; they'll deduct about $10 per night.

If you want to stay at a Victorian guesthouse, reservations are a must. Even the larger ones, like the Mainstay, have no more than 12 rooms; most have less, and they're snapped up quickly in season and, more and more, out of season too.

I've previewed below first all the establishments that provide room and breakfast—the traditional bed-and-breakfast accommodations (as you'll find, many also serve tea-and in the afternoon too). Next is a preview of the guesthouses that provide only accommodations. The three old Victorian hotels are described next, and the chapter concludes with the oceanfront motels and the less-expensive properties off the beach.

The Bed-and-Breakfast Victorian Guesthouses

The Mainstay Inn, 635 Columbia Ave., Cape May, NJ 08204 (tel. 609/884-8690)

You may have seen photos of Tom and Sue Carroll's Mainstay inn. It's been on the cover of one national magazine and featured in many others, praised as "the most lavishly and faithfully restored guesthouse" and "the most beautiful conservative Victorian home in a town full of lovely old high-style places." That it is, and more, due to the efforts of the Carrolls who, 16 years ago, were the first of the young couples who fell in love with Cape May and decided to spend their lives there. They first came when Tom, a Coast Guardsman, was stationed at the local training center. They owned a smaller house on Jackson Street, and later sold it to buy the Mainstay. They've been working on it ever since, restoring its splendor and preserving the elegant Italianate villa.

You'll see a magnificent example of their refurbishing effort when you first enter the house: The wallpaper patterns and colors in the foyer and throughout the first floor rooms are truly stunning. Even if you don't stay here, it's worth taking the house tour just to see the results of their inspired efforts.

Set behind a buff-and-green painted picket fence in a garden blooming with pink and orange flowers, the Mainstay has a gracious wrap-around veranda with white columns, its stately proportions topped by an ornate cupola. The house, painted buff and white with dark-green shutters, was built in 1872 by two gamblers as an exclusive clubhouse in which their friends could gamble and pursue other gentlemanly pleasures. The first-floor drawing room has 14-foot ceilings and black cast-iron gasolier chandeliers; there are ornate plaster molding and ceiling medallions throughout the downstairs rooms. The Carrolls have retained much of the original richly ornamented furniture and added antiques that gracefully blend in. The entrance foyer has a 12-foot-high pier glass and an enormous black walnut chest. In the drawing room there is room for several Victorian sofas, side chairs, globe lamps, a grand piano, and a game table. Beautiful Oriental rugs and window treatments of lace and heavy silks are in every room. The dining room's ornate brass chandelier is centered over the polished wood table that seats 12 at each of the two breakfast sittings, at 8:30 and 9:30 a.m.

In cool weather Sue's hot breakfasts approach the multicourse Victorian meals of that well-upholstered era. Fresh fruit or juice, baked pineapple, sausage patties, Bavarian cheese puffs, and coffee and teas comprise a sample menu taken from Sue's own cookbook of breakfast treats. From mid-June to mid-September a continental breakfast of fresh fruit and juice, cold cereal, homemade breads or cakes, and coffee or tea is offered. Guests may help themselves and eat in the dining room or on the veranda, weather permitting. Tea is served daily in the dining room with cookies or some sweet tidbit; in summer it's iced tea on the veranda. On Tuesday, Thursday, Saturday, and Sunday tea follows the house tour given to the public; tour guests join the house guests for refreshments. Tours are given at 4 p.m. and are $4.

Mainstay guests can enjoy great variety in their accommodations. Many of the rooms are very large, furnished with massive Renaissance Revival beds with carved headboards and marble-topped tables and dressers. The rooms are wallpapered with dramatic colors complementing the custom-made draperies and pretty quilts and coverlets. A less formal room has colorful painted cottage-style furniture, with flower-patterned wallpaper and matching bedcover. Old-fashioned prints and globe lamps with colored glass are the perfect period accessories for these individually decorated rooms. In all there are six guest rooms, each named for a famous American who spent time in Cape May—Abraham Lincoln, Clara Barton, etc. Two rooms have private bath; the rest share baths.

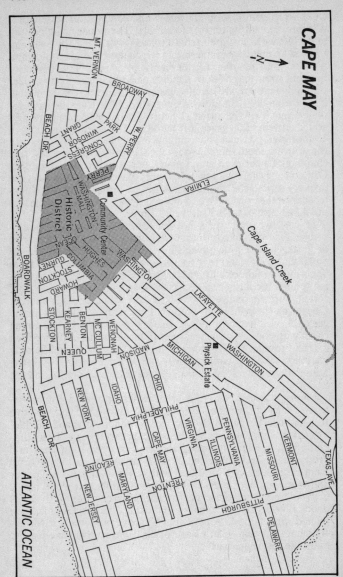

Next door on Columbia Avenue is a two-story gingerbread cottage that is also part of the Mainstay's accommodations. These rooms all have private bath; the guests have breakfast and tea in the main building.

The rooms in either house range from $55 to $95, including breakfast, tea, and beach passes. Deduct $10 for single occupancy. Open from April through November, the Carrolls request a three-night minimum stay in season. Advance reservations are imperative. The inn does not provide parking, so you'll have to find a space on the street.

The Brass Bed, 719 Columbia Ave., Cape May, NJ 08204 (tel. 609/884-8075)

This Carpenter Gothic Victorian "cottage" was built as a summer retreat in 1872 for a Philadelphia businessman, Lewis Dannenbaum. When the present owners, John and Donna Dunwoody, bought the house in 1980, they discovered that most of the bedroom furniture was original, with the builder's and owner's names on shipping tags still attached. All that furniture has been restored and remains in the rooms.

The Dunwoodys, and their three children, were introduced to Cape May, as were several other innkeeper families, during John's service at the local Coast Guard station, although Donna remembers coming to the resort as a child. The town's care and respect for its architectural heritage, the small-town friendliness of the other families that had ventured into the innkeeping business, and the opportunity to leave big-city life, where the prevailing values did not put a high priority on the quality of life, inspired the Dunwoodys to buy the old house. Their pride in what the whole family has accomplished in restoring the house and its period furniture is very hospitably shared with their guests in this very charming Victorian retreat.

In keeping with the Victorian spirit, and the house's location, one block from the ocean, it's painted cream (for sand), with deeper yellow (for sun) on the shutters, roof brackets, and porch rail trim. The public rooms, where the guests gather before breakfast or in the evenings, are the cozy parlor and the dining room. A settee with matching chairs, a marble-topped table with Cape May—related books on architecture and history, and an upright piano with sheet music invite guests into the parlor. John Dunwoody, if coaxed, will crank up his old Grafonola for your entertainment. The Dunwoodys are thoughtful hosts, and in the foyer are a collection of menus from local restaurants that they'll look at with you, if you like, to help decide where to go for lunch or dinner.

They serve breakfast in the dining room at a long, lace-covered table. The Queen Anne dining chairs are heirlooms from Donna's family; the Indian rug was Donna's mother's. The brass gasolier (electric and gas) chandelier has its original etched-glass bell-shaped bulbs. Old photos and prints and flowered wallpaper decorate the walls. Teddy Roosevelt is a particular hero of the Dunwoody family; the hall wallpaper is a reproduction from TR's Sagamore Hill estate, and there's a photo of him in the front hall.

Upstairs there are eight bedrooms, five on the second floor, three on the third; the rooms are named for the old hotels of Cape May. The Congress, on the second floor, has a private half-bath (toilet and sink, a shared shower is in the hall). It's got floral wallpaper with a deep-blue ground, a shining brass bed near the bay window, and white lace-trimmed comforter and pillow shams. Two needlepoint cushioned side chairs and a graceful table are at another window. There's a big wardrobe, an oak dresser, and a mirror. All the rooms are individually decorated, the polished brass beds and colorful wallpapers in each of the rooms are complemented by pretty white organdy curtains and oak or walnut dressers. One room has an old trunk; another has period theatrical posters. Marble-topped washstands, rockers, and other period furnishings create a unique environment in each room. On the second floor two rooms each have a private half-bath; the other two rooms share a bath. On the third floor one room has a private bath, the other two rooms share a bath. Ceiling fans and louvered doors keep the fresh air moving under the eaves.

Rooms with shared bath are $45 to $60, depending on the season and the size of the room. Rooms with private bath are $60 to $80. There are outside hot and cold showers for the convenience of bathers returning from the beach (and inside facilities too).

These rates include a full breakfast in the fall, spring, and winter, a continental breakfast in summer. There are two seatings, one at 9 a.m., the other at 9:45 a.m., at the dining room table. Donna is a skilled cook, and her hot breakfast features a hearty main dish, which might be a casserole of eggs, cheese, and sausages, preceded by both fresh fruit or fruit compote and fresh juice. Croissants or muffins accompany the main dish, and there's homemade coffeecake and coffee or tea. Except for the hot main dish, the continental breakfast has the same components.

In the afternoons the Dunwoodys serve tea in the dining room; in the summer it's iced tea on the porch. If you're there on St. Patrick's Day, John will ask you to join him in celebrating his Irish heritage with an afternoon treat of Irish coffee topped with fresh whipped cream.

The Brass Bed is open year round; ask about special off-season rates. Parking is on the street here.

The Queen Victoria, 102 Ocean St., Cape May, NJ 08204 (tel. 609/884-8702)

The Queen Victoria looks so traditionally Victorian that it could serve as a model typifying that era's architectural hallmarks. It's painted a dramatic and authentic green and crowned with a fish-scale-tile patterned mansard roof pierced with round dormer windows topped by little Gothic gables. Carved brackets decorate the roof line and the two-story corner bays. On the front and side porches columns topped with intricately carved woodwork support the roof. A pretty flower garden and lawn surround the house, which is separated from the street by a cast-iron fence.

The owners of this wonderfully showy Victorian inn spent many hours working to achieve such splendid results. Both Dane and Joan Wells were well equipped to do the job—Joan was executive director of the Victorian Society of America, and she and Dane had been looking for an old house to restore and open as a country inn. Their place is a delightfully old-fashioned retreat, with a personal hospitality as warm as it is rare.

The living room is furnished with the Wellses' handsome collection of Mission pieces. On a cold winter's day it's a pleasant spot to sit in front of the crackling fire and leaf through some of the volumes in Joan's collection of books on art, architecture, decorative arts, history, and fiction. There's a neighborly cat that may join you.

Breakfast is served in the dining room, on the sideboard. After helping themselves, guests may eat at the big table or outside on one of the porches. Fresh juice and fruit, a main dish such as Joan's crustless quiche, made with eggs, cheese, and spinach, a fruit or nut bread, coffee cake or muffins (all breads and cakes are fresh and hot every morning), special coffees sent by Joan's aunt in South America, and teas start your day with a flourish. In the afternoon, tea is offered at the dining room sideboard with a sweet (cookies) and a savoury (a cheese or meat spread and crackers). The Wellses have bicycles that guests may borrow to explore Cape May, and the hosts also provide beach tags.

All 12 of the Queen Victoria's guest rooms can accommodate at least two people; eight of the rooms have private bath and the rest all have sinks in the room. Joan has a crib that she'll lend your infant, but toddlers are discouraged. In harmony with the inn's ambience, the bedrooms are named for eminent Victorians like Disraeli, Lillie Langtry, and the Prince of Wales. The queen's namesake room has a king-size bed with a lacy spread, a Victorian sofa, and side chairs. In all the rooms guests will find fresh-cut flowers and colorful quilts handmade by Mennonite women. There's a handsome four-poster in the Prince Albert room. Plants, oriental rugs, lace curtains, and carved rocking chairs attest to the Wellses' tasteful attention to the period decor.

From Easter to Columbus Day, and weekends year round, rates at the Queen Victoria are $59 for medium-size rooms with shared bath, $79 for medium-size rooms with private baths, and $89 for large rooms with private bath and small refrigerators. Weekday rates from Columbus Day to Mother's Day are 20% to 25% cheaper. There's limited parking on the property for $2. The Wellses have leased a nearby lot for guest parking, and if you don't mind walking, those spaces are free for guests.

The Abbey, Columbia Avenue and Gurney Street, Cape May, NJ 08204 (tel. 609/884-4506)

Victorian opulence infused with the humor and friendliness of owners Marianne and Jay Schatz welcome you to the beautiful Gothic villa facing the monument park on Gurney Street. Don't be surprised if the person at the front door is wearing a straw boater or an engineer's railroad cap. It's Jay, whose irrepressible good spirits may just be his way of expressing his continuing pleasure at having left the corporate hassle to do what he loves. In fact, he and Marianne, between them, accumulated 29 years in the chemical and steel industries before they began their loving restoration of the 1869 building that is considered the finest example of Gothic Revival architecture in the East.

Jay's entertaining ways begin at breakfast, at the big table that seats the 14 guests the house can accommodate, and continue to his lawn croquet games in the late morning, and the afternoon refreshments and house tours, where Jay has a whole new group of people to amuse.

The house was built for a wealthy Pennsylvania coal baron, John B. McCreary, by a famous architect of that era, Stephen Button. The result was the Abbey, with its imposing 60-foot tower, stenciled- and ruby-glass arched windows, large comfortable rooms, and shaded verandas. The house's furnishings were assembled by the Schatzes on forays to auctions and estate sales in nearby Delaware, Pennsylvania, and south Jersey. Their acquisitions are impressive: in the front and back parlors are two matching sets of carved Victorian sofas and side chairs, beautiful globe lamps, and high mirrors. An antique harpsichord sits framed by a windowed alcove. Oriental rugs, potted plants on old walnut stands, and hand-stenciled wall borders dress the room with color and warmth. Original window treatments, with elaborate valences and swags of beautiful fabric, were hand-fashioned and sewn by Marianne, who is a talented needlewoman.

The guest rooms upstairs are on different levels, with several short flights of stairs leading in different directions. Each of the rooms is named for a historic Victorian city—Charleston, Saratoga, Newport, etc.—and each decorated a bit differently; carved wooden headboards, elaborate dressers, old-fashioned table lamps, and pretty coverlets and curtains are the rooms' principal furnishings. Most of the rooms have private baths. For those that do not, there is a bathroom the size of a bedroom, outfitted with a handsome tub and Victorian furnishings. For those who wish to see the Abbey but are not able to stay there, the Schatzes offer a tour ($2) at 5 p.m. on Thursday, Saturday, and Sunday. Tower tours (for guests only) take you up on the roof, where you can see Delaware, 9½ miles away.

Rates at the Abbey are $55 to $88 a night, with prices depending on the size of the room and bath facilities. Deduct $10 a night for single occupancy. The inn is open April to November. The price includes a home-prepared breakfast, served buffet style in the dining room (in summer it's outside on the veranda). Fresh juice or fruit, eggs, quiche, home-baked rolls or bread (blueberry muffins and Irish soda bread are among Marianne's specialties), cereal, a cheese board with cream cheese, edam, Swiss, and gouda are some of the fine ingredients you might expect to see at an Abbey breakfast.

On-site parking is an added convenience. The Schatzes also provide their guests with beach passes and, as noted earlier, there is a late-afternoon refreshment.

The Summer Cottage Inn, 613 Columbia Ave., Cape May, NJ 08204 (tel. 609/884-4948)

The first thing you'll notice on entering this delightful Victorian cottage (as it was called in that era) is the warm, congenial atmosphere which can be attributed to hosts Nancy Richfortn and Bill March.

In the tradition of the Cape May guesthouse, the inn was designed in 1867 as a family summer vacation cottage by Cape May's renowned architect Stephen Decatur Button. Built in the Italianate style with a two-story veranda, the house is topped by a picturesque cupola. On the ground-floor veranda are an old-fashioned porch swing, rockers, flowering plants, and ferns. White wicker furniture grouped around the fireplace make for a relaxed front sitting room where guests can meet and read. An elegant parlor and the dining room display a handsome collection of Victorian pieces, family heirlooms, and lots of pretty extra touches like the fresh flowers and plants you'll see throughout the house.

Upstairs the nine guest rooms are each furnished in a different Victorian mode—Eastlake, Renaissance Revival, etc. Most rooms have private sinks and sitting areas, with bath adjoining or nearby. The rooms cost $50 to $65 a night for a shared bath, $65 to $75 for private bath.

Breakfast is made and served by the owners, whose homemade offerings feature quiche, crêpes, egg entrees, freshly baked warm breads and pastries, fine local fruits, their own jams, coffee, and imported teas. We tasted Nancy's unique chocolate bread and noted the recipe in her collection of Summer Cottage recipes.

Beach passes and hot and cold outdoor showers and dressing rooms are also available.

The Victorian Rose, 715 Columbia Ave., Cape May, NJ 08204 (tel. 609/884-2497)

If you're looking for a romantic seaside setting, come to the Victorian Rose, where Linda and Bob Mullock have tempered the Victorian Gothic architecture of their beautifully restored inn with some 1920s and 1930s furniture and accessories—including recordings of big-band music to dance to in front of the white living room fireplace. The Mullocks are particularly happy to entertain honeymooners or anniversary couples. They recall with nostalgia the couple whose children had given them a week at the Victorian Rose as a 50th-anniversary present.

The Carpenter Gothic–style inn is painted a striking gray-blue, which is set off in summer by the blooming profusion of 125 rosebushes that Bob tends. Gingerbread fretwork, hanging plants, rockers, and a hammock decorate the veranda, where guests can sit and enjoy the refreshing ocean breeze. The inn is strategically situated at the head of Howard Street, facing the ocean at the other end of the street.

Eight well-appointed bedrooms, several with private bath, are in the main house. There's a little cottage with a kitchen in the yard behind the house, and apartments for weekly rentals. Ceiling fans and louvered doors waft the ocean breezes through the second and third floors. The largest room (on the second floor), has a king-size bed and private bath. The guest rooms are all furnished with old pieces, but the emphasis is on country-style comfort rather than authentic-to-the-period decor.

A light breakfast is served in the dining room, which is furnished with a massive carved wooden table, sideboard, and chairs. Dishes from Linda's collection of antique floral patterns set a pretty table for the fresh fruit salad, quiche or homemade breads, coffee and teas.

Summer rates at the Victorian Rose range from $53 to $85, depending on size of room and bath facilities. In winter and spring the rates drop to $50 to $80 a room. Inquire directly for rates for weekly rental of the cottage and apartments.

Captain Mey's Inn, 202 Ocean St., Cape May, NJ 08204 (tel. 609/884-7793 or 884-9637)

I'm sure Cape May's founder would feel greatly complimented that a fellow Hollander, Carin Fedderman, and co-owner Millie LaCanfora named their inn in his honor. Owning a bed-and-breakfast guesthouse was a longtime ambition of these two hard-working women, and they've put in long hours scraping away the layers of paint to reveal the warm golden tones of chestnut oak paneling that distinguish the interior of their handsome inn.

Carin has enriched her adopted land and made a unique contribution to the inn's decor with family heirlooms. Her pewter mug collections, a blue Delft-plate collection, the carved wood bookcase, and the wood-framed lace screens that ornament Dutch windows and afford privacy to the living room are all Dutch imports. Another typically Dutch touch is the rear courtyard, where over 600 tulips bloom in the springtime.

Captain Mey's Inn is conveniently located right near the Washington Street mall. Built at the turn of the century, it's simpler in design than earlier Victorian houses. A wrap-around veranda with wicker furniture is the beige and tan inn's principal ornament. In the little foyer the original pastel-colored wall tile has a shell motif that is repeated in the beautiful Tiffany-style stained-glass hall windows. An Eastlake design carved oak fireplace in the dining room is trimmed with an unusual delft blue-tile front that depicts the 12 trades—hunting and farming among them. Guests gather for breakfast at the massive oak table, where they'll enjoy fresh fruit, cheese imported from Holland, home-baked breads or cakes, jellies made from beach plums, and coffee or tea. Afternoon tea or sherry is served around the fireplace or, weather permitting, outside on the veranda.

The bedrooms on the second and third floors are tastefully furnished with an eclectic mixture of marble-topped dressers, white wicker, floral wallpaper, lace curtains, and carved headboards. All rooms have coverlets handmade by Millie's mother. A huge bathroom on the third floor has a big clawfoot tub and a variety of interesting objects, including a sled, a school desk, and old Raggedy Ann dolls.

The cost of a room at the inn ranges from $70 to $95, depending on whether or not the room has a private bath. There are special weekly and off-season rates. A large parking lot adjoins the inn and guests have free parking privileges.

Barnard-Good House, 238 Perry St., Cape May, NJ 08204 (tel. 609/884-5381)

The comfort, decor, and setting of the Barnard-Good House is a tribute to the imagination, talent, enthusiasm, and hard work of Nan and Tom Hawkins. Set behind its original picket fence, the three-story Victorian cottage has a mansard roof, typical of the French Second Empire style so popular in 1868 when the house was built. Guests relaxing on the wrap-around veranda can admire some of the best gingerbread decoration in Cape May (and that's quite a compliment in this curlicued town). The house was recently painted a soft purple, with blue and deep-red trim to show off the intricate architectural details. Hanging plants and wicker rockers on the veranda and pansy-filled window boxes complete the picturesque façade.

In the dining room, Nan's whimsical "Turkish Corner" exemplifies the Victorian interest in faraway places. A charming tent effect of fabric and lace curtains is draped over a fringed and tufted Victorian sofa and matching side chairs. The lace-covered dining table is centered under an eye-catching iron, brass, and pewter gasolier. A marble-topped server and a sideboard with solid-brass pulls in the shape of griffins contribute to the rooms' solid Victorian charm.

Guests can play the old organ in the adjoining parlor or just enjoy the glow of the carved and tiled gas fireplace. It's a good room for relaxation, with the light softly filtered through the white lace curtains that you'll find throughout the house, and plants and unusual objets d'art collected by the Hawkinses.

The Barnard-Good House has four bedrooms and two baths on the second floor; on the third floor there are one bedroom, a suite with private bath, and a house bath. The house bath is one of the inn's top attractions—it's got a huge copper tub and a wooden john with a pull chain, all in good working order. The rooms vary in size and decor, but you'll note polished-wood floors and Oriental rugs throughout the house.

One room is decorated in white and gold, with a handsome brass-and-iron bed, antique painted washstand, and small oak dresser. A half-bath was recently added to another room, which is comfortably furnished in old oak. Toile wallpaper and a four-poster bed are featured in another bedroom. On the third floor, another of Nancy's decorating fancies is the "Purple Passion" room, a composition of lavender and white that has iris-print wallpaper, a lavender and white lace counterpane, a white wicker and painted washstand, and a king-size brass bed. The Hawkins suite, decorated in pink and green, is romantically private, with its own sitting room.

From her store of over 100 cookbooks, Nan's creative cookery is sure to surprise and please you. A full breakfast is served from April 1 to June 1 and September 15 to November 1. One of her recent menus included strawberry-orange juice, buttermilk fruit ring, cheese puffs filled with ham and topped with Mornay sauce and garnished with a spiced peach, tomato wholewheat bread, and apple cake and coffee. From June 15 to September 15, a lighter repast with a menu comprising the likes of tangerine-lime juice, crêpes filled with apples and raisins and garnished with sour cream, cottage cheese rolls, and peanut-butter bacon muffins would be served.

To work off the happy effects of these breakfasts, the Hawkinses have bicycles that guests may use to explore Cape May. If you're back by 5 p.m. or so, on Saturday night the Hawkinses serve a convivial libation of wine, with cheese and crackers, to while away the time before dinner.

Rates range from $60 to $80 a night at the Barnard-Good House (named for a great-grandparent on either side of the family), which is open from April 1 through November. Beach tags are included in the rate, as is free parking on the grounds.

Albert G. Stevens Inn, 127 Myrtle Ave., Cape May, NJ 08204 (tel. 609/884-4717)

Alice and Paul Linden run the Albert G. Stevens Inn, which is a few blocks from the center of town overlooking the triangular green Wilbraham Park. As you come from town on West Perry Street, look for Myrtle Avenue to your right. The house, which dates from 1900, was commissioned by a local physician as a wedding gift to his bride.

As you approach the inn, you'll see a wrap-around veranda. Though the main entrance is in the front, the veranda is also accessible from the two dining rooms on the side, and you can usually find guests enjoying a second cup of coffee there in the late morning.

A spectacular floating staircase rises from the entrance hall all the way up to the tower room. To the left of the staircase is the double parlor, which preserves the antique flavor of the house. One room has the original mother-of-pearl inlay parlor suite that Dr. Stephens gave his wife. The other parlor has an oak mantel over the gas fireplace that's always lit on cool spring and autumn days.

Breakfast is served in the double dining room at 9 a.m. It's a homemade meal, with fresh, natural ingredients, starting with fruit of the season or juice, then a main dish of quiche, pancakes, waffles, or eggs, and coffee cake, plus tea or coffee.

All six guest rooms have double beds and private bath. On the ground floor is a small apartment with private bath that could comfortably accommodate two couples. All the rooms are individually decorated; antique furniture, beautifully patterned imported wallpapers coordinated with pretty spreads (many 1930s-vintage chenille), a country cottage set, brass and iron beds are some of the features of the decor.

Rooms cost from $65 to $80 per night, depending on size, floor, and time of year. Breakfast, beach passes, and parking are included.

The Gingerbread House, 28 Gurney St., Cape May, NJ 08204 (tel. 609/884-0211)

The Gingerbread House is one of the eight original Stockton Row cottages designed by Stephen Button and built in 1869 as summer rentals for wealthy families who traveled with their servants to summer in Cape May.

There are six guest rooms, three with private bath. The master bedroom has two double beds, a spacious porch, and a private bath. Country Victorian-style wicker and wood, with floral wall-papers, green plants, and ceiling fans characterize the rooms' understated charm.

The handiwork of Fred and Joan Echevarría, the couple who own and operate the inn, lends a unique personal style to the decor. Fred's photographs and woodcarving, Joan's needlework and shell collection, plus original watercolors, plants, and fresh flowers from the garden are all part of the return to simple pleasures that a stay in Cape May offers.

The inn is open year round and provides a continental breakfast made by Joan. Fresh juice or fruit, homemade bread or cake, and coffee or tea are served in the parlor, where there is a lovely fireplace and a Victorian sofa and side chairs. In the summer it's pleasant to eat al fresco on the front porch.

In-season rates are $58 to $85 a night; the off-season rates are about 25% less. Well-behaved children over 7 years old are welcome.

Duke of Windsor, 817 Washington St., Cape May, NJ 08204 (tel. 609/884-1355)

Late Victorian houses, built at the turn of the century, no longer were profusely decorated with gingerbread and Gothic details. Although the houses were just as large or even larger, with spacious parlors and dining rooms, the façade was simpler in concept. A three-story bay capped by a peaked tower and a simple columned porch, like the Duke of Windsor's, is characteristic of the period.

Located about midway between the Washington Street mall and the Physick estate, and just four blocks from the ocean, the Duke of Windsor is a large, rambling old house. The interior is grander than the outside—it's got a wealth of architectural detailing that owners Fran and Bruce Prichard have brought to light in their careful restoration. Wood paneling, stained-glass landing lights, plaster ceiling medallions, a spectacular open staircase, and tile fireplaces have been carefully cleaned or scraped down to their original beauty and are shown to good advantage in the comfortable period setting.

Each of the nine guest rooms has its own personality and is decorated with furniture and accessories that evoke the Victorian era. My favorite was the third-floor tower room, although it is among the smallest. It's five sided, with lace-curtain-hung windows on each side, a pretty matching comforter and bed linen, and a low pointed entrance that you have to duck down under to avoid banging your head. It's very private, light, and airy.

The price of the room also includes a breakfast (made by Bruce) of fruit, cereal, eggs, bacon, fruit or nut bread, and coffee or tea. In summer it's lighter fare, without the eggs and bacon. Afternoon tea is served in the parlor or on the porch, depending on the season.

The Duke of Windsor is open from April through December, and for the February holiday weekends. Before too long Fran and Bruce hope to keep the inn open year round. Their rooms cost $45 to $80 a night, depending on the size of room and bath facilities. Parking is provided for, and there are house bikes that guests may borrow. Beach tags are provided.

Alexander's Inn, 653 Washington St., Cape May, NJ 08204 (tel. 609/884-2555)

Alexander's is a very elegant inn, with a fine restaurant (see Chapter XI) and four guest rooms. Each of the rooms is furnished with Victorian antiques in a distinctive color scheme of bronze, silver, rose, and green. The rose and bronze rooms have their own sinks and share a bath; the other two rooms have private baths. The rooms cost from $70 to $85 per night. Guests are treated to breakfast of juice or fruit, croissants, and coffee in their rooms. Afternoon tea is served in the parlor. Beach passes are a convenient extra. Alexander's is open from February to December 15.

Humphrey Hughes House, 29 Ocean St., Cape May, NJ 08204 (tel. 609/884-4428)

The buff-colored brick foundation, wrap-around veranda, and brown shingled upper stories of this turn-of-the-century home are the hallmarks of the late Victorian era, although the house bears the name of one of Cape May's earliest families. Capt. Humphrey Hughes settled in Cape May in 1692, and his son Humphrey Hughes II purchased the ground on which the house now stands. The first structure on the property was moved to another location, and the present building was erected in 1903 for Henry Justi, a wealthy Philadelphian.

The house's public rooms on the first floor are magnificently paneled and carved with American chestnut burnished to a warm golden color. Oriental rugs, plants, gilt frames, and carved Victorian sofas and chairs decorate the rooms in a grand manner. In the dining room, three massive pieces that originally belonged to the house seem in proportion to the room's vast size. The glass-enclosed veranda next to the dining room is a pleasant place to read, relax, and play backgammon on a breezy evening.

Up the beautiful chestnut wood staircase, the second and third floors have ten guest rooms, all extraordinarily spacious, and many-windowed for summer comfort. Mirrored wardrobes, carved headboards, oak and walnut dressers and washstands, lace or organdy curtains, floral wallpapers, and Victorian-style lamps are used in the rooms to create an ambience faithful to the late Victorian era. Three of the rooms have private baths; the others share three baths outfitted with period decor (but updated plumbing).

A buffet-style continental breakfast is on the sideboard from 9 to 10:30 a.m. daily. Juice, home-baked rolls or sweet breads, coffee or tea, plus an afternoon tea and light tidbits are included in the rates. House tours are given on Friday, Saturday, and Sunday at 4 p.m., followed by tea and snacks. The tour is free to house guests; a $2 donation is requested of others.

The Humphrey Hughes House is open from May to October, and rates range from $50 to $90 a night. Credit cards are accepted.

The Manor House, 612 Hughes St., Cape May, NJ 08204 (tel. 609/884-4710)

Without stepping outside Mary and Tom Snyder's recently restored guesthouse you'll find many wonderful things to see, not least of which is their player piano. Their decor is an eclectic mix of country Victorian, with an especially inviting sitting room where guests can read or just relax and stare into the fire on a cool evening.

The inn seems perfect in every detail. Each of the ten guest rooms has one of the quilts that Mary collects. The room's color schemes generally follow the quilt's. Some beds are brass, while others have carved-oak headboards. Oriental rugs, marble-topped dressers, fringed lampshades, and unusually carved or painted wardrobes are combined in an ambience of country comfort and Victorian detail. The bedrooms are exceptionally cheerful and inviting, clean, and comfortably furnished.

Mornings begin with a full breakfast that alternates among a variety of juices, homemade breads, cheese, cereals, eggs, meat, fish, coffee, and tea. Breakfast and afternoon tea can be enjoyed in the dining room or on the wide shaded veranda, where I recommend you sit, to take in the beauty of Hughes Street, one of the prettiest in town. Smoking is permitted only on the veranda.

The rates at the Manor House range from $70 to $95 a night and include beach tags and a parking permit with a refundable deposit. Winter rates are $58 and up.

Hanson House, 111 Ocean St., Cape May, NJ 08204 (tel. 609/884-8791)

The sprawling Dutch Colonial Hanson House is big, comfortable, and unpretentious. It's exceptionally well located, a few steps from the Washington Street mall and a block and a half from the beach.

Vera and Alfred Hanson were longtime Cape May vacationers, as were their families before them. When they were thinking about retirement, it seemed quite natural to return to Cape May and run a guesthouse, which they have been doing with ease and charm since the early 1970s.

The living room is furnished with a happy combination of antiques, comfortable chairs, and a couch of more recent vintage. Some wonderful family portraits have an interesting story behind them (ask Vera to tell you about them). Souvenirs, all sorts of memorabilia, and knickknacks are displayed in old-fashioned glass cabinets. It's like being in a fascinating antique store to view the variety of objects the Hansons have inherited or acquired and are loath to part with.

Upstairs are the four very comfortably appointed guest rooms, two with private bath. The carpeting is specially luxurious: Oriental rugs over wall-to-wall carpets. In the summer, a dining room is converted into a fifth bedroom, with a private bath and entrance.

The breakfast menu has fresh orange juice or grapefruit (in season); a main dish such as bacon and eggs, pancakes, or waffles with maple syrup; sweet buns or raisin toast; and coffee or tea. Breakfast on the porch is a refreshing way to start the day, and if you return in the late afternoon, there's light refreshment to enjoy while you plan your evening activities.

You'll pay $55 to $85 for a room at the Hansons', depending on the season and the bath facilities. Hanson House is open year round.

The Manse, 510 Hughes St., Cape May, NJ 08204 (tel. 609/884-0116)

It's been called the Manse since 1908, when it was built as the church house for the Cape Island Presbyterian congregation. When Dorothy and Nate Marcus bought it and opened their guesthouse, it seemed appropriate to keep the name and the house's historic identity.

It's a very comfortable and homey guesthouse, furnished with a combination of family heirlooms, antiques, Oriental carpets, and traditionally styled contemporary furniture. Polished wood floors and woodwork are especially handsome in the dining room, where there's a sparkling crystal chandelier.

The guest rooms have the warmth of a family home, with flowered wallpaper, comforters, and flower prints on the walls. Look for the fleur-de-lis that is worked into the elaborate stained-glass windows at the stair landings.

An antique player piano provides some musical entertainment for the guests. A full breakfast is served in the dining room in winter, on the veranda in summer.

The guest rooms are $55 to $60 on the third floor, $65 to $75 on the second floor. There's free parking on the property, and complimentary beach passes.

The Delsea, 621 Columbia Ave., Cape May, NJ 08204 (tel. 609/884-8540)

A well-run, friendly guesthouse, the Delsea has some of the finest gingerbread ornamentation in town. It adorns the two verandas, the roof line, and the balustrade of the front steps. Not wanting to hide any of its glory, the owners, Rosemary Stumpo and Suzanne Littell, put in roll-up blinds instead of awnings to shade the verandas. If you're lucky enough to stay in one of the second-floor front rooms, you'll have private access to the second-floor veranda.

The house is painted Delsea gold, with blue shutters, and the gingerbread is white—it makes a very pretty picture with the nicely tended flower garden and apron of green lawn in front of the house. Floral wallpaper color coordinated with the rug, white woodwork, and ball fringe curtains are standard throughout. The rooms are furnished with a mixture of antiques and contemporary pieces for an informal country Victorian air, accented with marble-topped tables and nostalgia pieces.

A continental breakfast is served in the front parlor, or on the veranda. Juice, coffee, and something delicious from a local bakery are on hand for a leisurely start to the day. The daily rates charged are from $45 to $70, depending on size of room and bath facilities. The Delsea is open from May through October. Youngsters are welcome.

Victorian Guesthouses—Accommodations Only

Seventh Sister Guesthouse, 10 Jackson St., Cape May, NJ 08204 (tel. 609/884-2280)

That the front of the Seventh Sister Guesthouse faces the ocean doesn't sound unusual, until you learn that the ocean is behind its Jackson Street address. When Stephen Button designed the row of three-story frame cottages to be erected near the widest bathing beaches in town, he very sensibly put the front porches where they would be most useful, along a little private lane, Atlantic Terrace, facing the ocean. Strictly speaking, the Jackson Street entrance is the back door.

You'll find an interior of brilliant light, white wicker, green plants, and the exciting colors of contemporary paintings by Jo-Anne Echevarría Myers. Jo-Anne and Bob Myers own and operate the inn year round, and have furnished it with some 50 wicker pieces from their collection. In the guest sitting room you can see the original coal grate fireplace. Don't miss Jo-Anne's funny and insightful books, especially the one containing her dollar-bill mail art project. A spectacular circular staircase joins the three floors.

The six guest rooms are bright and sunny. They're decorated with plants, antique wicker, and Jo-Anne's paintings, and most have ocean views. Room rates vary with the season: in March, $44; in April, $48; in May, $50; in June, $52; in September, $50; in October, $48. In July and August rooms are $55 a night.

Although there's no cooking on the premises, you're 30 seconds away from the Mad Batter restaurant and a short walk from the mall and all major restaurants.

Holly House, 20 Jackson St., Cape May, NJ 08204 (tel. 609/884-7365)

Appropriately painted in light green, dark green, and bright red, Holly House is one of the seven Victorian cottages famous as Cape May's Seven Sisters. Facing away from Jackson Street, the Renaissance Revival cottage is owned by Corinne and Bruce Minnix. It was during Bruce's tenure as mayor of Cape May that the city acquired landmark status, purchased the Physick Estate (the mansion was to be demolished), and passed the zoning regulations to preserve the character (and buildings) of Cape May.

If you sit on Holly House's porch swing, you have a view of the ocean and the Acroteria, a little group of cabaña-like buildings decorated with pointed ornaments (acroteria) at the peaks of their roofs. In the summer, shops occupy the Acroteria.

The Minnixes share their comfortable living room with guests. On one side of the room is the fireplace with its original coal grate, flanked by two comfortable chairs. A pretty green velvet Victorian couch faces the fireplace from across the room. Guests are invited to use the piano.

Holly House has six light and airy guest rooms, informally decorated in a lighthearted Victorian country style. One of the rooms has two iron beds, painted blue, with white spreads and a washstand. When the cottages were built, they were rented as furnished units, much as today's motels or summer rentals. The Minnixes have several journeyman's chairs that were among the original cottage furnishings. There are two baths, shared by the six bedrooms, that are nicely outfitted with gleaming tile. Be sure to see the house's architectural highlight, the graceful curving staircase that winds up all three stories.

There is no cooking, but restaurants from inexpensive to gourmet are steps away. Children over 3 are welcome. The rooms cost $50 a night in summer. Off-season rates are $40 per night. On holiday weekends, add $5 per night.

Poor Richard's Inn, 17 Jackson St., Cape May, NJ 08204 (tel. 609/884-3536)

Harriett and Richard Samuelson's guesthouse strikes a good balance between present-day informality and Victorian charm. The distinctive exterior of their Second Empire house has a five-color paint scheme chosen to accentuate the arched gingerbread, brackets, cornices, friezes, and other wonderful architectural ornaments that were stylish in 1882 when the house was built. Inside the inn, that same attention to detail is pointed more toward country-style comfort than to recreating the past. The effect is totally charming, due to the Samuelsons' artistic talents and their collections of patchwork quilts, baskets, oak and pine furniture, blanket chests, and hooked rugs. That is not to say that they don't have elements of more traditional Victorian decor—in some of the rooms you'll see marble-topped bureaus, ornate beds, floral wallpaper, Lincoln rockers, and the like. You'll also see examples of the Samuelsons' own work hanging throughout the house (they're expatriate artists from New York and have been in Cape May since 1977).

All the rooms have fans and are well ventilated; most have windows on three sides. There are two porches where guests can sit and look out at busy Jackson Street (the Mad Batter is next door) and the ocean. In the morning the Samuelsons provide a big 30-cup coffee urn for guests to help themselves; they can take the coffee back to their rooms or sit out on the porch.

For the five rooms that share two baths, in-season rates are $39 to $52 a night. The one room with private bath is $67 nightly. There are two apartments available also, a one-bedroom and a two-bedroom; each has a well-equipped kitchen and private bath. Off-season rates and cost of the apartments are given on request. Children are expected to be well behaved. The inn does not have parking facilities.

Windward House, 24 Jackson St., Cape May, NJ 08204 (tel. 609/884-3368)

This guesthouse is a typical shingle-style cottage with curved bay windows and upper and lower porches, a late Victorian design that you'll find in other coastal resorts like East Hampton and Newport. Owned by Owen and Sandy Miller, the inn retains much of its lovely original stained- and beveled-glass panes and polished oak panels and doors.

The guest rooms are furnished with family heirlooms and antiques, except for the efficiency apartment which has more of a contemporary look. The apartment has a convertible living room/bedroom, a galley kitchen, bath with shower, cable TV, ceiling fan, and a sliding glass door that opens to a small deck and private entrance. Of the seven guest rooms, two have air conditioning; the others, ceiling fans. The Cottage Room is an especially appealing accommodation. There is a comfortable window seat at the curved bay windows overlooking Jackson Street, two double brass beds, and French doors that open to a porch. All the rooms have refrigerators.

A double room with private bath is $60 to $75; with a shared bath it's $60. Off-season rates are discounted 5% to 10%. Beach passes are an added convenience. The Windward provides private parking and complimentary breakfast except in July and August when only coffee is served.

The Carol Villa Hotel, 19 Jackson St., Cape May, NJ 08204 (tel. 609/884-5970)

The Carol Villa, right in the heart of Cape May, offers simple and handy accommodations for anyone on a budget. The country Victorian furnishings are not elaborate, but the large, airy rooms are pleasant, some with ocean views, and the halls are well maintained.

It's owned by Vickie Seitchik and Harry Kulkowitz, who also

operate the wonderful Mad Batter restaurant on the first floor. They offer 30 immaculately kept rooms; four have private baths, and all the rooms have sinks. There are a couple of single rooms, some triples, and the majority doubles. The rooms start at $17 for a single, and the price ranges up to $50 for the triple with private bath. I recommend that you use the money you save staying here at the Mad Batter for one of their great brunches.

Woodleigh House, 808 Washington St., Cape May, NJ 08204 (tel. 609/884-7123)

Run by the same family for over 20 years, the Woodleigh House has four guest rooms. The white clapboard house was built in 1866, and a recent addition has enlarged it considerably. The addition is for family use only, and the guests will continue to stay in the main section.

Patricia Wood Jackson and her brother, Edwin Wood, along with his wife Jan, are continuing the tradition of "guest housing" launched by their mother, Mabel Wood.

All the guest rooms have baths. Rates range from $35 to $70 per night, with the seventh night free for a week's stay. Coffee and juice are served in the dining room between 7:30 and 10:30 a.m. Guests are invited to help themselves. Tea drinkers and decaf-fers are accommodated if they make their wishes known!

Belmont Guesthouse, 712 Columbia Ave., Cape May, NJ (tel. 609/884-7507)

Right on Columbia Avenue, in the heart of the historic district, the Belmont is an unpretentious but comfortable guesthouse. Built as a private summer home in 1879, the house has a spacious porch for relaxing. The friendly owners, Mr. and Mrs. Magee, offer neat, airy rooms at $35 a night. The furnishings are simple, but the rooms are scrupulously clean. One room, on the first floor, has a private bath and rents for $40 a night; all the other rooms share baths. The Belmont is open May 1 through October.

Self-Sufficient Apartments

Although many of the motels have efficiency units or apartments that are preferred by those who like the privacy of home living, the **Dormer House International**, 800 Columbia Ave., Cape May, NJ 08204 (tel. 609/884-7446), offers one- and two-bedroom apartments right in the historic district.

The Dormer House was built in the 1890s for a Philadelphia

marble dealer, John Jacoby, and it retains much of its original marble and furniture. The house is a rambling, white clapboard structure, set on a corner lot with a big backyard where guests can picnic and use the family barbecue. You enter the house via the enclosed side porch, a long, plant- and white-wicker-lined solarium that's a delightful place to relax and read. The living room/lounge has an enormous fireplace and Colonial style settle.

The eight private apartments are cheerfully decorated and maintained in superb condition. The ones I saw were uniformly sunny, light, and airy. The furnishings blend period pieces with contemporary ones in a comfortable, homey way. Marble fireplaces, antique coverlets, wicker and bamboo couches and side chairs, plants, and fresh flowers decorate the rooms. The kitchens are modern and fully equipped with ranges, refrigerators, Formica counters, dishes, and appliances—toaster-ovens or toasters. Children of all ages are welcome, and there are cots and cribs available for guests' use. Each apartment has a private bath. A TV cable is provided in each apartment, but you have to bring your own TV set. The owners, Bill and Peg Madden, delight in showing off their house and sharing it with visitors.

In season, rates are $465 weekly for the apartments that sleep four, $560 for those that sleep six. Rentals in season are only by the week; out of season the apartments are available on a daily basis also. In December, January, February, and March, daily rates are $33 (for up to four) and $41 (for up to six); in late spring and early fall, rates rise to $58 and $70 respectively. These rates do not include linens (bath towels, sheets, pillowcases), which can be provided at an extra charge.

The Victorian Hotels

The **Colonial Hotel and Motor Lodge,** Beach Drive at Ocean Street, Cape May, NJ 08204 (tel. 609/884-3483), offers the charm of old Cape May in the full-service Victorian hotel and the conveniences of modern comfort in the motor lodge.

The twin towers of the Colonial Hotel, its magnificent oceanfront veranda, and the lawn have been on this site since 1894. The present owners, the Fite family, purchased the old hotel in 1928. Considered very modern in its time, the Colonial had such renowned guests as John Philip Sousa, who came to Cape May to lead his band in concerts on one of the old piers. Among the social events that took place at the hotel was the 1915 debut of Baltimore belle Wallis Warfield, who became the Duchess of Windsor, when the king of England renounced his throne to marry her, a divorced commoner. The Colonial had the first elevator in town. Another of its innovations linked the rooms to the front desk with electric bells.

Guests today have a choice of lodgings. If you elect to stay at the old hotel, between June 15 and September 4 a complete breakfast and full-course dinner are included in the room price. With private bath, a room for two is $88 a night, Modified American Plan; two rooms with a bath are $155 a night. The hotel rooms are quiet and comfortable, furnished with colonial-style maple, white organdy curtains, and white spreads. The rooms are of varying sizes and shapes, due to the hotel's Victorian configurations, and many have ocean views. Telephones and TV are in the lobby's lounge area.

In the motor lodge, rooms with two double beds cost $84 a night. Furnished in tasteful traditional-style furniture, the rooms have private balconies overlooking the pool and the ocean, sitting areas, color TV, telephone, and refrigerator. Motel guests may, if they wish, take breakfast and dinner in the Colonial's dining room for $16 a day per person.

There is a round children's pool adjoining the kidney-shaped pool and the sundeck. Lounge chairs and umbrellaed tables are comfortable poolside appurtenances. Parking is free for guests at either accommodation.

In the Colonial dining room (in the Victorian hotel), you'll sit on cane-bottom ladderback chairs at intimate tables for four, set with fine china and silver. The breakfasts are standard fare: juice, eggs and breakfast meats, rolls and coffee. Dinners begin with an appetizer of juice or homemade soup, and a tossed green salad. There is always a choice of entrees—perhaps roast beef, fried shrimp, broiled weakfish, and breast of capon—garnished with vegetable of the day and potato. Homemade desserts, pies or cakes, and ice cream or fruit, complete the menu.

The motor lodge is open from mid-April to the beginning of November; the Colonial Hotel has a shorter season, from Memorial Day through Labor Day.

The **Chalfonte,** 301 Howard St., Cape May, NJ 08204 (tel. 609/884-8409), is Cape May's oldest hotel. It has been open every summer since it was built in 1876 by the legendary Col. Henry Sawyer. Sawyer was taken prisoner by the Confederate Army in the Civil War and was sentenced to death. His mother, who had met President Lincoln when he vacationed in Cape May, appealed to the president to save her son's life. At this time the son of Robert E. Lee was a prisoner of the Union forces, so Lincoln effected an exchange of prisoners, and Sawyer came home to Cape May.

Ornately trimmed with intricately carved gingerbread between the arches and columns of its gracious two-story double veranda, the Chalfonte is crowned by a typically Italianate villa-style gabled cupola. On its Sewell Street façade, an elegant row of two-story-high thin columns support the portico outside the hotel dining room. Green and white striped awnings and green shutters enliven the white clapboard hotel's stately repose. Like many other Cape May houses of this period, the Chalfonte has a traditional southern elegance, and the building would not look out of place along the Gulf Coast.

The hotel's present owners, Judy Bartella and Anne LeDuc, acquired the property from Mrs. Calvin Satterfield, whose family bought the hotel from the Sawyer family in 1910. The new owners are dedicated to restoring and preserving the fine old hotel. They invite volunteers to join the restoration work on weekends in April, May, and early June. For a fee of $15 for the weekend, workers get two nights' lodging at the Chalfonte, plus the famous southern-style breakfasts and dinners that are prepared by the chef who has been cooking for the Chalfonte for over 40 years—she is the fourth generation of her family working at the hotel, and I understand that members of the fifth generation are waiting in the wings. Both the breakfasts and dinners feature regional specialties—fried fish, spoonbread, country-fried ham and eggs at breakfast; fresh vegetables, southern fried chicken, home-baked rolls, cakes, and pies at dinner. The dining room is also open to the public, and traditional weekly menus have a devoted following who come for their special favorites.

In the long dining room the ceiling is ornamented with plaster medallions painted a soft rose. Guests are seated communally at large tables covered with white tablecloths and set with china and silver. Also on the main floor are a writing room, a reading room, and the King Edward Room Bar. Guests check in at a huge oak roll-top desk.

The Chalfonte's 103 rooms are furnished very simply. Today it seems incongruous for a resort to have such a showy façade and spartanly furnished guest rooms. For the Victorian vacationer, however, the bedrooms were just for sleeping; the society of the other guests, conversation with new and old friends, was an important element of the vacation. The communal rooms—the lounges, the library, even the spacious verandas filled with rocking chairs—were where they spent most of their time. It was most unlike the modern taste for motel rooms that are completely fitted with TVs and private sitting areas, and the guests do not mingle at all.

Many guest rooms have iron beds and all have at least one antique piece often a marble-topped dresser or bureau. Four of the rooms have private bath, complete with old iron tubs. The shared baths are all modernized; some have showers, others tubs. Breakfast and dinner are included in the Modified American Plan rates. Single rooms range from $43 a night, double rooms from $59 nightly. The most expensive rooms, with two double beds, are $96 to $108 per night. Room sizes and accommodations vary, and cots can be put in at your request.

You may be able to take advantage of the special package rates. Mid-June to mid-July and most of September there is a 25% discount on weekdays. On weekends in June, if you pay for two nights the third night is free. Over the Fourth of July holiday, if you stay five to ten days, you'll get a 25% discount. There is also a 10% discount for groups of 15 or more.

The Chalfonte is open for guests on Memorial Day weekend, and then from mid-June through October (including the Victorian Week festivities), and for the work weekends in April, May, and early June.

Extensive renovations at the **Congress Hall,** Beach Drive at Congress Street, Cape May, NJ 08204 (tel. 609/884-8421), are aimed at restoring the hotel to its place as one of the most prestigious in town. In 1968 the hotel became part of the Rev. Carl McIntire's Beacon Conferences facility, and it has hosted many of its Bible conference activities, concerts, and dramatic performances, along with welcoming other summer vacationers.

Imposing 2½-story white columns form an elongated L-shaped portico that graces the pale-yellow facade of the hotel. Rooms facing the front have sweeping views of the extensive lawn, pool, and ocean. When the hotel was built in 1879, the owner deliberately had it set back into a corner of the property so that his daughter, who lived on Congress Place, could keep her ocean view.

Floor-to-ceiling windows, covered with lace curtains and adorned with pastel-colored swags of floral drapery, and cool marble floors promise a majestic conclusion to the lobby restoration. A curved staircase sweeps up to the guest room floors. In the renovated rooms modern comfort and Victorian charm combine to form a tasteful, airy atmosphere. Eastlake bureaus, some stripped to a lovely wood tone, others still painted in pastels, brass or iron beds, Victorian-style sofas and side chairs highlight the decor. All rooms have private bath. Smoking is not permitted, either in the bedrooms or the public spaces.

During July and August a single room, costs about $48, a double is $64. In May rates are $24 and $39 respectively. All rates include free parking and a full breakfast in the hotel dining room. The Congress is open seasonally.

On the Congress Place side of the hotel, facing onto Perry Street, the **Bayberry Inn** (tel. 884-8406) serves brunch and dinner, 11 a.m. to 2 p.m. and 5 to 9:30 p.m.

From Easter to New Year's the restaurant offers international cuisine on its summer porch or inside next to its antique fireplace. Brunches (or lunches, if you like) might consist of waffles, a salad, eggs, crêpes, or a variety of sandwiches (such as a grilled turkey and cheese). Prices range from $3.75 to about $6.50. The dinner menu is an eclectic selection of dishes from around the world. Spicy chicken wings in a Thai honey sauce ($3) or steamed clams and smoked chorizo in white wine sauce ($4) are among the appetizers. For entrees lamb brochette with a mustard peppercorn crust ($12) or woven salmon and flounder with saffron beurre blanc ($14) offer imaginative possibilities. Both the brunch and dinner menus change seasonally.

The **Christian Admiral,** Beach Drive and Pittsburgh Avenue, Cape May, NJ 08204 (tel. 609/884-8471), is under the same auspices as the Congress Hall. This monumental seven-story brick building looks more like a governor's palace or public institution than an oceanfront hotel. It was built in 1906 to 1908 and served as the Cape May Hotel. Severely battered in the great storm of 1962, it was vacant for a number of years before the Reverend McIntire's group took it over.

White limestone steps lead up to the first-floor terrace, where rows of rockers enable guests to survey the pounding ocean waves at the sea wall or, closer at hand, the hotel's pool. The hotel lobby is, in a word, magnificent. Quadruple sets of tan marble columns, a high ceiling pierced by a majestic stained-glass dome, a grand piano and huge marble fireplaces flanking the entrance doors emphasize the heroic scale of the room.

The hotel has over 300 rooms, and is often chosen as a meeting place for church or other private groups. Its auditorium can seat 1000 people, and is the only place in Cape May large enough to hold the Coast Guard band's summer concerts.

Individuals are accommodated as well as groups on a daily or weekly basis. Since this is a nonprofit ownership, guests must pay a $2 fee to join and promise not to use alcohol or smoke on the premises. Three meals a day (two on Sunday) are included in the daily rates of $60 for a room with private bath, $49 for a room with shared bath. The hotel is open from Mother's Day to the end of October.

Cape May Motels

ON THE OCEANFRONT: Motels on the beach are naturally more expensive. Prices change seasonally, so you can save money by coming before or after the peak season—around July 15 to August 20. You'll always save money by forgoing ocean-view rooms, which are always a few dollars more.

Upper Bracket

The **Marquis de Lafayette,** Beach Drive between Ocean and Decatur Avenues, Cape May, NJ 08204 (tel. toll free 800/257-0432, in New Jersey 800/582-5933, or 609/884-3431), has its own large pool and is right across the street from the beach. Its 74 rooms are nicely decorated, with a bow to the Victorian era—floral wallpaper, brass beds—but all the comforts of a modern motel (TV, private bath, room phone). A full breakfast is included in the price of the rooms, and is served in the Gold Whale restaurant on the first level. All the rooms face the ocean and have private balconies. The Marquis de Lafayette is a Best Western hotel and has a number of different package plans and special theme weekends, such as their Birdwatchers Weekend, with films and a field trip, or a riding weekend that includes horseback riding along Delaware Bay beaches. Be sure to ask for their special package rates.

The motel's two restaurants offer a choice of atmospheres: the Gold Whale is a café-like room, with an informal setting. Breakfast, lunch, and dinner are served, and there is late-evening entertainment. The Gold Whale features Italian specialties, sea-food entrees, sandwiches, and snacks. The Top of the Marq, on the motel's sixth-floor room overlooking the ocean, has more formal dining and dancing and a unique mural of Cape May.

The motel offers three kinds of accommodations. The Abbey rooms, with one double bed; the Victorian rooms, with two double beds; and the Marquis rooms, which can sleep six in a suite with a bedroom with two double beds, a living room with a convertible sofa, and a kitchen. There is a three- to four-night minimum stay in season, with rates starting at $108 per night for an Abbey room to $140 per night for a Marquis suite. Rates drop substantially, about 30% to 40%, before June 15 and after Labor Day.

First Class

The **Golden Eagle Inn,** Beach and Philadelphia Avenues, Cape May, NJ 08204 (tel. toll free 800/257-8550, in New Jersey 800/582-

5991, or 609/884-5611), overlooks the ocean and is open year round. It features efficiency apartments with one and two rooms as well as regular motel rooms. All units have ocean views. The two-room efficiency has bedroom, living room, dining area, and kitchen. All rooms are comfortably furnished and air-conditioned, and have refrigerators. The motel rooms cost $90 a night from June 15 to September 3, a one-room efficiency is $95, and a two-room efficiency is $118 a night.

The hotel has an indoor whirlpool and heated pool, as well as an outdoor heated pool and a kiddie pool. Ping-Pong and shuffle-board games are near the pool.

Facing the ocean, the **Coachman's Motor Inn & Beach Club,** 205 Beach Dr., Cape May, NJ 08204 (tel. 609/884-8463), is a prime location for lively activities. Tennis courts, a basketball court, shuffleboard, pitch-and-putt golf, and a spacious swimming pool are its outstanding recreation facilities. The Beach Club portion of the motel has been converted to a time-sharing plan with luxurious suites that are available for rental on a weekly basis. All boast a full-size living room (with a queen-size sofa bed), dining area, and a full kitchen. In addition there is a large bedroom, full bath, and closet area. The motel offers the two double-bedded rooms that are available to overnight guests and efficiencies that are rented only by the week during the summer.

From June 20 to Labor Day, motel rooms cost $80 to $90 a night. Efficiencies are $85 to $95 a night, and must be rented by the week. There is an added charge for each person over the two-person rate listed above.

A landmark with locals and tourists, the on-premises Rusty Nail restaurant serves breakfast from 8 a.m. to noon, dinner from 4:30 to 10 p.m. Weather permitting, lunch is available on the outside patio. The Rusty Nail is an informal, roomy place, with windows all around that let you look out on the ocean. Stop in for a drink in the lounge; their frosted mugs hit the spot on a hot summer's day. At night there's dancing in the lounge.

The **Montreal Inn,** Beach at Madison Avenue, Cape May, NJ 08204 (tel. 609/884-7011), is owned and run by the Hirsch family, who are on hand to keep things running smoothly. The motel is directly across from the beach. It has its own heated pool, game area with shuffleboard and mini-golf, restaurant, cocktail lounge, and a package store. Families will find a number of attractive features here—cots and cribs, a kiddie pool, babysitters, a washer and dryer, barbecue facilities, and a refrigerator in every room.

You'll be faced with a choice of eight different kinds of accommodations, ranging from a breezeway motel room (no ocean views) with two double beds, to efficiencies with balconies over-looking the pool and ocean beach, and deluxe efficiencies with two double beds and a sofa bed. The furnishings are clean and comfortable, some rooms are especially attractive with white painted French provincial-style table and chairs, flowered spreads, and tweed carpet. Color TV, off-street parking, and air conditioning are standard throughout the motel's 70 units.

Open from the beginning of March through November, the Montreal has a schedule of rates that range from $23 to $59 for the breezeway motel room to a high of $30 to $94 for the deluxe efficiency unit.

At the **Heritage Motor Inn,** Beach Drive and Stockton Place, Cape May, NJ 08204 (tel. 609/884-7342), you only need to cross the street to enjoy the nightly activities in Convention Hall. The motel's split-rail fence out front, gabled roof, and old-fashioned street lamps foretell the cozy Colonial-style decor of the 21 wood-paneled rooms, attractively furnished with Ethan Allen Early American furnishings accented with green and brown rugs, spreads, and draperies. The rooms all face the ocean; some are efficiency units, and all have refrigerators and color TVs. There's free off-street parking for guests, and it's open from Easter through November. The motel's rates vary seasonally. The highest rates, from mid-July to Labor Day, are $89 for a room, $94 for an efficiency. The least expensive rates, in early spring and late fall, are $37 and $41 respectively.

The **Stockholm,** 1008 Beach Dr., Cape May, NJ 08204 (tel. 609/884-5332), is an atrium-style motel built around a pool and grassy central lawns. The colors of its dark-brown arches and white columns at the entrance are repeated on the motel's fa-çade, which has decorative blue doors to each of the units. Inside, the rooms are pleasant but undistinguished—tweed carpets, or-ange spreads, contemporary furniture in wood tones.

Families should note that there is a children's pool next to the larger pool, and the hotel has a reliable sitter on call. The motel charges $82 for a room with two double beds in the high-season, mid-July through Labor Day, and $88 for an efficiency. Rates vary seasonally to a low of $40 and $42 respectively in early spring and late fall.

The **Stockton Manor,** 805 Beach Dr., and the **Stockton Motor Inn,** 809 Beach Dr., Cape May, NJ 08204 (tel. 609/884-4036), share the facilities of a swimming pool, off-street parking, and outdoor barbecue grill, but they certainly differ in ambience.

The Manor is a Victorian-era mansion (1872) with several fire-places, and it was built as a summer residence. Sitting on a rocker on the spacious veranda, guests can watch the sun setting over the ocean, the beach, and the sea-wall promenade. All the guest rooms on the second and third floors have ocean views. Individually decorated with period furniture, the rooms have the modern convenience of private baths and color TV. The rooms cost $75 to $95 per night. If you're planning a week's stay, inquire about the one-room efficiencies and three- and four-room suites that are available on a weekly basis. The Manor is open from Memorial Day weekend through September.

The two-story red brick Motor Inn, trimmed with white shutters and low shrubs, harmonizes well with the cedar-shingled Manor. The lawns and pool separate the two buildings. The motel has 32 units, decorated in tones of beige and rust. The accommodations range in size from a standard one-double-bedded room to a four-room suite. All units are equipped with refrigerators. In high season three kinds of accommodations are rented on a daily basis: rooms with one double bed, two double beds, and efficiencies. The rates are $85, $90, and $97, respectively. The rates descend seasonally to a low of $35, $39, and $45 in early spring, slightly higher in late fall.

La Mer Motor Inn, Beach Drive and Pittsburgh Avenue, Cape May, NJ 08204 (tel. 609/884-2200), is an attractive family resort. You'll find comfortable contemporary-style furnishings, matching draperies and bedspread in rooms that surround a central courtyard where a gleaming pool is the center of attention. For the kids there are a mini-golf course, playground, and pool slide, and for everyone there are outdoor barbecue grills and bicycle rentals. The accommodations range from a room with one double bed to a large efficiency with two double beds. The rates peak between mid-July and mid-August at $80 to $90 for the motel room, $110 for the large efficiency. Rates descend before and after that period to lows of $38 to $46 in spring, $60 to $71 in fall.

You won't have any trouble finding the **Atlas Motor Inn,** 1035 Beach Dr., Cape May, NJ 08204 (tel. toll free 800/257-8513, in New Jersey 800/642-3766, or 609/884-7000). Just look for the bright-orange panels that ornament the balconies of the six-story motel. Nice rooms feature a bright decor of orange quilted spreads color coordinated with the floral-print draperies; in some of the rooms the draperies and spreads have a matching floral print. In this resort you'll find an Olympic-size pool with a slide for adults and a separate shallow pool for kids, poolside cocktails and lunch service, and saunas. You can dine in the Crystal Room restaurant and enjoy dancing, entertainment, and late-evening refreshments in the cocktail lounge. Highest rates for a room with one double bed and a double Hide-a-Bed (the least expensive accommodation) are $85 in high season. A room with two double beds is $95. In winter the rates drop to $30 and $45. Suites with cooking facilities are available, as well as holiday weekend packages (off-season only).

Moderately Priced Motels

The **Jetty Motel,** 2nd Street and Beach Avenue, Cape May, NJ 08204 (tel. 609/884-4640), is nestled along the beachfront opposite the last fishing jetty of the town shore. It's a great location where you can walk out on the rocks and watch the sun set over the lighthouse on Cape May Point across a quiet inlet. The two-story motel, painted a sparkling white with nautical marine-blue trim, has motel rooms and efficiencies decorated in golden brown. The furniture is styled with a contemporary flair in wood tones and white Formica tops. You can cool off in the pool and watch the kids splash in their own spot or play shuffleboard. Fishing is right across the street. You can dine on favorite family fare at the popular Jetty Restaurant. Sandwiches are a reasonable $1.30 to $3.25 (for a many-layered hoagie); dinner entrees run from $7.50 to $12.95 (for a large plate of fresh fish and seafood). The Jetty Motel charges $79 to $83 for a motel room with one double bed and $84 to $86 for efficiencies (sleep four) in the high season; rates drop to $43 to $52 in late spring and early fall. The management does not accept credit cards; cash or travelers checks are preferred.

One of the motels I found most appealing is the **Cape Motor Inn,** Beach Drive and Grant Street, Cape May, NJ 08204 (tel. 609/884-4256). The beautifully landscaped entrance is planted with low junipers and pebbled areas. The three-story motel seems to rise harmoniously on its beachfront location with its clapboard façade painted a misty gray. The simplified gingerbread touches along the balconies pay homage to the town's Victorian past. Thoroughly modern rooms are decorated in pale beiges, light blue, and handsome Scandinavian-modern pieces. All of the motel rooms have ocean views, though some of the efficiencies do not. You'll find such amenities as a pool, Ping-Pong, and a barbecue area for guests' use. The Ocean View, a casual family-style restaurant, is right across the street. Double rates are $80 to $125 in summer. The rates vary seasonally to a low of $35 to $66 from October 28 to May 3.

Another very pretty place to stay is the **Sea Crest Inn,** Beach

Drive and Broadway, Cape May, NJ 08204 (tel. 609/884-4561). Beautifully landscaped gardens surround the property and a charming poolside gazebo graces the front lawn. The extra-spacious rooms are decorated in sunny yellow, with bamboo-look painted furniture adding to the tropical ambience. Window-walls with balconies overlook the pool and the ocean. Some efficiencies have fully equipped kitchens and dining areas. Wherever you stay, you'll enjoy such amenities as off-street parking, cable color TV, shuffleboard, and a barbecue and picnic area. Two people pay $76 from mid-July to Labor Day, $81 for a room with full kitchen facilities. Rates drop considerably in winter and the rooms cost $43 a night.

The **Surf Motel & Apartments,** 200 Beach Dr., Cape May, NJ 08204 (tel. 609/884-4132), is a modest-size tranquil motel tucked away on pretty grounds across the street from the beach. Old-fashioned flowerbeds line your path to the heated pool, which is sectioned off at one end for youngsters. You'll retire to good-sized carpeted rooms furnished with light, contemporary wood pieces. Both motel rooms and efficiencies have cable color TV, air conditioning, and ceramic tile baths. Director's chairs on the balconies and redwood lounge chairs are inviting spots to relax and read. In summer, charges are $75 to $77 from mid-July to Labor Day for a motel room, $80 to $82 for a room with kitchen-ette. Winter rates are $36 and $39 respectively.

Sage-green wrought-iron railings add a trim touch to the **Colton Court,** 105 Beach Dr., Cape May, NJ 08240 (tel. 609/884-5384), a two-story red brick motel with spacious rooms over-looking the kidney-shaped pool and sun patio. You'll find the refrigerators furnished in all the rooms a handy extra for snacks or lunch fixings. A room for two with two double beds is $75 from July 4 to Labor Day. An efficiency with kitchen facilities is $85 in the same time period. In slow months rates drop to $40 for a double, $45. Each additional person is $7 per night, year round.

IN TOWN: The **Victorian Motel,** Perry Street and Congress Place, Cape May, NJ 08204 (tel. 609/884-7044), is Victorian in name only, but it's an attractive place nonetheless. A conventional three-story red-brick-with-white-trim motel, the rooms all open onto private balconies that overlook the patio and pool. Its location, right at the head of the picturesque Washington Street mall, means that it's steps away from restaurants and shops. The beach is close by (only a block away), and there's ample off-street parking.

You can take your choice of accommodations—a motel room with two double beds that sleeps two or four, a one-room efficiency that sleeps four to six, or a two-room efficiency that has a private bedroom and also sleeps four to six. Fully equipped kitchens are in all efficiencies. All 38 units of the motel feature cable color TV, room phones, and individually controlled heat and air conditioning. The rooms are comfortable and well furnished in contemporary color schemes. There is elevator service.

The rates are moderate, especially if you're traveling with a party of four. In season, from June 25 to September 16, the rooms are $70, one-room efficiencies are $80, and two-room efficiencies run $95. Between May 21 and June 24, and September 17 to May 20, rates are $42, $52, and $60 respectively. The rest of the year prices drop to $32, $39, and $44.

Under the same ownership, the **Camelot Motel,** at Howard and Stockton Streets, Cape May, NJ 08204 (tel. 609/884-1500), is slightly more expensive, on a quiet street near the ocean, which is in view from the motel's rooms. Painted a sunny yellow with green trim, the motel offers 38 units, all with balconies overlooking the pool, the children's pool, and a sundeck. The interior of the rooms and apartments effectively uses contemporary furnishings—beige tweed couches, parsons tables, leather-upholstered armchairs—to create a clean, uncluttered look. The motel offers a choice of accommodations—one- or two-bedroom apartments, a two-room or two-bedroom efficiency suite, plus the regular motel rooms. All the units have cable color TV and air conditioning. In season, motel rooms are $68 a night; the efficiencies and apartments range from $95 to $135. Off-season, rates are $34 for the rooms, and $44 to $75 for the accommodations with kitchens. The off-street parking facilities are limited to one car per motel unit. The motel is open year round.

BUDGET BESTS: The **Madison Motel,** 601 Madison Ave., Cape May, NJ 08204 (tel. 609/884-4838), has simply furnished rooms, but for the money it's hard to beat this one-story 12-room motel, decorated inside in hues of orange and brown. There's a fenced-in swimming pool, and gas lamps in the front garden add a nice touch. The Madison's highest rate for a room with two double beds is $73 during August. The rate drops to $68 the last two weeks of July, and continues downward to a wintertime low of $35.

Back to back with the Madison, the **Blue Amber Motel,** at Madison and Virginia Avenues (across from the water tower), Cape May, NJ 08204 (tel. 609/884-8266), is another money-saver.

The rooms are basic but serviceable. There's a regular family clientele that returns year after year. No doubt the big lawn, pool, picnic tables, and barbecue (not to mention the prices) have a lot to do with that. In peak season rates are $74 a night (July 22 to August 20); they drop about $5 to $7 every two-week period to opening day on May 1 and the late-fall closing.

Chapter XI

DINING IN CAPE MAY

RESTAURANTS IN CAPE MAY run the gamut with an extraordinary range of options. Whether you're in the mood for nouvelle cuisine in an elegant candlelit room, brunch in a lively café, or casual family dining in an informal seafood bar overlooking the water, you'll find it, in abundance, and fairly priced for the quality.

With so many people coming to a town as small as Cape May, you may have to wait a while to get into the town's restaurants in the summer season (or for that matter, in the spring and fall too). It's worth the wait, however, for there are some talented cooks. I've categorized the restaurants by cuisine, and since most of the restaurants are à la carte, I've noted prices for some appetizers and entrees so you can estimate what the cost of a dinner will be.

INTERNATIONAL / AMERICAN: The **Mad Batter,** 19 Jackson St. (tel. 884-5970), is everybody's favorite Cape May restaurant since it opened ten years ago. Oh, there are other renowned restaurants in town now, some serving elegant French cuisine in hushed surroundings, or offering truly creative dishes inspired by the local fish and produce, but none has surpassed the Mad Batter in its inspiration, personal warmth, lively ambience, and, lest I forget, its cooking. It's all there, whether you eat in the skylit main dining room, under the yellow-striped awning of the front porch, or through the French doors onto the brick patio of the Garden Terrace.

Many find it hard to believe that a restaurant that can seat 180 people can maintain the level of quality and relaxed charm of the Mad Batter. It's due in no small measure to the energy and acumen of its owners, Harry Kulkowitz and Vickie Seitchik, whose commitment to their remarkable staff of chefs and wait-persons is returned by an amazing flow of creativity that's made their restaurant *the* place to go, and to go back to.

Before they opened the restaurant, Vickie was a dancer and Harry ran an art gallery; actually he still does, as you'll see by the work of local artists that hangs in the main dining room. The restaurant is open from the middle of March through November, although they plan to keep it open year round eventually. Whether or not they do, they'll still take their off-season trips to faraway places, looking for exotic new dishes to please their customers. That's the kind of caring that makes this such a great place to eat.

The only warning I'll drop before telling you just what all the fuss is about, is this—all the food is cooked to order, and the service is, well, leisurely. Take that into consideration if it's going to bother you. I hope it won't, for you'll miss a good meal, beginning with breakfast or brunch.

(No one, by the way, seems to remember how the restaurant got its name. According to the *New York Times,* which awarded it two stars, the Mad Batter specialized in crêpes when it first opened, hence its whimsical name.)

The orange juice is freshly squeezed, and so is the apple, pineapple, or pear juice ($1.25 to $2.50). If you'd like an offbeat start to the day, the Mad Porridge is a delicious and healthful combination of oats, wheat flakes, malt barley, brown sugar, hazelnuts, and raisins. Bagels, muffins, croissants, homemade whole-grain bread, or sweet pumpkin bread might be just the right accompaniment for your morning cuppa Java (blended with Mocha and Colombian coffee beans to produce the Mad Batter's special brew).

Closer to midday you'll probably add on a main dish, soup, or salad, and call it brunch. Prices are moderate for the crêpes ($4.75), egg dishes ($5.75), salads ($4 to $7), and soups ($2.25 to $3.50) on the menu. The pancakes with sautéed fruits are outstanding. If you choose an omelet, the variations are your options —bacon, vegetable, cheese, or duxelles. Try either the shrimp quenelle and watercress soup in a wine and fish broth or the curried butternut squash soup—you'll be glad you did. Chilled soups are equally dreamy—the shrimp in a cool puree of avocados and cream, for example. The "3rd & 4th" is a delightful selection of three cheeses served with fruit and homemade bread. For pasta lovers, a lunch of fresh spinach pasta with roasted green peppers, havarti cheese, and walnut sauce ($6.25) will be just right.

Breakfast, lunch, and dinner menus change every few weeks. In addition to the printed menus, specials are posted daily on blackboards in the main dining room and on the front porch. There are two soups that have been on the dinner menu that I especially recommend—the unusual Ashoka velvet, a smooth blend of crabmeat and corn with sherry and ginger ($3.50), and the zuppa de clams, which is not really soup at all but six luscious clams steamed in a rich sauce of fresh tomatoes, wine, garlic, parsley, fresh fennel, and basil ($4.25). Salade chinoise is a tangy combination of broccoli, cashew nuts, water chestnuts, and Mandarin oranges with an oriental dressing. The only complaint I have about another appetizer—the tender Maryland crabfingers served with homemade mustard sauce ($4.75)—is that the dozen morsels served disappeared too quickly.

The eclectic and delicious variety of entrees reflects the influence of Harry and Vickie's travels. You can trace the origin of at least two dishes to their trip to Thailand: the crispy lichee duck ($14.50) and a flavorful Siam shrimp, a stew spiced with chili peppers and lemon grass and cooked in coconut milk with mushrooms and crisp snow peas ($14.75), both entrees served with rice. A nouvelle cuisine entree of grilled boneless chicken breast with fresh apple and green peppercorn sauce ($11.50) is as tasty as it is unusual. The Petrograd vegetarian pie shows how well the chefs meet the challenge of preparing an exciting meatless entree —a whole-wheat-crust-covered dish of cream cheese, hard-cooked eggs and sauteed onions, cabbage, and walnuts ($9.25). Pork ribs smoked with aromatic woods and covered with orange plum sauce ($14.75) and steak marinated in oyster sauce and charcoal grilled will be pleasing to the meat-eaters on hand.

No matter how you slice it, the Mad Batter's desserts fall in the superior category. All the cakes, pies, sorbets, and ice creams are made at the restaurant. And how does one choose between boccone dolce (almond meringues layered with almond Amaretto buttercream and served over caramel sauce); chocolate pear puddle (a pear poached in red wine, filled with chocolate, walnuts, and brandied currants, chocolate glazed and served over crème anglaise); and di pie (a fruited sour cream custard pie topped with walnut streusel)? The only answer I could come up with is to go with obliging friends who'll let you taste their desserts.

The Mad Batter is open seven days, for breakfast, brunch, and lunch from 8 a.m. to 2:30 p.m. Dinner is 5:30 to 10 p.m., till 10:30 p.m. on Friday and Saturday.

Louisa's, 104 Jackson St. (tel. 884-5882), occupies a tiny, shingled house with about a dozen tables set with brightly colored tablecloths, fresh flowers, and candle lamps for a warm, informal bistro setting. Skilled cookery draws such crowds that no reservations are accepted—just join the line outside. While you're waiting in line, your companion can buy a bottle of wine to accompany what will be a really superior meal. You might start with a smoked sea trout rillette ($4) or hot and spicy ginger sesame peanut noodles ($3.50). Snapper bluefish with parsley, capers, and lemon sauce ($9.50) is a perfectly cooked entree. Watch for the homemade pasta dishes—like the fettuccine with spring vegetables ($8.50). The restaurant's chocolate black-bottom cake has a devoted following, though I'm devoted to the crème brulée myself (both are $2.75).

CONTINENTAL/FRENCH: Maureen's, 429 Beach Dr. (tel. 884-3774), opens onto one of the most spectacular vistas of any Cape May restaurant. Sitting on its glass-enclosed terrace, you can enjoy magnificent panoramic ocean views and eat continental cuisine of a very high standard. The restaurant is on the second floor, upstairs from Summers (see Seafood section below) (see Chapter XII).

Young owners Steve and Maureen Horn opened their first restaurant in Philadelphia, where Steve, a Cordon Bleu graduate, was the chef. Their venture was so successful that they branched out to a Cape May restaurant as well. The Horns sold the Philadelphia place, moved to Cape May, and now own the restaurant downstairs as well.

Maureen is usually at the door to greet you; Steve is the chef, who not only oversees all the cooking but personally selects all the food, and even butchers his own veal to be sure of the quality.

Before dining you can have an apértif at the little bar, paneled in wood and ornamented with stained glass, around to the left as you enter. You can eat indoors or on the enclosed terrace. The decor is classically elegant. White linen tablecloths, candles on each table, floral wallpaper, swagged draperies, paintings, plants, and sparkling chandeliers create the ambience of a fine traditional European restaurant.

The menu, while it has some elements of classic cuisine, is quite adventurous, and shows the influence of the Horns' interest in traveling and studying exotic fare. I'd suggest that you begin with the lobster and shrimp bisque. Fresh tortellini with prosciutto is another fine way to start your dinner.

In the realm of entrees, medallions of veal au bec rouge ($19.50) is one of Steve's most popular creations. The veal is served on a bed of lobster, shrimp, and crab with a sauce St. Milo. Some of the flavorsome fish entrees show the influence of the nouvelle cuisine philosophy; others are in the classic French mode. The poisson jardinière ($17) is modern and light, consisting of a selection from the best of the day's fish baked with aromatic vegetables and lemon and served in a reduction sauce of the natural juices. Crab Versailles ($16) is more richly sauced and seasoned with sherry, Dijon mustard, and gruyère cheese. Fresh sea scallops, local flounder, and seafood cassolette make first-rate entrees too.

If none of the above tempts you, surely the porterhouse steak will ($22). Another favorite is the poulet africaine ($14.75). All entrees are served with a house salad and fresh vegetables of the season.

The pastry chef, Ron Jackson, came with the Horns from Philadelphia, and I'm glad he did. Though the dessert offerings vary daily, I hope you'll have a chance to order his cheesecake topped with raspberries; it's scrumptious. Ron's past creations have included such treats as a coconut mousse, served on a homemade mint sorbet, and topped with a puree of fresh strawberries. For chocoholics, the chocolate praline torte is a worthy contender. All desserts are $3.75.

Maureen's is open daily for dinner from 5 until 10 p.m., on Sunday from 4 to 8 p.m., from March to November.

Alexander's, 653 Washington St. (tel. 884-2555), is in a charming, 2½-story French Second Empire-style Victorian house that's painted a soft smokey blue. Set in an old-fashioned flower garden behind its original cast-iron fence, the building's lacy gingerbread trim, bay windows, and mansard roof epitomize the glories of Victorian architecture.

Inside you're greeted by fresh flowers, Oriental rugs, lace curtains, antiques, and oil paintings in the Victorian parlor that's furnished with a yellow upholstered settee and side chairs. The house was built in the 1880s for a local family who kept it until the mid-1960s. Diane and Larry Muentz, who own it now, undertook and completed the job of renovating the property, restoring its original detailing and opening a fine restaurant and guest house (see Chapter X). Diane studied at the Restaurant School of Philadelphia, and her culinary skill has earned Alexander's reputation as one of the top restaurants in the area.

Dinner at Alexander's is a relaxed, leisurely affair recalling the life-style of an earlier era. Don't be surprised if it takes 2½ hours or so. The tables are deliberately set apart, with enough space in between so that you don't have to listen to other people's conversations, or worry about putting your elbow in someone else's soup. The dining rooms accommodate only 38 guests, so you'll have attentive service. The tables are set with linen and lace, silver and crystal, and in the flickering candlelight you'll think there couldn't be a more romantic dinner in Cape May—and you'll be right.

Diane Muentz carefully selects the dinner menu and uses the best ingredients available. Her appetizers are prepared with imagination. You might begin with an original recipe of sausage nut strudel, layers of pastry encasing sausage, cream cheese, and nuts.

There are unique main dishes on the menu, such as shrimp with mushrooms, shallots, garlic, and wine, and Cornish game hen Su Ling, roasted and basted with plum and raspberry bordeaux. A flavorful rabbit stew is prepared the country French way with onions, pine nuts, bacon, parsley, and red wine.

Those who want meat can choose between filet mignon, steak au poivre, or loin lamb chops. If local seafood is appealing, there's always a fish du jour or the oysters Cajun, poached in cream and sherry with subtle spices and served in a puff pastry shell.

If it's possible to consider dessert after this feast, I'd ask for the bananas Foster. Prepared at tableside, the bananas are flambéed in kirsch, dark rum, and carmelized sugar, and presented over vanilla ice cream. Another house specialty is a frozen white chocolate brandy Alexander pie.

Dinner is served from 6 p.m. daily June to September. Expect to pay about $30 per person. From mid-April to Memorial Day and from September through December dinner is served only on weekends. On Sunday there's a five-course brunch from 10 a.m. to 1 p.m.

You can choose from a whole variety of imported and/or decaffeinated teas, brewed decaffeinated coffee, or a heady brew of Alexander's own coffee, served in an individual heavy silver pot that's left on your table with a warmer. Chilled juice and fresh seasonal fruits precede the entree, which has a globe-circling list of candidates: scrambled eggs and bacon; southern fried fish with eggs; Belgian waffles with melted butter, maple-honey rum syrup, and sausage or bacon; pecan buttermilk pancakes; or eggs Alexander, two poached eggs with filet mignon. Homemade desserts are included in the $14.95 prix-fixe meal. Hazelnut cheesecake, homemade ice cream, and brie cheese are among the possibilities.

Alexander's doesn't have a liquor license, and you may bring your own wine or liquor; there's a 75¢-per-person service charge for set-ups.

The Swallows, 400 Broadway (tel. 884-0400), a five-minute walk from the Washington Street mall, is an elegant restaurant that's one of my personal favorites. Set back on a pretty lawn, it occupies the first floor of a lovely old house originally built in the late 1700s, with later Victorian-era additions. Its young owners, Barry Marron and Anthony Casasanto (who is also the chef), have created a charming atmosphere in which to serve their exquisite specialties. There are three dining rooms, one in the old Colonial part of the house. It's a cozy-warm room, with a fireplace, beamed ceilings, and wide-plank floors. The other rooms are decorated in rose and green, with plump banquettes and Victorian side chairs. In the hallway is a handsome pier glass that's always adorned with floral arrangements of the season, as are the fireplaces. The walls are bright with art posters and Anthony's original paintings.

Only dinner is served, from 6 to 10 p.m. The menu changes often, so Anthony can keep his culinary skills sharply honed. His special appetizers might include a choice of pasta salad with shrimp tossed in lemon and olive oil ($5), Roman broccoli soup ($3), or mushroom pâté ($4). There are usually three entrees, such as a veal of the day, baked tilefish with fresh chives and mushrooms ($14), and breast of duck in strawberry-blackberry glaze ($15). Enticing desserts are the chef's specialty, and they look as good as they taste. Champagne mousse, English trifle, and chocolate walnut cannoli merit your attention. The Swallows is open from the beginning of May to the end of October; reservations are suggested.

Peaches, 322 Carpenter's Lane, at the Washington Mall and Sawyer Walk (tel. 884-0202), serves brunch from 11 a.m. to 2:30 p.m. and dinner from 5:30 p.m. It's a cozy spot, tucked away behind the mall, and there are just nine tables in the restaurant. The brunch menu has salads, sandwiches, and specialties—banana french toast, mesquite grilled catch of the day, or vegetarian lasagne. At dinner the entree choices might number grilled Thai duck ($12.95), fettuccine with smoked salmon, and daily specials as well.

Le Toque, 210 Ocean St. (tel. 884-1511), is a very casual bistro. Pretty pastel tablecloths and napkins decorate the tables and travel posters extolling the beauties of France adorn the walls. Breakfast, served daily from 9 a.m. to 9 p.m., offers croissants in a variety of styles (almond, with chocolate, etc.). A continental breakfast is $3.50. Lunch features salads, quiche, croissant sandwiches, and soups. Dinner, from 5 to 9 p.m., might feature roast duck ($14.95) or blackened redfish ($14.95).

CAJUN/CREOLE: On the Cape May scene for just three years, **410 Bank Street** (tel. 884-2127) has a light, casual environment in which diners can feast on the trendiest of Cajun specialties. Located in a two-story sage green and buff Victorian house, the restaurant occupies the screened-in front porch, the rear courtyard, and the front parlor. While waiting for dinner, patrons can use the crayons provided at each table to decorate their heavy white paper tablecloth. Outstanding artworks are pinned up in the restaurant. But let's get to the food, which is top drawer, an eclectic selection of New Orleans favorites, with the accent on fresh ingredients, mesquite grilling, and lovingly prepared desserts. For an appetizer you might choose Lake Pontchartrain blue crab claws or mesquite-grilled shrimp. Specialty entrees like blackened gulf redfish and Cajun shellfish gumbo filé are favorites. There are usually chicken, beef, veal, and lamb entrees as well. House salad, fresh bread, and vegetables accompany each entree. The chocolate cake will delight your sweet tooth, or you might opt for another New Orleans treat—bread pudding with bourbon cream sauce. With entrees in the $12.95 to $17.95 range, expect to pay about $30 per person for a three-course dinner.

410 Bank Street is open for dinner daily from 5 to 10 p.m. Reservations are a good idea.

AMERICAN/TRADITIONAL: One of the best dinners I've eaten in Cape May was at the **Washington Inn,** 801 Washington St. (tel. 884-5697). My first impression of this charming restaurant was favorable, when I walked under the marquee up to the enclosed veranda and peeked in to see the pretty pastel tablecloths and napkins, white wicker settees, blue flowered-print chair covers on white bentwood chairs, and hanging plants. It wasn't open when I first stopped by, but I'm glad I went back early. The restaurant doesn't take reservations, and even though it can seat 130, if you come after 6:30 p.m. on a weekend night you'll probably have to wait. You could have a predinner drink in the bar, paneled with wood salvaged by Mr. Craig, the owner, from old chestnut doors that had been in a local house. The leaded-glass panes behind the bar are actually part of an old German wardrobe, which was brought to this country by the owner's grandmother at the turn of the century. There are several dining rooms: the central room with a classical brick and white-manteled fireplace that's especially attractive on a cool night, the aforementioned glassed-in terrace, and a room that adjoins a spectacular greenhouse display of so many orchids it's almost like a tropical scene. Whichever room you dine in, it will be nicely lit with a pretty hurricane glass lamp on your table.

The food is authentic American fare, served by friendly waitresses who'll see that you get a deliciously warm loaf of fresh pumpernickel with a tangy swirl of rye through it and a big scoop of butter. The main dishes are surprisingly moderate. The prices range from $13.95 for stuffed flounder to $17.95 for surf and turf—a petite filet mignon and a lobster tail. The house salad, a potato, and vegetable of the day are served with the entree.

The appetizers are very good. Cold seafood cocktail ($5.95) was the most expensive appetizer on the menu. Other traditional appetizers, include homemade clam chowder and onion soup.

The menu has many beef, veal, chicken, and seafood choices, including lobster tails, seafood en brochette, and ocean scallops. Homemade pastries and ice cream are good desserts to try—if you have the room. Dinner will cost about $25.

The Washington Inn is open from 5 to 10 p.m. daily June through September. It's closed in January and February, and open weekends only the rest of the year.

It's hard to imagine any nicer combination of food and decor than **Watson's Merion Inn,** 106 Decatur St. (tel. 884-8363). In the summer of 1885 Patrick Collins opened on Decatur Street a "fine marine boarding villa . . . a first-class establishment." By 1900 Collins Café was advertising whiskies, fresh seafood, and beer. When the steward of Philadelphia's Merion Cricket Club bought the café in 1906, he changed the name to the Merion, and so it has remained, with the owner's name preceding its historic one.

The two-story white frame building has a striped awning out front, and a side terrace for dining al fresco, but I hope you'll take a look inside too. The foyer is engagingly papered with a green and rose floral pattern and decorated with old photos of Cape May. Swinging doors of dark wood inset with beautiful stained-glass panels lead into the bar and restaurant. It's the oldest bar in Cape May, and a real work of art, with carved wooden trim, columns, and mirrors set against a richly burnished wooden background. Heavy gilt-framed oil paintings, brass-and-glass chandeliers, green wainscoting, and flowers on the pink-clothed tables evoke a cozy turn-of-the-century ambience with remarkable fidelity. You may be seated in one of several dining rooms, but all have an intimate, warm quality that's very easy to take.

The dinner menu is carefully selected and prepared with the finest ingredients. Dinner is served daily from 4:30 to 10 p.m. If you're seated before 6 p.m. you can take advantage of the early-bird special. The night I was there it was broiled fresh weakfish with Mornay sauce for $7.95 ($10.95 after 6 p.m.). All entrees include a relish tray, green salad, fresh bread basket, and two vegetables. There's a good selection of seafood entrees; broiled salmon ($15.95) and crab imperial ($13.95) are two favorites. You might also try the honey-glazed ham steak ($11.95) or the veal Merion style, with white wine and mushrooms ($14.95). The spectacular dessert is the old-fashioned strawberry shortcake with real whipped cream ($3.50). The Merion Inn is open seven days a week Memorial Day to Labor Day; weekends only in April and May, October and November. No credit cards, but travelers checks are accepted.

SEAFOOD: The **Lobster House,** Fisherman's Wharf, Cape May (tel. 884-8296), just across the bridge from the end of the Garden State Parkway, is located on a working fishing dock. If you're there early in the morning, you can see the fishing fleet docking and unloading a full cargo of fresh fish. It's a fascinating place to look around, talk to the oldtimers, and really feel what it's like to be part of a tradition that goes back thousands of years.

Fish lovers will have a field day at the Lobster House, which is really a complex consisting of a retail fish market and clam bar, a coffeeshop, a cocktail lounge that's aboard an old schooner, and the famed Lobster House, a seafood restaurant with a very nautical air, complete with candlelight and soft dinner music.

The retail fish market stocks a full line of condiments and relishes along with oysters, scallops, and the other freshly caught fish of the day. The market has a take-out kitchen with a counter facing the wharf where you can buy all the expected seafood treats, and they're guaranteed fresh! Fried shrimp are $4.50 for six; fried clams are $2.75 for a half pound; fried scallops are $4 a half pound. Softshell crabs are $2.35 each. Snapper soup and clam chowder are available by the pint or the quart. After you've assembled your picnic, sit on the wharf and enjoy your fresh-cooked feast in view of the passing boats.

The schooner *American,* docked at the fisherman's wharf, has a cozy cocktail lounge below deck. It's a pleasant place to go for a drink and snack while waiting for your table at the restaurant (which doesn't take reservations). An intercom calls you when your table is ready. The main bar in the restaurant also serves cocktails.

Colonial waterfront decor characterizes the Lobster House's dining rooms. Polished dark-wood paneling, red-checked tablecloths, Windsor chairs, cut-glass tumblers, and ship's-wheel chandeliers provide a nostalgic, seafaring ambience. Try to get a table along the window-wall overlooking the wharf and inlet. Wherever you sit, you'll be amused and amazed by the eclectic displays of nautical objects. I saw a full-size ship's figurehead, duck decoys, ship models, stuffed game fish, and a canoe paddle.

To get right to the main event, the broiled lobster tail with drawn butter is luscious, moist and sweet ($21.95). Steamed or broiled lobsters are priced according to market, as are the Alaskan king crab claws. The lobster is just about the most expensive item on the menu. The other entrees range from $9.50 to $14.25, and include such choices as fresh scallops; baked, fried, or broiled flounder; broiled bluefish; and stuffed shrimp. Landlubbers have several possibilities—broiled filet mignon, chopped sirloin, and chicken breast among them.

All entrees are served with the house salad, a potato with a large dollop of sour cream or french fries, and a choice of the day's vegetables. A warm loaf of french bread and a crock of butter accompany the dinner. You may decide to skip the appetizer —the dinner entree is quite generous. If the clams or oysters on the half shell seem very appealing (and they are), it might be a good idea to share a plate before embarking on the entree. If you're really hungry, the clam or fish chowder or oyster stew, or seafood cocktail are fine for starters.

The desserts are traditional and homemade—apple pie, cheesecake, rice pudding, and chocolate mousse—the perfect way to end a traditional seafood meal.

The Lobster House is open for lunch daily from 11:30 a.m. to 3 p.m., for dinner from 5 to 10 p.m., 2 to 9 p.m. on Sunday.

Owners Steve and Maureen Horn, not content with their superb continental restaurant (Maureen's) upstairs, have opened **Summers,** also at the corner of Beach Drive and Decatur Street (tel. 884-3504), specializing in seafood favorites. A casual spot with red-checked tableclothes, wood paneled walls, a raw clam/oyster bar near the entrance, and a convivial bar, Summers serves lunch, brunch, and dinner. The lunch menu lists clams casino, oysters on the half shell, and clam chowder, among the oldtime shore favorites. Hot entrees feature crab fritters, seafood pasta Alfredo, and beef Burgundy. For brunch you might try the eggs Rockefeller, a concoction of poached eggs served on a bed of oysters Rockefeller and covered with a Mornay sauce. Entree prices are $6 to $8.50; sandwiches are $2 to $4 less. At dinner grilled or baked fish of the season and lobster, shrimp, or crab entrees are top choices. Steaks and pasta specialties round out the main offerings. After 10 p.m. there's entertainment. With entrees ranging up to $17, a full dinner will be around $20 to $30.

Summers' lunch/brunch is served from 11:30 a.m. to 3 p.m.; dinner from 5 to 10 p.m. The bar is open till 2 a.m. Dress is casual.

A & J Blue Claw, on Ocean Drive about a quarter of a mile before the toll bridge to Wildwood Crest (tel. 884-5878), is a family dining spot noted for its raw bar and Maryland blue claw crab. It overlooks the fishing fleet at rest in the inlet and is a comfortable, low-key place to dine. Hanging plants, and hurricane lamps on the polished wood tables enliven the simple setting. You might start with a cold appetizer of clams ($3.50) or oysters ($5.50) on the half shell. Lobster tail is $21.95, if you're feeling flush. Scallops, broiled or fried, are a perennially popular favorite at $13.95. Lunch is served till 3 p.m. and dinner till 9 p.m., till 10 p.m. on weekends. There's a bar-lounge that's open all day until the early hours of the morning.

ITALIAN: The **Trattoria,** 312 Carpenter's Lane, next to the Pink House (tel. 884-1144), which opened in spring 1983 under the direction of Marie and Gene Gallagher, seats 20 in a casually chic atmosphere. You'll sit on white garden-type chairs at a candlelit table covered with a pink tablecloth and set with white china and green napkins. In summer the restaurant spreads out onto the open-air deck. For good-tasting *cucina italiana,* and some of the friendliest people around, you'll do well here.

Dinner might start with stuffed mushrooms ($3.75) or Cape May crab soup ($2.75). The entrees are first-rate: shrimp marinated in olive oil, garlic, and basil ($12); chicken Tuscany ($10.25); tortellini in tomato and cream sauce ($9.50). If you can handle dessert, try the Mona Lisa torte—it'll make you smile. Dinner is served from 5:30 to 10 p.m. The Trattoria offers a lunch menu from 11:30 a.m. to 2:30 p.m. featuring soups, salads, pasta, and fish entrees. Prices range from $2.75 (a tarragon tuna sandwich) to $5.50 (baked fresh flounder).

Owned by Janice Merwin and Stephen Miller, also proprietors

of 410 Bank Street, next door, **412 Bank Street** (tel. 884-2127) offers an imaginative array of Italian specialties in an intimate room and adjoining porch of a typical Cape May Victorian house. The dining room walls are painted in a wholly unusual blue-green that suggests the Mediterranean in an offbeat way. On the menu pasta and seafood reign. Appetizers feature buffalo mozzarella cheese with sun-dried tomatoes, radicchio and arugula in a tossed salad, and fresh calamari. Vegetarian entrees and pastas in all shapes and sizes from manicotti in fresh tomato sauce to tagliatelle in a delicately seasoned cream sauce are the specialties. Tartufo, Italian cheesecake, and hazelnut cake are what you'll see on the dessert menu. If the crowds next door are any indication, this new venture should be a big hit.

A Ca Mia, on the Washington Mall next to La Pâtisserie bakery (tel. 884-1913), offers northern Italian dinners in a simple setting of white tablecloths and blue-painted chairs. You'll pay $12 plus the cost of the entrée for a full course dinner—choice of two appetizers, a pasta, the entrée, dessert, and coffee or tea. Entrees range in price from $8.95 (for a giardino fantasia—broccoli and cauliflower in puff pastry) to $16.95 (lobster in Marsala sauce).

A Ca Mia is open for dinner from 5:30 to 10 p.m. every night except Tuesday.

TAVERN FARE: Here are two friendly places that serve lunch, dinner, and late-night snacks year round. Live entertainment after 9 p.m. adds to their popularity.

Naturally the **Pilot House,** 142 Decatur St. (tel. 884-3449), at the mall, has a nautical decor. There's even an anchor out front at the wooden deck. Inside you'll find a telegraph (an old ship instrument), an aquarium, mounted game fish, captain's chairs, and polished wood tables with hurricane lamps carrying out the theme. A brick fireplace adds cheer in the winter. Sandwiches, burgers, salads, and several Mexican specialties are on the lunch menu. The chef's repertoire at dinner features special seafood combinations, such as a broiled quartet of shrimp, scallops, crabmeat, and flounder for $15.95. The creamy and well-seasoned deviled crab ($10.25) is another house specialty. A limited selection of pasta, beef, chicken, and veal entrees are also well prepared. With all entrees (except pasta) you'll get a salad, choice of potato and vegetable or spaghetti. The Pilot House is open for dinner from 5 to 10 p.m., for lunch and snacks from 11:30 a.m. to 5 p.m., and for late-night snacks from 10 p.m.

On the mall at Decatur Street, the **Ugly Mug** (tel. 884-3459) has good food at low prices. Tan drinking mugs hang on the ceiling beams and hark back to the days when they belonged to members of the Ugly Mug Club. According to legend, the club's most memorable event was a contest to see who could blow the most foam out of a beer glass. Today both locals and visitors congregate at the big U-shaped bar in the middle of the room and the surrounding booths. Mahogany wainscoting and red-flocked wallpaper evoke a turn-of-the-century ambience in this busy, convivial restaurant. The best chili in town is $1.55 for a cup, $2.25 for a bowl. Sandwiches in all the standard combinations are tasty and filling; ham and cheese is $3.15. Their famous platters feature seafood—scallops, shrimp, crab, and flounder—and cost from $6.25 (a flounder casserole) to $10.35 (seafood combo). Homemade chocolate-chip cake and cheesecake (each $1.75) are excellent. The Ugly Mug is open seven days, year round, from 11:30 a.m.

BUDGET BEST: The friendly owners of the **Filling Station,** across from the Acme on Lafayette Street (tel. 884-2111), took over an old filling station (Sinclair—remember the sign of the dinosaur?) and daringly converted it into an excellent restaurant whose good food at reasonable prices has made it one of the best liked in Cape May, and one of the most frequented by locals. Each of the three cozy rooms is decorated a bit differently. I preferred the garden-like setting in the room with pretty flower paintings, park-bench-style seats, and ceramic tile floors. As you enter you can't miss the salad bar; after one look it's a sure bet you'll add it to your dinner entree for a dollar extra. Nightly blackboard specials offer good value. I had the broiled flounder ($8.65); it arrived hot and fresh with a flavorful broccoli quiche-like casserole as garnish. The local favorite is the seven-ounce serving of filet mignon for $9.95. You might like to start off with the hearty fish chowder ($1.95 for a bowl). Families will gravitate to the fried chicken—served for three to five people with french fries and cole slaw for $18.95. The Filling Station is open April to October from 4:30 to 10 p.m. Tuesday through Sunday.

It pays to dine early at the Filling Station. Come anytime between 4:30 and 5:59 p.m., punch the time clock at the door, and that's the price of your "Beat the Clock" dinner special. Arrive at 4:32 and your dinner costs $4.32; the earlier you come, the greater your savings. The Filling Station is a two-minute walk from the mall.

FOR LIGHT MEALS: Fresh-squeezed lemonade is a refreshing drink at the **Lemon Tree,** on the Washington Mall (tel. 884-2704). You can have breakfast from 8 a.m., and lunch—soup and sandwiches —in a simple, attractive setting for prices in the $2.50 to $5 range.

And don't miss a stop at **Svensk,** 108 Jackson St. (no phone), a cozy café with outdoor tables that serves fresh-from-the-pan crêpes with sweet or savory fillings from 95¢ to $3.75.

Chapter XII

WHAT TO SEE AND DO IN CAPE MAY

STROLLING OR BIKING the old-fashioned streets of Cape May is the best way to see the largest collection of authentic Victorian structures in the nation. What makes this historic district so exciting is that it's not a modern-day re-creation or an impersonal museum-like assemblage of architectural styles. Cape May is a real, functioning town whose hotels, guesthouses, restaurants, and shops happen to represent a romantic and picturesque era of American history.

Most of these lovely old houses were built after the town's great fire in 1878. Their architects were commissioned by wealthy Philadelphians and southerners who wanted their summer houses to flaunt their recently acquired fortunes. Many of these newly rich had taken the Grand Tour through Europe, where they saw the grandeur of Gothic cathedrals, Italian villas, Renaissance palaces, and medieval fortresses. When they came home they wanted to show off their sophistication. So their architects found favor by adding an electic mixture of decorative features that were based on old styles—massive chimneys, French Empire mansard roofs, Gothic towers, medieval gables, Renaissance balconies, and Elizabethan paned windows, among them.

Not all the houses in Cape May were built for rich people, but even the simplest dwellings of that era had some ornament. The carpenters decorated the little frame buildings with the products of their new bandsaws that could mass-produce intricately carved designs in wood that were called carpenter's lace or gingerbread.

Seeing the Sights

Begin your visit at the very charming little information booth on the Washington Mall, where you can pick up guided tour information and brochures to help see it yourself. The booth was moved here from Philadelphia's Fairmount Park, where it was built for the 1876 Exposition. The booth dispenses information from 10 a.m. to 5 p.m. in summer.

GUIDED TOURS: While you might think that a guided tour of a little town like Cape May is superfluous, I hope you'll consider taking one of the trolley or walking tours sponsored by the **Mid-Atlantic Center for the Arts (MAC),** 1048 Washington St., Cape May, NJ 08204 (tel. 609/884-5404), the local restoration-minded group that has played a leading role in Cape May's renaissance.

Aboard a trolley tour, you'll get a comfortable ride and an entertaining account of Cape May's past and present as you travel through the streets. Tickets are $3.50 for adults, $1 for children, and the tour lasts about 30 minutes. In July and August children's trolley tours are given every Thursday at 9:30 a.m.; tickets are $2 for adults, $1 for children.

Walking tours are especially designed for those who like their history close up and in detail. The guides are townspeople whose informed, anecdote-filled talks about Cape May and Victorian customs are infused with such enthusiasm that you'll really find them spellbinding. The walking tours take about 1½ hours and begin at the mall information booth. The cost is $4 for adults, $1 for children.

To get an idea of what the interiors of these middle-class mansions and picturesque cottages were like, you can go inside with one of the house tours. The **Mansions by Gaslight** tour starts at the Physick estate, 1048 Washington St., where you can buy tickets from 7:30 on every Wednesday evening from mid-June to mid-September and on most holiday weekends, at $10 for adults, $5 for children. Tours are from 8 to 10 p.m. and also visit the Abbey, the Mainstay, and the Wilbraham Mansion for a rare and intriguing view of how the Victorians lived.

The **Cottages at Twilight** tour visits four other interiors on Monday evenings from 8 to 10 p.m. Purchase tickets—$10 for adults and $5 for children—at the Dr. Henry L. Hunt House, 209 Congress Pl., from 7:45 p.m.

All of the foregoing tours are offered in July and August. In the winter, weekend tours offer a money-saving combination of an hour-long trolley tour, a guided tour through the lavish interior of the Physick house, and a festive ending with hot cider and doughnuts in the Physick house kitchen. The combination tour lasts two hours and costs $8 for adults, $4 for children. The walking tours are given on Sunday morning, weather permitting, at 10 a.m.

During Cape May's **Victorian Week** festivities, usually beginning the weekend before Columbus Day and continuing through the holiday weekend, evening stained-glass tours and self-guided tours of Victorian homes are added to the festive schedule. The **Christmas Candlelight Tour** is self-guided through more than a dozen homes and churches specially decorated for the season. A spectacular gingerbread house contest brings out a display of charming edible edifices in the houses you'll tour.

A private outfit, the **Cape May Carriage Company** (tel. 465-9854), will take you on a half-hour horse-and-carriage ride through Cape May at $5 for adults, $2.50 for children. The carriage leaves from Ocean Street and Washington Mall on weekends in spring and fall, daily in summer.

A HISTORICAL WALK: If you're sightseeing on your own, start at the **Old Bank Building,** next to the information booth on Washington Mall and Ocean Street. This 1895 three-story Renaissance Revival building has a formal, dignified look suitable to a place where people entrusted their money. Today it houses McDowell's gift shop. Notice the Greek key design that ornaments the buff brick building with a classical decoration.

One of the few buildings that survived the 1878 fire that devastated some 30 acres of Cape May, **208 Ocean Street** is a rather seedy-looking 2½ -story clapboard house with a front porch. Proof that the building existed before the fire is displayed in a stereopticon view showing the house standing amid the ruins of the town. Step up onto the porch to see the photo in the window of Cohen's jewelry shop, the present owner and occupant of number 208.

Turn left at the corner to **Hughes Street,** which wins my vote as the prettiest street in town. It's like an old country lane, narrow and curvy, with tree-lined front gardens and a wonderful assortment of houses from different periods of Cape May history. You can see the old carriage mounts and cast-iron horse ties along the street. If you come by at dusk, when the street's gas lamps are lit, you'll imagine you can hear the clip-clop of the horses that used to stop here.

The Greek Revival, white two-story house with black shutters at **609 Hughes Street** dates back to 1838. Mrs. Hughes, who first lived there, was married to a sea captain. She wrote in her diary how frightened she was to be alone in the house in the woods when he was at sea. Strange to think that 14 years later Cape May was a thriving resort!

One of the guest houses described in the accommodations section, the **Manor House,** 612 Hughes St., is a massive example of the American shingle style, a popular design for resort "cottages" in the early 1900s. There's an especially pretty flower garden that I hope is in bloom when you're there.

The various shades of green fish-scale tile on the mansard roof at **619 Hughes Street** are, if you look carefully, arranged in a flower pattern, and the roof is bordered with a scalloped tile design. Towers and turrets abound on Hughes Street; see number 626.

The **Joseph Hall House,** 645 Hughes St., offers a brilliant display of Victorian color that highlights the elaborate gingerbread trim. The owner of this 1868 cottage feels that the strong yellows are much closer to the paint colors of the era than white—the one color Victorians most disliked.

Turn down Stockton Place to Columbia Street. On Stockton you can peek into a backyard, on your left, to see a green and white gazebo, the only authentic one surviving in Cape May, I'm told. Not only did these airy little structures provide a shaded seat for a summer afternoon. They were much sought after by courting couples who could take advantage of the closest approximation of privacy afforded in this staid era to steal a kiss or two away from their chaperone's watchful eyes.

The **Mainstay Inn,** 635 Columbia St., is an elegant 1872 villa with original furnishings and gasolier chandeliers. It was originally a gambling house and gentleman's club known as Jackson's. If you stand on the corner of Stockton and Columbia and look toward Ocean Street, you'll find that all the front porches are perfectly aligned—truly a reflection of the Victorian spirit.

The yellow-painted **Brass Bed,** 719 Columbia St., is a fine example of Carpenter Gothic style, as is the blue with cream trim of the **Victorian Rose,** 715 Columbia. All three are guesthouses described in Chapter X.

Take Howard Street a few steps toward the ocean and you'll see the double verandas, gables, and cupola of the **Chalfonte,** 301 Howard. It's Cape May's oldest continuously operated hotel, open every season since it was built in 1876 by Col. Henry Sawyer, who was a prisoner of the Confederacy, later exchanged for Col. Robert E. Lee, Jr., son of the general. The Chalfonte's guest rooms and restaurant are described in Chapter X.

Turn right onto Kearny Street and continue two blocks to Gurney Street. Facing you are the seven identical cottages built in 1871 and named in honor of the old Stockton Hotel. The **Baldt House,** 26 Gurney St., retains most of its original wealth of wood ornaments. Built as summer rental units, each cottage cost $2,000 a season—not exactly a budget price for the time. The row was designed by Stephen Decatur Button, an architect whose work is very evident throughout Cape May.

At the corner of Gurney Street, at the monument park, is the **McCreary House,** beautifully restored and open as the Abbey guesthouse. Note its 60-foot tower with round ruby-glass windows and iron cresting. The vertical emphasis of the house's design is evident in the Gothic arch repeated in the doors, windows, and porch brackets.

Turn left onto Columbia Street, and as you walk toward Ocean Street you'll see a number of unique gingerbread patterns along the way. The **Delsea,** 621 Columbia St., built in 1867, is a good example. Don't miss the old-fashioned flower garden at number 609.

The **Queen Victoria,** 102 Ocean St., is painted a beautiful shade of green that's authentic to the Victorian period. It's surrounded by an old cast-iron fence, as are two other houses on the corner of Columbia and Ocean.

Take another left down Ocean Street to Beach Drive. The massive **Colonial Hotel** is best viewed from across the drive if you stand on the promenade. It was a modern wonder, filled with such newfangled inventions as an elevator, when it was built in 1894. Henry Ford was one of its distinguished visitors.

Walk 2½ blocks along the promenade and stop between Jackson and Decatur Streets. Here you'll have a good view of the **Seven Sisters,** the Renaissance Revival cottages designed by Stephen D. Button. Five of the cottages have their backs to Jackson Street; all face Atlantic Terrace, a private lane, and the **Acroteria,** a semicircle of tiny cabaña-like structures that house shops.

Continue another block to Perry, and turn up to number 9, and note the blue and green ceramic blocks inset in the porch railing. The tiles were purchased at the Philadelphia Exposition in 1876.

The **Congress Hall Hotel,** at Beach Drive and Congress Street, is the third hotel of the name on this site. The original hotel was called the Big House, but its name was changed to Congress Hall when the owner decided to run for Congress. Gen. Stonewall Jackson and Henry Clay were among its renowned guests.

Numbers 22 and 24 Congress St., the **Joseph and John Steiner Cottages,** were originally owned by two brothers and had a connecting second-floor veranda.

The blue and yellow trim on numbers **203 and 207 Congress Place** distinguish the houses built in 1876 by E. C. Knight. His daughter Annie occupied number 203. Knight owned the Congress Hotel also, and he had a special covenant in the hotel's deed that nothing would ever obstruct his daughter's view of the ocean. He even had the hotel originally built at the corner of the property so her view would be open. Note the two-story verandas on the Knight house and the captain's walk on the roof.

The **Dr. Henry Hunt House** illustrates the Victorian motto—the more decoration the better. The house could serve as a catalog of the period's architectural ornaments—Gothic gables, a balcony, bays, a turret, and patterned shingles, to name a few.

Continuing along Congress Place to Perry Street, you'll come to the most photographed house in Cape May, the 1879 **Pink House,** 33 Perry St., that looks more like a pink and white valentine than a building.

THE PHYSICK ESTATE: Both symbolically and literally, the impressive Emlen Physick House and Estate, 1048 Washington St. (tel. 884-5404), are important to Cape May. It was the threat of demolition that brought together the community to save the old house. The ensuing restoration effort and formation of the Mid-Atlantic Center for the Arts have led to the renaissance of Cape May as a seashore resort and its emergence as a National Historic Landmark site, as important to the nation as Bunker Hill, the Alamo, and Mount Vernon.

This architectural monument was designed by Frank Furness, a famous Philadelphia architect, in 1879. Furness also designed the High Victorian-style Academy of Fine Arts in Philadelphia. Both structures bear such hallmarks of Furness's work as elaborate chimneys that are wider at the top than at the bottom, dormers, and lavish use of trim. The building was commissioned by Dr. Emlen Physick, a Philadelphia doctor, who, on gaining his degree, came to live here with his mother. He never practiced medicine for the rest of his life.

The house has 16 rooms and visitors can see the exquisite furnishings, many original to the house. Dr. Physick's bedrooms still have the old family photographs on display. Maintained by MAC, the house is open to visitors for daily tours except Monday during the summer, on a more limited schedule the rest of the year, for a charge of $4 for adults, $1 for children. Call for complete information.

Evening Entertainment

Cape May offers old-fashioned family-style summer entertainment. MAC's **Mid-Atlantic Stage** group (tel. 884-ARTS) has a full season of theatrical productions on the outdoor stage on the Physick Estate. Bring the children and a beach chair or blanket to enjoy the program.

The **Jersey Cape Performing Arts Guild** presents dramatic productions at the Cape May City Hall Auditorium on Washington Street (tel. 884-0054) and other locations in the area. Tickets cost $4.50 for adults, $2.50 for seniors and students.

At the Rotary bandstand behind the mall, **band concerts** enliven the summer nights.

John Philip Sousa conducted his band on the lawn of the Congress Hall, and Cape May hopes to renew that tradition with gala Fourth of July concerts by the New Jersey Pops orchestra.

Film programs, dances, and other special events are held at the **Convention Hall** on Beach Drive.

NIGHTLIFE: The population of Cape May is not much given to a fast-paced nightlife scene, but you can enjoy a convivial evening of music and dancing in several of the motels and restaurants.

The **Top of the Marq,** Ocean Street and Beach Drive (tel. 884-3431), the rooftop restaurant of the Marquis de Lafayette motel, has dinner and dancing to piano music nightly from about 8:30 p.m. In spring and fall the music is on weekends only. Both the **Crystal Room** at the Atlas Motor Inn, Beach Drive near Madison Avenue (tel. 884-7000), and the **Rusty Nail** lounge at the Coachman Motor Inn, 205 Beach Dr. (tel. 884-0220), have music for listening and dancing nightly.

Summers, at the corner of Beach Drive and Decatur Street (tel. 884-3504), has a small dance floor, revealed when several tables are pushed back after 10 p.m. A trio provides the smooth sounds. When the trio is off, you'll probably hear blues or light jazz to help while away the evening hours. **Carney's,** next door (tel. 884-4424), is a popular watering hole for both locals and vacationers.

At the **Old Shire Tavern,** Washington Mall (tel. 884-4700), affectionately dubbed the Shire, frosted mugs of beer and light bites are a fine accompaniment to the area's hottest jazz sounds.

The **Ugly Mug** and the **Pilot House** are pubby spots that have late-night snacks and entertainment (see Chapter XI). Country and western blue grass is featured at the Mug after 9 p.m., and there's a duo at the Pilot House after 10 p.m.

Atlantic City Excursions

The allure of Atlantic City extends to Cape May, and the casinos know it. Bus service is available for the one-hour trip. The **Casino Bus Co.** departs from the Golden Eagle Inn, Beach Drive and Philadelphia Avenue (tel. 884-4343). Casino bonuses will more than pay you back for the cost of the trip; check with the tour operator for the latest offers.

Shopping

The **Washington Mall** is Cape May's original downtown shopping street. Many of the shop buildings have been standing since the days of wooden sidewalks and dirt streets. In 1971 the city closed Washington Street to traffic between Ocean and Perry Streets, put out park benches, and planted flowers, shrubs, and trees on the new mall. Today it's a lovely promenade lined with boutiques and restaurants, nearly 50 establishments, some of them tucked away in little mini-malls off the main street. Awnings are cranked down to keep the sun off the merchandise, and shopkeepers can be seen sweeping the sidewalks in front of their stores. In spring you'll find the cherry trees in glorious bloom on the mall. At Christmastime the mall is bedecked with garlands and wreaths, gaslights, lighted trees, and candlelit storefronts.

You can find charming presents in the Old Bank Building, at the corner of Ocean Street and the mall, in **McDowell's Gallery.** They display a stunning assortment of kites and will be happy to give you their "Guide to Safe and Sure Kiting" brochure with your purchase. Hand-thrown pottery, fine jewelry, art glass, posters, and regional books are popular mementos of a Cape May visit. Next door is **La Pâtisserie** bakery, the right place for a midmorning croissant or pain au chocolat. There's coffee to go. The bakery is open from 7 a.m. to 5:30 p.m.

Keltie's newsstand is the place to buy your New York, Washington, Philadelphia, or Atlantic City newspaper. You can also pick up magazines, paperback or hardback books, and stationery supplies in this useful spot.

You can watch candles being hand-dipped at the interesting **Flim-Flam Candle Shop,** 106 Jackson St. The owner himself dips the candle wick into several vats with varying hues of hot wax to make a candle that's always a bit different from the one before. On the shelves stand unusual candles that are hand-carved after many dippings to show off the rings of color. Some of these are expensive, but they can be refilled at home and make beautiful garden ornaments on a summer night.

You may not have time to go out to Sunset Beach to look for Cape May "diamonds," so stop in at the **Treasure Cove,** 312 Washington Mall, to get some to take home. Handcrafted leather is the bailiwick of **The Baileywicke,** 656 Washington St. (across Ocean Street). Jack Bailey, who is a member of the prestigious Guild of Master Craftsmen, Sussex, England, is in charge here.

If it's time for an ice-cream cone, **Uncle Charlie's,** 310 Washington Mall, has old-fashioned ice cream and sugar cones. **Laura's Fudge,** across the way will keep your sweet tooth happily at work.

Sports

The Delaware Bay and Atlantic Ocean waters meet at Cape May, and yield over 30 varieties of fish here. If you've never gone fishing before, this is the place to start. You'll also find tennis, nearby golf courses, riding, and biking vying for your pre- or post-swimming hours.

FISHING: The best fishing season is the summer, when you can fish for fluke, weakfish, sea bass, porgies, tuna, bluefish, bonito, albacore, white and blue marlin, and a host of other game fish. If you've got your own rod, just head out to the jetty across from the Jetty Motel, past Second Avenue, at the end of Beach Drive.

Capt. Bob Schumann's *Sea Star II* is a party boat (tel. 884-4671) that sails daily at 9 a.m. from the **South Jersey Fishing Center,** Route 9, at the entrance to Cape May. His six-hour expeditions will cost $17 for adults, $9 for children.

GOLF AND TENNIS: There are three golf courses in Cape May County, but that covers a lot of territory. Closest to Cape May city is the **Stone Harbor Golf Club,** Route 9, 1½ miles north of exit 10 off the Garden State Parkway (tel. 465-9270). Call in advance for guaranteed starting time. In season, greens fees are $14 daily and $8 after 4 p.m. Electric carts cost $16 for 18 holes. Golf lessons are available. The club also has two outdoor tennis courts.

In Cape May, right next to the Physick Estate on Washington Street, the **William J. Moore Tennis Center** (tel. 884-8986) has 13 clay courts. You'll pay $4 an hour for a court. Contracts for two weeks are $45; monthly and seasonal arrangements are also offered.

RIDING: The **Hidden Valley Ranch,** 4070 Bayshore Rd., Cold Spring (tel. 884-8205), is open year round (closed Sunday). If you like, they'll take you riding on the beach.

BIKING: Delighted to put their cars aside for a few days, many Cape May visitors choose to explore the area by bike. The **Village Bike Shop,** on Ocean Street across from Washington Mall (tel. 884-8500), is centrally located and has coaster brakes, five-speeds, ten-speeds, and bicycles built for two for hire. Open from 6:30 a.m. to 8 p.m., they charge $2.50 an hour, $7 a day, and $20 a week for rentals. There's free parking for as long as you're riding their bikes.

SWIMMING: The Victorians loved sea bathing; they called it hydrotherapy, and made it a part of their health regimen. To acquire a tan, however, was déclassé, strictly for the lower classes. And, of course, mixed bathing was a real no-no. To keep the sexes properly separated the Cape May beaches had strict bathing hours: a white flag on the beach from 7 to 8:30 a.m. and 6 to 7:30 p.m. meant the ladies were bathing; they got the least sun. A red flag waved for the gents from 8:30 to 10 a.m. and 4:30 to 6 p.m. How did mixed bathing ever evolve? Well, one story goes that all the heavy woolen clothes the women wore dragged them down in the water, they (rightfully) feared drowning, and sought a manly arm to keep them afloat. Soon all ladies were coming to bathe with their escorts.

The best swimming beaches today begin at about Perry Street and continue to the fishing jetty.

The Nearby Sights

CAPE MAY POINT STATE PARK: In the park's 300 acres of freshwater marshland, woodland, and beaches, you can picnic, fish, or hike. Birders know that spring and fall migrations are the best times to spot song birds, waterfowl, shore birds, birds of prey, and sea birds. For the latest news in avian happenings, the New Jersey Audubon Cape May Bird Observatory has a **birding hot line** (tel. 609/884-2626). Take the **self-guided nature tour** for a look at all the representative species of birds, plants, trees, mammals, reptiles and amphibians, and wildflowers of the area. At the observation platform you'll have a good opportunity to see the creatures of the marshes, if you are patient and quiet. Coded markers along the nature trail correspond with the free tour booklet you can pick up at the visitors center. You'll be able to identify the bayberry shrubs, wax myrtle, eastern red cedar, pitch pine (the predominant pine of the pine barrens), oak, and cattails that all flourish in the Cape May meadows and marshlands.

To reach the state park (tel. 884-2159), which is three miles west of Cape May, take Lafayette Street to Sunset Boulevard. Turn left onto Lighthouse Avenue and follow it to the park entrance. You'll pass the Cape May lighthouse, built in 1859 and still in operation.

CAPE MAY DIAMONDS: You won't have to go mining for Cape May diamonds; they're lying on Sunset Beach waiting for tourists to sift the semiprecious quartz stones from the sand. Some of the shops along the Washington Mall sell jewelry made from the polished stones, and this is where the raw material comes from. The concrete hulk rising out of the water a few yards offshore is what remains of the S.S. *Atlantis,* which was constructed during World War I and was sunk in 1926. Sunset Beach is at the end of Sunset Avenue.

CAPE MAY–LEWES FERRY: A 70-minute mini-cruise connects the historic towns of Cape May and Lewes, Delaware. Taking along your bike will cost $6 but it's a pleasant ride to the ferry, at the end of Ferry Road, and you'll be able to explore Lewes. The ferry also accommodates cars for $14 one way.

COLD SPRING VILLAGE: This is a recreation of a south Jersey farm village. Although it never existed as a real village, the 15 buildings—the craft shops, a country store, and the Old Grange restaurant—are old structures that were moved here from their original sites. From May to October there's a full schedule of events, such as the strawberry festival, sheep-shearing demonstration, antique car show, square dancing, and harvest festival. To reach historic **Cold Spring Village** (tel. 884-1810), you can take Broadway from Cape May; past Ferry Road it becomes Seashore Road, and the village will be on your right shortly after that intersection with Ferry Road.

A SCHOONER CRUISE: You can take a three-hour cruise aboard the *Delta Lady,* an authentic replica of a Chesapeake Bay oyster schooner whose rose-colored sails have been a familiar sight for the last ten years. Departure times are 10 a.m. and 2 and 6 p.m. from **Miss Chris Fishing Center,** 3rd and Wilson Dr. (tel. 884-

1919). Wind and tide determine the ship's course; the cost is $20 per person.

CAPE MAY COUNTY MUSEUM: Housed in a white clapboard pre-Revolutionary farmhouse, the museum is a fitting showcase for memorabilia of the region. Among the exhibits are an 18th-century kitchen and bedroom, a collection of medical and pharmaceutical objects, and a period dining room. There are many Indian artifacts, early tools, decoys, and a nautical collection of ship models. The museum (tel. 465-3535) is on Route 9, north of the Stone Harbor Boulevard exit of the parkway. Hours are 10 a.m. to 4 p.m. Monday through Saturday from mid-June to mid-September. The museum is closed January, February, and March, and on Monday the rest of the year. Admission is $2 for adults, 75¢ for ages 12 to 18, and free for under-12s accompanied by an adult.

LEAMING'S RUN: Twenty acres of beautiful gardens offer a delightful respite whose tranquility is broken only by the distant call of a bird. A sandy winding path weaves through the gardens so the visitors can see each separate garden from different vantage points. Each of the gardens has a theme—such as the English cottage garden or the evening garden, designed with blue and white flowers to be at its loveliest in morning and evening. There are an orange garden, whose brilliant display includes dahlias, gladiolus, coleus, nasturtiums, and in the fall pumpkin; a reflecting garden that has a pond with Egyptian lotus with huge pink flowers; a ferny vista that provides a shady walk; and a bridal garden, all in white, of course. The Cooperage gift shop in an old barn has dried flower baskets and a variety of dried materials for making old-fashioned dried arrangements. The Cooperage is open from May 15 until Christmas and may be visited apart from the gardens by its entrance on Route 9. It is open daily 10 a.m. to 5 p.m. Leaming's Run Botanical Gardens is open daily from 9:30 a.m. to 5 p.m. May 15 until October 20. Admission is $3; children 6 to 12 $1, under 6 free. The gardens (tel. 465-5871) are on the west side of Route 9, Swainton, between Avalon (exit 13 of the parkway) and Sea Isle City Boulevard.

GUS YEARICK'S HEDGE GARDEN: The nearly lost art of topiary—training and cutting shrubs into unusual and ornamental shapes—is on display near Cape May, in Fishing Creek. Ninety-three-year-old Gus Yearick has been sculpting privet hedges into a life-size clipper ship (36 feet long and 7 feet high), Santa and his reindeer, animals, and other unique pieces for over 50 years, and his garden reflects the endless hours he has spent trimming and cutting. To reach the garden at 158 Fishing Creek Rd., take Route 47 west at exit 4 of the parkway; turn left at Old Shore Road, right onto Fishing Creek Road. The garden is open from the first of May to November; donations are accepted.

Chapter XIII

A SOUTH JERSEY DAY TRIP

NOT ALL THE THRILLS of a south Jersey vacation are at the seashore. Using Cape May as your base, a one-day circle tour can take you to historic Bridgeton, a remarkable monument to 19th-century industry and the state's largest historic district; one of the country's last free zoos; and Wheaton Village, where you can see what a working 1888 glass factory was like, visit the outstanding Museum of American Glass, and stroll around the nicely landscaped grounds that re-create a way of life that existed a century ago.

The route is about 90 miles, to Bridgeton and back, so you can allow about two hours for driving, and many others for rambling and discovery.

From Cape May, take the Garden State Parkway to exit 4, and follow Route 47 west to Millville. Follow the signs in Millville to Wheaton Village.

Wheaton Village

The first successful glass factory in America was founded by Caspar Wistar, a German immigrant, in Salem, New Jersey, in 1739. Numerous other glasshouses were soon operating in the area, particularly in Millville, where Dr. T. C. Wheaton bought an existing factory in 1888.

Carl Sandburg wrote a poetic evocation of the glass workers' life in *In Restless Ecstasy*. It begins, "Down in southern New Jersey, they make glass. By day and by night, the fires burn on in Millville and bid the sand let in the light . . . Big, black fumes, shooting out smoke and sparks, bottles, bottles, bottles, bottles, of every tint and hue, from a brilliant crimson to the dull green that marks the death of sand and birth of glass."

A gala festival celebrating south Jersey's heritage of glassmaking, Wheaton Village is a spacious 88-acre park-like setting for the picturesque buildings, re-creating the architectural styles of the late 1880s, that house a glass factory, craft studios, gift shops, and the renowned **Museum of Glass.** Entering at the front gatehouse, you'll be right at the Village Green.

The best place to begin is the museum. In its grand foyer, decorated in the manner of an opulent lobby at one of the great Victorian resort hotels such as were found in Cape May or Saratoga Springs, New York, you'll see the magnificent chandeliers that were rescued from Atlantic City's famous Traymore Hotel before its destruction. Costumed hostesses in the museum will be glad to answer your questions. Ask the hostess to play the music box or the parlor organ for you.

The museum displays, beautifully illuminated to catch the facets of color and graceful forms, begin in the earliest period of American manufacture with the bottles, window glass, and rarer decorative items from the first successful factories—Wistar's in south Jersey, Steigel in eastern Pennsylvania, and Amelung in Maryland. The aqua color of the bottles is, I understand, due to the iron in the unprocessed sand. Decorative artistry flourished around the middle of the 19th century, and the characteristic south Jersey looped pattern became popular. To obtain the looped effect, glass threads of one color were looped in a ball of glass that was of a different color. This pattern was often used in pitchers, bowls, and vases. The brilliant colors and graceful shapes of the late-19th-century glass factories produced such glasses as Amberina, Rubina, Spangled Glass, and Latticino. A re-creation of an 1890s country kitchen shows how various glass products were used at the time.

Glassblowers in the early south Jersey factories were allowed to use the glass at the end of the day (or more likely their lunch hours) to make items for themselves. This type of glass, known as "end-of-day" or whimseys, are on display in the form of canes, fish, turtles, pipes, hats, and paperweights. The colors of Carnival glass shimmer in iridescent splendor in the art nouveau displays that have glass by Tiffany and other early 20th-century designers.

Located directly behind the museum, the **glass factory** is in continuous operation during the day. The exterior of the factory building has been copied from old photographs of the original Wheaton Glass factory that was destroyed by fire in 1889. In the main furnace area visitors can watch the glassblowers work. Three times daily, at 11 a.m. and 1:30 and 3:30 p.m. there is a special working demonstration with narration. The factory is in continuous operation, and you may visit whenever you like, but these special demonstrations are especially informative.

Crafts and Trades Row, your next stop, is also in continuous operation, except from noon to 12:30 p.m. The craftspeople employ centuries-old techniques in their trades—pottery, tinsmithing, spinning, and woodcarving. A miniature train ride and a playground nearby will catch your children's eye, while you may be curious to see the 1876 Centre Grove schoolhouse that was moved here in 1970.

A whole row of shops along the **Main Promenade** faces the museum. The paperweight shop carries examples of Wheaton-made glass as well as foreign paperweights from Scotland, Italy, and France, which range in price from $5 to several hundred. A general store has a friendly cracker-barrel atmosphere plus old-fashioned housewares and penny candy. The **Brownstone Emporium** has gift items both charming and original in glassware, brass, and pewter, wooden ware, and china. If you'd like to know more about glass, collecting it, its history in south Jersey and worldwide, visit the **bookstore,** which has an in-depth selection of titles on the topic, as well as a good number of books about the region.

If you've brought along a picnic lunch, there's a shaded grove with tables; or you can have a pleasant, inexpensive lunch at the small cafeteria.

Wheaton Village is open year round, seven days a week, from 10 a.m. to 5 p.m.; closed all major holidays. Admission is $4 for adults, $2 for students (ages 6 to 17), $3.50 for seniors, $9 for a family (parents and children). Children 5 and under are free. In the winter months the admissions and schedules are subject to change; it's a good idea to call ahead (tel. 609/825-6800).

Bridgeton

Continuing on Route 49, a 15-minute drive will bring you to Bridgeton. Stop in at the **Tourist Center,** at the crossroads of Routes 49 and 77, 50 East Broad St., Bridgeton, NJ 08302 (tel. 609/455-4802), for a map of the state's largest historic district (over 2,200 sites). The information center also has brochures about the buildings in the historic district and facts about the sites. Here's a quick rundown so you'll know what there is to see.

The charm of the past lives on in downtown Bridgeton. It was first settled in 1686, and the town grew along both banks of the Cohansey River. By the time of the Revolution, Bridgeton had about 200 inhabitants. At least two buildings, Potter's Tavern, at

49 West Broad St., and the Ebenezer Miller House, remain from pre-Revolutionary times. The town prospered mightily in the 1800s. Well-to-do businessmen, whose fortunes came from the iron and nail factory, the 12 gristmills, and a lumber mill, built elegant homes in the latest architectural styles—Federal, Colonial and Greek Revival, Italianate, and Gothic Revival. Atlantic Street and Commerce Street have the greatest concentration of historic houses.

The Riverfront Promenade and the Fountain Plaza provide a pastoral setting, and tables, for a picnic. In summer concerts and art exhibits are held here. The Cohanzick Zoo, open from daylight to dusk year round, houses birds and animals from all over the world in the natural setting of the park. Over 20 different kinds of waterfowl play and swim in the raceway. Children can come up close and touch a barnyard assortment of lambs, goats, and burros. There is no admission charge.

If you have time for only one of the abundance of museums and historic sites in Bridgeton, make it the **Nail Mill Museum** (tel. 455-4100) in the City Park. This 1815 building served as the office for the old Cumberland Nail & Iron Works, the principal industry in town from 1815 to 1899. Local historians note that probably every house in town built in that period is held together with the locally made nails. Many of the exhibits relate to the nail factory, but there are also displays about other early industries in Bridgeton, notably glass and pottery, some examples dating back to the pre–Civil War era. The Nail Museum is free of charge; it's open weekends only or by special arrangement.

The whole family will enjoy the **George Woodruff Museum,** 150 East Commerce St. (tel. 451-2620), with its over 20,000 artifacts from the Nanticoke–Leni Lenape Indians who lived in the area (closed Sunday); the 1899 Firehouse that has an 1877 Old Silsby fire engine; and the **Sports Hall of Fame** (tel. 451-7300). Schedules vary, so check with the Tourist Center for hours of opening.

Meals En Route

Setting out at lunchtime from Cape May will bring you to **Menz's** (tel. 886-5691) in a matter of minutes. It's on Route 47 and Fullingmill Road, about two miles past exit 4 on the parkway, on your way to Millville. The restaurant was a south Jersey tradition for over 40 years in a different location, but it's now moved to the shore, where it keeps hungry travelers happy in a bright, family-style series of dining room. Windsor chairs, wooden tables, Tiffany–style lamps, and a great collection of shore and country memorabilia—a spinning wheel, elk heads, buoys, a uni-cycle, stained-glass objects, and an 1831 dried wreath presented by a grateful customer—decorate the rooms. You'll be grateful too, not only for the hearty home-cooking, but for the reasonable prices at Menz's. The Sunday special of rolled-out old-fashioned chicken pot pie will set you back $6.50, deviled crab is $7.95, and broiled flounder is $8.95. Any one of the above could serve as your main meal of the day. There's also a good children's menu with a number of choices, and homemade desserts. Menz's is open Monday to Friday from 3:30 p.m. to 9 p.m., from noon on weekends.

Going off the beaten path to Fortescue, a small fishing town on Delaware Bay, the **Hotel Charlesworth's** dining room specializes in fresh seafood. Overnight accommodations are also available here (tel. 609/447-4928).